Contents

ABOUT SOURCEBOOKS MEDIAFUSION

Launched with the 1998 *New York Times* bestseller
We Interrupt This Broadcast and formally founded in 2000,
Sourcebooks MediaFusion is the nation's leading publisher
of mixed-media books. This revolutionary imprint is dedicated
to creating original content—be it audio, video, CD-ROM,
or Web—that is fully integrated with the books we create.
The result, we hope, is a new, richer, eye-opening,
thrilling experience with books for our readers.
Our experiential books have become both bestsellers
and classics in their subjects, including poetry (*Poetry Speaks*),
children's books (*Poetry Speaks to Children*),
history (*We Shall Overcome*), sports (*And The Crowd Goes Wild*),
the plays of William Shakespeare, and more.
See what's new from us at www.sourcebooks.com.

About the Text

There are two key versions of *King Lear*, a quarto of 1608 (the First Quarto or Q1) and the Folio version of 1623 (F1). There are significant differences between the First Quarto and the First Folio, and each version of the play has a claim upon our attention. While the Oxford editors Wells and Taylor (1988) have argued that the two versions of *Lear* are separate and equally authentic, most editors, dating as far back as Alexander Pope (1725), have opted for a composite text, combining the beauties of both versions. This edition follows in that tradition.

However, my sense of "Shakespearean" differs, and given the changes in aesthetics over the centuries, it is no great surprise that my text looks very little like Pope's composite. I have used, for the most part, the early performance-based Q1 for reasons I articulated in an article about the "Good" quarto of *Lear*, and I have added passages from the longer F1. This text is an edition for the present and does not claim to have solved the "mystery of things" relating to *Lear*. My choices are explicit, and I encourage the reader who wants to explore the text to go online to the Sourcebooks Shakespeare web site, where it is reproduced with enhanced color-coded features that show my Q1 and F1 selections clearly.

I have modernized Shakespeare's spelling and punctuation along the principles espoused in Stanley Wells' *Modernizing Shakespeare's Spelling* (1979) and his *Re-Editing Shakespeare for the Modern Reader: Based on Lectures Given at the Folger Shakespeare Library, Washington, D.C.* (1984). However, where modernization strips a word of its original meaning, the archaic spelling has been retained: see, for example, "villein" (3.7.74).

Like any composite text, deciding what to keep and what to let go is a fraught and time-consuming process. Conflating Q1 and F1 has necessitated some relineations, but lineations are already suspect; editors regularly turn two half-lines into one full line, etc. I have, however, attempted to retain the Quarto's transitions from prose to verse, hoping, perhaps fruitlessly, that some of Shakespeare's original intention survived the various exigencies of the journey it was compelled to take from the playhouse to the printing house.

Douglas A. Brooks

On the CD

1. Introduction to the Sourcebooks Shakespeare *King Lear*: Sir Derek Jacobi

ACT 1, SCENE 1, LINES 44-106

2. Narration: Sir Derek Jacobi
3. Trevor Peacock as Lear, Penny Downie as Gonoril, Julia Ford as Cordelia and Samantha Bond as Regan
   The Complete Arkangel Shakespeare • 2003
4. Paul Scofield as Lear, Harriet Walter as Gonoril, Emilia Fox as Cordelia, and Sara Kestelman as Regan
   Naxos AudioBooks • 2002

ACT 1, SCENE 1, LINES 136-176

5. Narration: Sir Derek Jacobi
6. Anton Lesser as Kent and Trevor Peacock as Lear
   The Complete Arkangel Shakespeare • 2000
7. David Burke as Kent and Paul Scofield as Lear
   Naxos AudioBooks • 2002

ACT 1, SCENE 2, LINES 1-22

8. Narration: Sir Derek Jacobi
9. Simon Russell Beale as Edmund
   Naxos AudioBooks—Great Speeches and Soliloquies • 1994
10. Toby Stephens as Edmund
    Naxos AudioBooks • 2002

ACT 1, SCENE 4, LINES 249-264

11. Narration: Sir Derek Jacobi
12. Laurence Olivier as Lear
    Granada International • 1984

ACT 1, SCENE 5, LINES 6-36

13. Narration: Sir Derek Jacobi
14. Paul Scofield as Lear, David Burke as Kent, and
    Kenneth Branagh as the Fool
    Naxos AudioBooks • 2002
15. Laurence Olivier as Lear, Colin Blakely as Kent,
    and John Hurt as the Fool
    Granada International • 1984

ACT 2, SCENE 1, LINES 13-36

16. Narration: Sir Derek Jacobi
17. Gerard Murphy as Edmund and David Tennant as Edgar
    The Complete Arkangel Shakespeare • 2003
18. Toby Stephens as Edmund and Richard McCabe as Edgar
    Naxos AudioBooks • 2002

ACT 3, SCENE 2, LINES 1-24

19. Narration: Sir Derek Jacobi
20. Donald Wolfit as Lear and Job Stewart as the Fool
    Living Shakespeare • 1962
21. Paul Scofield as Lear and Kenneth Branagh as the Fool
    Naxos AudioBooks • 2002

ACT 3, SCENE 4, LINES 37-69

22. Narration: Sir Derek Jacobi
23. David Tennant as Edgar, John Rogan as the Fool, Anton Lesser
    as Kent, and Trevor Peacock as Lear
    The Complete Arkangel Shakespeare • 2003
24. Richard McCabe as Edgar, Kenneth Branagh as the Fool,
    David Burke as Kent, and Paul Scofield as Lear
    Naxos AudioBooks • 2002

Act 3, Scene 7, Lines 47-90

25. Narration: Sir Derek Jacobi
26. Samantha Bond as Regan, Rob Edwards as Cornwall, and
    Clive Merrison as Gloucester
    The Complete Arkangel Shakespeare • *2003*
27. Sara Kestelman as Regan, Jack Klaff as Cornwall, and
    Alec McCowen as Gloucester
    Naxos AudioBooks • *2002*

Act 4, Scene 7, Lines 42-73

28. Narration: Sir Derek Jacobi
29. Rosalind Iden as Cordelia and Donald Wolfit as Lear
    Living Shakespeare • *1962*
30. Julia Ford as Cordelia and Trevor Peacock as Lear
    The Complete Arkangel Shakespeare • *2003*

Act 5, Act 3, Lines 258-279

31. Narration: Sir Derek Jacobi
32. Paul Scofield as Lear, David Burke as Kent, Richard McCabe
    as Edgar, and Peter Blythe as Albany
    Naxos AudioBooks • *2002*
33. Sir John Gielgud as Lear, Lines 258–279 and 306–312
    Sir John Gielgud Charitable Trust

34. Introduction to Speaking Shakespeare: Sir Derek Jacobi
35. Speaking Shakespeare: Andrew Wade with Myra Lucretia Taylor

36. Conclusion of the Sourcebooks Shakespeare *King Lear*:
    Sir Derek Jacobi

Featured Audio Productions

NAXOS AUDIOBOOKS (2002)

King Lear	Paul Scofield
Gonoril	Harriet Walter
Regan	Sara Kestelman
Cordelia	Emilia Fox
Duke of Albany	Peter Blythe
Duke of Cornwall	Jack Klaff
Earl of Gloucester	Alec McCowen
Edgar	Richard McCabe
Edmund	Toby Stephens
Earl of Kent	David Burke
Fool	Kenneth Branagh
Duke of Burgundy	John McAndrew
King of France	Simon Treves
Oswald	Matthew Morgan

THE COMPLETE ARKANGEL SHAKESPEARE (2003)

King Lear	Trevor Peacock
Earl of Gloucester	Clive Merrison
Earl of Kent	Anton Lesser
Gonoril	Penny Downie
Regan	Samantha Bond
Cordelia	Julia Ford
Edmund	Gerard Murphy
Edgar	David Tennant
Fool	John Rogan
Duke of Albany	David Horovitch
Duke of Cornwall	Rob Edwards
Oswald	Jonathan Tafler
Gentleman	Clifford Rose
King of France	John McAndrew
Duke of Burgundy	Christopher Gee

LIVING SHAKESPEARE (1962)

King Lear	Donald Wolfit
Gonoril	Coral Browne
Regan	Barbara Jefford
Cordelia	Rosalind Iden
Earl of Kent	Derek Francis
Earl of Gloucester	Joseph O'Conor
Duke of Burgundy	Mark Kingston
King of France	Brian Spink
Duke of Albany	David Dodimead
Duke of Cornwall	Peter Eyre
Fool	Job Stewart
Edgar	Thomas Johnston
Edmund	Mark Brackenbury

GRANADA INTERNATIONAL (1984): Laurence Olivier as King Lear

Naxos AudioBooks—Great Speeches and Soliloquies (1994): Simon Russell Beale as Edmund

Note from the Series Editors

For many of us, our first and only encounter with Shakespeare was in school. We may recall that experience as a struggle, working through dense texts filled with unfamiliar words. However, those of us who were fortunate enough to have seen a play performed have altogether different memories. It may be of an interesting scene or an unusual character, but it is most likely a speech. Often, just hearing part of one instantly transports us to that time and place. "Friends, Romans, countrymen, lend me your ears", "But, soft! What light through yonder window breaks?", "To sleep, perchance to dream", "Tomorrow, and tomorrow, and tomorrow".

The Sourcebooks Shakespeare series is our attempt to use the power of performance to help you experience the play. In it, you will see photographs from various productions, on film and on stage, historical and contemporary, known worldwide or in your community. You may even recognize some actors you don't think of as Shakespearean performers. You will see set drawings, costume designs, and scene edits, all reproduced from original notes. Finally, on the enclosed audio CD, you will hear scenes from the play as performed by some of the most accomplished Shakespeareans of our time. Often, we include multiple interpretations of the same scene, showing you the remarkable richness of the text. Hear Paul Scofield's authoritative and measured Lear banish Kent in the 1962 Living Shakespeare series. Compare the same speech to the wrenching rendition by Laurence Olivier in his 1984 performance. The actors create different meanings, different characters, different worlds.

As you read the text of the play, you can consult explanatory notes for definitions of unfamiliar words and phrases or words whose meanings have changed. These notes appear on the left pages, next to the text of the play. The audio, photographs, and other production artifacts augment the notes and they too are indexed to the appropriate lines. You can use the pictures to see how others have staged a particular scene and get ideas on costumes, scenery, blocking, etc. As for the audio, each track represents a particular interpretation of a scene. Sometimes, a passage that's difficult to comprehend opens up when you hear it out loud. Furthermore, when you hear more than one version, you gain a keener understanding of the characters. Is Lear a greedy patriarch or a misunderstood father? Are his daughters the victims of his misogynistic cruelty or the deserving targets of his ire? The actors made their choices and so can you. You may even come up with your own interpretation.

The text of the play, the definitions, the production notes, the audio—all of these work together, and they are included for your enjoyment. Because the audio consists of performance excerpts, it is meant to entertain. When you see a passage with an associated clip, you can read along as you hear the actors perform the scene for you. Or, you can sit back, close your eyes, and listen, then go back and reread the text with a new perspective. Finally, since the text is a script, you may find yourself reciting the lines out loud and doing your own performance!

You will undoubtedly notice that some of the audio does not exactly match the text. Also, there are photographs and facsimiles of scenes that may not be in your edition. There are many reasons for this, but foremost among them is the fact that Shakespearean scholarship continues to progress, and the prescribed ways of dealing with and interpreting texts are always changing. Thus a play that was edited and published in the 1900s will be different from one published in 2007. Finally, artists have their own interpretation of the play, and they too cut and change lines and scenes according to their vision.

The ways in which *King Lear* has been presented have varied considerably through the years. We've included essays in the book to give you glimpses into the range of productions, showing you how different artists have approached the play and providing examples of what changes were made and how. Bradley Ryner writes of Michael Kahn's compelling 1999 interpretation, performed by the Shakespeare Theatre Company, in which the deaf actress Monique Holt plays a deaf Cordelia. He discusses how her deafness textures the father-daughter relationship, creates closeness with the Fool (who interprets her sign language), and emphasizes one of the play's thematic concerns: the breakdown of communication. "In Production," an essay by our text editor, Douglas Brooks, provides an overview of how the play has been performed, from Nahum Tate's early adaptation that created a long-standing tradition of *Lear* ending happily to Paul Scofield's seminal performance in the 1962 RSC production that reversed that trend. Exploring the origins and legacy of the happy ending, Brooks examines its effect on the relationship between the text and the realization of the play in performance. In his essay on *King Lear* in popular culture, Douglas Lanier cites adaptations of Lear's story, introducing productions that alter the play's geographic or chronological location while retaining the central themes of fatherhood, inheritance and the melodrama of familial relations. In *Broken Lance* (1954), for example, Lear's daughters are supplanted with cattlemen's sons; *Harry and Tonto* (1974) replaces the Fool with a cat; *My Kingdom* (2001) sets the drama of *Lear* in the context of a Liverpudlian mob family. The list goes on. Finally, for the actor in you, (and for those who want to peek behind the curtain), we have an essay that you may find especially intriguing. Andrew Wade, voice coach of the Royal Shakespeare Company for sixteen years, shares his point of view on how to understand the text and speak it. You can also listen in on him working with Myra Lucretia Taylor on a speech from the play; perhaps you too can learn the art of speaking Shakespeare. The characters come to life in a way that's different from reading the book or watching a performance.

One last note: we are frequently asked why we didn't include the whole play, either in audio or video. While we enjoy the plays and are avid theatergoers, we are trying to do something more with the audio (and the production notes and the essays) than just presenting them to you. Our goal is to provide you tools that will enable you to explore the play on your own, from many different directions. Our hope is that the different pieces of audio, the voices of the actors, and the production photos and notes will engage you and illuminate the play on many levels, so that you can construct your own understanding and create your own "production," a fresh interpretation unique to you.

Though the productions we referenced and the audio clips we have included are but a miniscule sample of the play's history, we hope they encourage you to further delve into the works of Shakespeare. New editions of the play come out yearly; movie adaptations are regularly being produced; there are hundreds of theater groups in the U.S. alone; and performances could be going on right in your backyard. We echo the words of noted writer and poet Robert Graves, who said, "The remarkable thing about Shakespeare is that he is really very good—in spite of all the people who say he is very good."

Dominique Raccah

Marie Macaisa

Dominique Raccah and Marie Macaisa
Series Editors

track 1

Introduction to the Sourcebooks Shakespeare **King Lear**
Sir Derek Jacobi

In Production

Douglas A. Brooks

Few records of the earliest performances of Shakespeare's plays have survived, but we are fortunate in the case of *King Lear*. The title page of the play, as it was initially published in 1608, provides us with some important details about the first performance of the play, who was in the audience, and even the basic plot of the play. While we have come to see *Lear* as one of Shakespeare's greatest tragedies, the title page of the 1608 edition (Q1) refers to the play not as a tragedy, but as the *"True Chronicle History of the life and death of King Lear, and his three Daughters"*, adding that it also tells the story of *"the unfortunate life of Edgar, sonne and heire to the Earle of Glocester, and his sullen and assumed humour of TOM of Bedlam"*. Whoever might have had an interest in purchasing a printed version of the play in 1608 certainly knew what to expect. Such a potential reader would have also learned that not only was the first performance of *Lear* "plaid before the Kings Majesty at White-Hall, upon S. Stephens night, in Christmas Hollidaies," but also that it was performed by "his majesties Servants, playing usually at the Globe on the Banck-side." In other words, the first performance of *King Lear* was a special production by Shakespeare's company, The King's Men, for James I at Whitehall Palace on December 26, 1606. The only other thing we know for certain about this performance was that Shakespeare's friend and fellow actor, Richard Burbage, one of the great tragedians of the English Renaissance stage, played the role of Lear that night.

Our good fortune begins and ends there. Apart from a production of the play that may have been put on in Yorkshire in 1610 (1), there is no reliable evidence that the play was performed again during Shakespeare's lifetime.

"BUT NOW IN THE DIVISION OF THE KINGDOMS"
When the theaters reopened shortly after the ascension of Charles II to the throne in 1660, *Lear* returned to the stage and was performed only twice in

the next decade or so in ways that Shakespeare might have recognized, once in 1664 and then again in 1675. The playwright, William Davenant, was

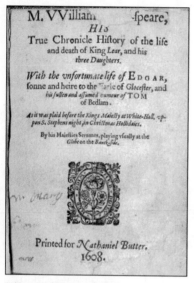

M. VVilliam.   -fpeare,
HIs
True Chronicle Hiſtory of the life
and death of King Lear, and his
three Daughters.

With the vnfortunate life of EDGAR,
ſonne and heire to the Earle of Gloceſter, and
his ſullen and aſſumed oumour of TOM
of Bedlam.

As it was plaid before the Kings Maieſty at White-Hall, vp-
pon S. Stephens night, in Chriſtmas Hollidaies.

By his Maieſties Seruants, playing vſually at the
Globe on the Banck-ſide.

Printed for Nathaniel Butter.
1608.

Title page of *King Lear* (1608)
Courtesy of the Horace Howard Furness Memorial Library, University of Pennsylvania

behind the first of these two largely unsuccessful attempts to put on stage what Shakespeare had written. Such an adherence to the playwright's text was to be short-lived. Along with the restoration of England to monarchic rule came an intensive effort to adapt and change Shakespeare's plays both for theater audiences and readers, and *Lear* did not escape unscathed. In 1681, Nahum Tate's now infamous adaptation appeared in print as *The History of King Lear* and proclaimed itself as containing the play as "acted at the Duke's Theater", a production mounted by the Duke's Company at their playhouse, with Thomas Betterton in the title role. I used the word "infamous" because although Tate's version greatly appealed to Restoration theater-goers and was more or less the only *Lear* audiences saw during the eighteenth and early nineteenth century, it has not fared well with Shakespearean critics. Rather, such critics have often disparaged the profound distortions Tate's adaptation imposed on the original—distortions, as Tate himself indicated, aimed at "making the Tale conclude in a Success to the innocent distrest Persons: Otherwise I must have incumbred the Stage with dead Bodies" (2). It is hard to imagine how some of the great, dark, often proto-existentialist early twentieth-century criticism of *Lear* by G. Wilson Knight or A.C. Bradley, for example, could have been written had they been responding to a play that concludes, as Tate's does, not only with Lear restored to the throne of the realm he had torn asunder, but also with Edgar and Cordelia destined for conjugal bliss. How odd all of this might seem to modern audiences who are sometimes taken aback by the crude and bawdy language that characterizes the banter between Edmund, Gonoril, and Regan. On the other hand, it would have surprised Shakespeare to see three female actors on stage playing Gonoril, Regan, and Cordelia in performances of Tate's *Lear* at the Duke's Theater. Prior to the closing of the theaters in 1642, numerous, widely circulated anti-theatrical pamphlets repeatedly upbraided players and playing companies for promoting wickedness, lewd behavior, and Papist (Catholic) beliefs. "Proper" women attended plays at their own moral peril, and no woman of any class would have been allowed to appear on stage, all female parts being played by boy actors. Indeed, it has been speculated that the Fool mysteriously vanishes from the play after the mock-trial scene (in Q1) because Shakespeare knew that the same boy actor playing him would also play Cordelia. When the Fool disappears after 3.6, Cordelia reappears. In Tate's *Lear*, which gives Cordelia more prominence than Shakespeare's, such juggling of roles would not have been necessary for two reasons: 1) an actress played Cordelia, and 2) Tate cut the role of the Fool altogether because he felt that such a character had no place in tragedy, regardless of the fact that his adaptation turned the play into a comedy.

Writing nearly a century after the earliest performances of Tate's play, Samuel Johnson noted what eighteenth-century audiences wanted from their *Lear*: "the publick has decided. Cordelia, from the time of Tate, has always retired with victory and felicity. And, if my sensations could add any thing to the general suffrage, I might relate, that I was many years ago so shocked by Cordelia's death, that I know not whether I ever endured to read again the last scenes of the play till I undertook to revise them as an editor" (3). Given the chaos that threatened to engulf England during the interregnum (1649-60), perhaps Tate's Lear best expresses the yearnings of Restoration audiences when he exclaims to Kent near the conclusion of the play, "Why I have News that will recall thy Youth; / Ha! Didst Thou hear't, or did th'inspiring Gods / Whisper to me Alone? Old *Lear* shall be / A King again" (5.6.104-7 in Tate's edition).

Perhaps the most celebrated productions of *Lear* in the eighteenth century starred David Garrick (1717-79), the actor, playwright, and theater mogul who dominated theatrical practices and tastes during his lifetime and after. Prior to Garrick, performers commonly declaimed their lines, rarely feeling compelled to modulate their approach for the sake of representing the nuances of a role. Garrick introduced theater-goers to a more natural approach to acting, one that sought to realistically communicate the shifting emotional registers of a part. Audiences loved what they saw. Describing the final scene of a performance of *Lear* (Tate's version) he attended in 1747, the actor and theater critic Thomas Davies (1712-85) wrote, "The half breathing and panting of Garrick, with a look and action which confessed the infirmity of old age, greatly heightened the picture...Who could possibly think of depriving an audience, almost exhausted with the feelings of so many terrible scenes, of the inexpressible delight which they enjoyed, when the old King, in rapture, cried out – 'Old Lear shall be a king again!'" (4). Another audience member (Thomas Wilkes) who saw Garrick perform Lear some years later, wrote, "his old grey hair standing, as it were, erect on his head, his face filled with horror and attention, his hands expanded, his whole frame actuated by a dreadful solemnity...methinks I share his calamities, I feel the dark drifting rain and the sharp tempest" (5). The natural style had literally taken the theater by storm, and Garrick's approach to preparing for the role suggests that method acting, so popular with contemporary film actors, has important antecedents in the performance history of *Lear*. On Garrick's assertion that his portrayal of Lear's madness was based on the real-life tragedy of a father who accidentally dropped his baby daughter out of a window and killed her, Thomas Davies reports that Garrick, "frequently went to see his distracted friend, who passed the remainder of his life in going to the window, and there playing in fancy with his child. After some dalliance, he dropped it, and, bursting into a flood of tears, filled the house with shrieks of grief and bitter anguish. He then sat down, in a pensive mood, his eyes fixed on one object, at times looking slowly round him, as if to implore compassion" (6). And so, art, it would seem, was imitating life.

Nevertheless, Garrick's portrayal of Lear was not without its detractors. In a review of Garrick's performance in the same production Davies found so moving, Samuel Foote (1720-77), a playwright, actor, and theater manager well-known in his day for penning popular farces, criticized Garrick's naturalistic style of acting as inadequate for representing the grandeur of kingship. Especially troubled by Garrick's handling of Lear's madness, Foote asserted that everything an actor does onstage to play the king "should express an Extravagance of State & Majesty...but no Sign of Equality, no Familiarity, no sitting down Cheek by Jowl" (7). Foote, whose 1741 performance of Shylock in *The Merchant of Venice* mesmerized London audiences, was in direct competition with Garrick, though he was far less financially successful. As such, professional bitterness may have fueled his critique. Whichever critic is more credible, there is no disputing Lear earned Garrick more acclaim than perhaps any other role he attempted, and he performed it regularly for more than three decades.

It is important to remember here that all such eyewitness accounts of *Lear* in the theater describe performances of what was essentially Tate's version of the play. During the many years he portrayed the king, Garrick increasingly incorporated more and more of Shakespeare's play into the performance texts he and his fellow actors relied on for a given production, but he could not bring himself to do without Tate's happy ending. Nor was he willing to allow the Fool to return from the exile imposed on him since 1681 because, as he put it, "the feelings of Lear would derive no advantage from the buffooneries of the parti-coloured jester" (8).

Garrrick's successor, John Philip Kemble (1757-1823), who first performed the role on January 21, 1788, agreed with him. Indeed, Kemble not only kept Tate's ending, but also restored some of the plot twists that Garrick had deleted, including Cordelia's marriage to Edgar. The theater critic George Daniel did not approve. Although Daniel praised Kemble for the realism of his performance, noting how the actor's "figure, countenance, and manner all conspired to give truth to the resemblance..." he was less moved, however, by Kemble's choice of Tate's version. Critizing the marriage that Tate created, which erased Cordelia's death, Daniel observed, "The daring presumption that marred this glorious drama, deprived us of Mr. Kemble's exertions in the scene where Lear enters bearing in the dead body of Cordelia. What this would have been in the hands of *such* an actor, we can only anticipate. But we deeply regret that Mr. Kemble's correct taste did not brush away this vile interpolation, and restore the original text of Shakespeare" (9). If only, as we shall see, Daniel could have avoided seeing *Lear* for another eight years.

Beginning in 1810 performances of *Lear,* regardless of the text on which they were based, were banned for the next decade out of concern that the representation of a monarch descending into madness would be insensitive at a time when King George III (r. 1760-1820), who suffered from recurrent bouts of mental illness in the later years of his reign, lapsed into a permanent state of incompetence during the final ten years of his rule. Upon his death in 1820, *Lear* would return, though not quite Shakespeare's *Lear.* In the year the ban was lifted, the widely acclaimed nineteenth-century English actor Edmund Kean (1787-1833) mounted a production of the play that relied heavily on the original texts, but still followed Tate in terms of its comic ending. Kean's performance was celebrated by a number of critics, but it was his portrayal of Lear's madness that was singled out for critical praise. One reviewer writing in the *New York Post* about Kean's 1820 production observed: "Nature, writhing under the poignancy of feeling, and finding no utterance in words or tears found a vent at length…in a spontaneous, hysterical, idiot laugh. The impressions made upon all who were present, will never be forgotten. His dreadful imprecations upon his daughters, his solemn appeals to heaven, struck the soul with awe" (10). Like Garrick before him, Kean had done a little preparation of his own, for it was widely reported at the time that "he was studying the character [of Lear] with great care, even visiting lunatic asylums to observe the effects of madness…He disturbed [his wife] Mary by wandering about the house with his eyes alternately vacant and filled with fierce light" (11). Emboldened by the favorable reception of this production and hoping to display fully his virtuosity as an actor by plunging himself into the depths of Shakespeare's *Lear*, Kean staged the play with its tragic ending in 1823. Virtuosity or not, the production proved so unpopular with audiences that after only three performances Kean was forced to return to Tate's version for the remainder of the run.

Despite this brief debacle, Kean's acting style continued to have a profound impact on stage actors in general, and on those who played Lear in particular. The impact extended to America, where the actor Edwin Forrest (1806-1872) fashioned himself Kean's disciple, even emulating his approach to preparing for a role as he readied himself to portray Lear's madness for a production during the 1827-28 theater season in New York. As a friend of the American actor recalled, "Mr. Forrest had studied the theory of insanity with a student's care...visited insane asylums and other places both here [in America] and in Europe, and with artistic exactness, carried out in his renditions all those mental peculiarities and eccentricities that critics recognize as truthful, and not as the mere ebullitions of a disposition and temper naturally fiery and irritable" (12). It was only a matter of time before Freud would come to rely on Shakespeare for some of his own theories of insanity.

"MEANTIME WE WILL EXPRESS OUR DARKER PURPOSES"

King Lear, as Shakespeare wrote it, would not return to the theater successfully until William Charles Macready (1793-1873) mounted a production, replete with the Fool and all of those "dead bodies" with which Tate had been loath to encumber the stage, in Drury Lane on January 25,1838 (13). An English actor who made his debut at the age of 16 playing Romeo at a theater in Birmingham, Macready went on to have a long and successful acting career, including three separate tours in America. While there, Macready attended performances of *Lear* starring Forrest. The English snob or the Shakespeare purist in him must not have liked what he saw, especially in front of the stage, because he later wrote, "The audience were very liberal, very vehement in their applause; but it was such an audience! – applauding all the disgusting trash of Tate as if it had been Shakespeare, with might and main" (14). It is unclear why Macready so disliked Tate's *Lear*, and why he subsequently expunged all of Tate's distortions from what amounted by now to a 150-year long performance tradition, but critical tastes were certainly shifting in the direction of his decision. And surely Daniel's rather damning review of Kemble's Tate-ish *Lear* could have made a persuasive case to anyone who might be planning to mount a production, like Macready, that it was time to bring Shakespeare back alive.

Perhaps the century that would produce the likes of Nietzsche, Marx, and Freud was finally ready for the "darker purposes" of the play Shakespeare gave us. Indeed, a work whose rallying cry seems to be, "Now gods, stand up for bastards" had suddenly become prescient of the decentering and illegitimacy that characterized the human condition in the West after Nietzsche's announcement of God's death had begun to ring in our ears.

Whether it was the critical winds that caught theatrical sails, or the proto-psychologism of the Romantic movement compelling us to look evermore inward to the point where God, if not dead, had at least been marginalized by our own self-deification—either way, the stage was being set for the moment when once again it would be littered with corpses, when once again Cordelia and Edgar would never speak to each other, when once again the king's initial longing to be "unburdened" so he can "crawl toward death," would, in his final dying words, be reduced to begging for help to "undo this button." Even the Fool would reappear, though in Macready's production it was a female character played by actress Priscilla Horton. It may not have been exactly what Shakespeare had in mind, but according to one reviewer, Horton brought the long-absent Fool back with a certain élan: "hers is a most pleasing performance, giving evidence of deep feeling; and she trills forth the snatches of song with the mingled archness and pathos of their own exquisite simplicity" (15). Significantly, all of the figurative hand wringing that brought Tate's *Lear* into the world and helped it to thrive so robustly on so many stages for so many years seems to have been for naught. As one reviewer who saw Macready's production on opening night made clear, a fully tragic *Lear* could make the journey from the page to the stage quite successfully.

Not only had Macready restored *Lear* to the theater in a form its playwright might have called his own, he was also inadvertently laying the foundation for a new set of performance traditions that would last well into the present. But beyond the textual choices that engendered this production, its back-to-the-futurism was also embodied in an important sense by the decisions that Macready made with regard to the play's setting. Now that "old Shakespeare" had finally returned, it was perhaps only fitting that his elderly king return to a stage that approximated the historical moment of his reign. Thus, as one reviewer who attended opening night appreciatively noted, the scenery "corresponds with the period, and with the circumstances of the text. The castles are heavy, sombre, solid; their halls adorned with trophies of the chase and instruments of war; druid circles rise in spectral loneliness out of the heath; and the 'dreadful pother' of the elements is kept up with a verisimilitude which beggars all that we have hitherto seen attempted" (16).

Lear was back in his element, and Macready's scenic efforts to re-locate the play in its mythic past proved infectious. Indeed, his attention to period details, "hitherto" unseen during the age of Tate, soon became *de rigueur* in a number of productions that were mounted during the second half of the nineteenth century, sometimes to the point of obsession. In one such production, Edmund Kean's son, Charles Kean (1811-1868) set out at mid-century to stage a *Lear* so heavily invested in recreating the King's Dark Ages that during rehearsals, he reportedly scolded the actor playing Edmund for inadequately denoting the play's historical moment. When that actor handed his key to Edgar, according to one account Kean exclaimed, "Good heavens! You give it to him as if it was a common room-door key. Let the audience see it, sir; make 'em feel it; impress upon 'em that it is a *key of the period*, sir" (17). Nature, it has been said, abhors a vacuum, and so with Tate's efforts to "rectifie what was wanting in the Regularity and Probability of the Tale" now expunged completely, this new fixation with making "'em feel" the temporal divide between their present and the play's present stepped in. It is probable that the great twentieth-century Shakespeare critic A.C. Bradley was hoping to un-fix this preoccupation when, in 1904, he essentially made *Lear* a refugee: "This world, we are told, is called Britain; but we should no more look for it in an atlas than for the place, called Caucasus, where Prometheus was chained by Strength and Force and comforted by the daughters of Ocean..." (18). If, like Prometheus, Shakespeare's *Lear* was homeless, then it was also timeless, and any theatrical attempt to shelter it within England's times of yore was likely to be as unaccommodating as the hovel into which the King and company escape from the storm. By deracinating the play from the moorings that had become ever more sturdy since Macready, Bradley was loosing the play onto the twentieth century. *King Lear*, to borrow from the title of Jan Kott's important critical study of Shakespeare, was about to become "our contemporary." The timing could not have been better.

In a production of the play that was first mounted at the Lyceum Theatre (London) on November 10, 1892 by the famous Victorian actor, Sir Henry Irving (1838-1905), what might be called the Macready curse—those who think they know *Lear*'s past are condemned to repeat it on stage as realistically as possible—was taken to something like its logical conclusion. Born, coincidentally, in the same year that Macready issued this curse, and dying a year after Bradley attempted to undo it, Irving was very clear about when he thought his *Lear* should be. Writing in the preface to an edition of the play he published in conjunction with the London premiere, Irving observed: "As the period of *King Lear* is fabulous, I have chosen, at the suggestion of Mr. Ford Madox Brown (who has kindly designed three scenes in the First and Second Acts) a time shortly after the departure of the Romans, when the Britons would naturally inhabit the houses left vacant" (19). Accordingly, Irving's Lear divested himself of his rule over a desolate fifth-century wasteland, peopled by hordes of barbarians and squatters making do among Roman ruins. No matter that one of the key historical references from which Shakespeare drew the basic elements of the story, *The History of the Kings of Britain* (1138) by Geoffrey of Monmouth ((c.1100-c.1155), tells of a King Leir who reigned from 861 BCE to 801 BCE, but then lost his kingdom when he attempted to divide it amongst his three daughters. In other words, nearly thirteen hundred years separate Geoffrey's historical Leir from the Lear imagined by Irving and Brown. Charles Kean, who was comparably concerned with accurately staging the play's historical moment, set his production in 800 AD, some 1600 years after the reign of the historical king. As if all of this emphasis on making the play "of the period, sir," as Kean put it, was not confusing enough, one of the painted backdrops Brown designed for Irving's Lyceum production consisted of "huge stones roughly laid upon each other in the Stonehenge fashion" (20). But if the anachronisms that inevitably emerged out of Macready and his successors' efforts to get it right bothered the audiences that attended Irving's *Lear*, they did not let on: the play ran for 76 performances, closing on February 1, 1893. And although the craving for historical authenticity that accompanied the return of Shakespeare's tragic *Lear* to the theater in the mid-nineteenth century did not completely disappear after Irving's production—indeed there was no shortage of period productions that were to follow—there was a significant shift in the locus of that craving from the stage to the page.

Within the same decade that Irving's *Lear* appeared, a newly intensified effort at getting Shakespeare right was underway. Textual scholarship, which began to emerge as a coherent discipline not long after Macready resurrected Shakespeare's *Lear*, had spent much of the second half of the century focusing its attention on Biblical texts. By the end of the century, that scholarly project well established, its various methodologies tried and tested, a new set of "sacred" texts was needed. Enter Shakespeare. Thus began an intensive scholarly effort, led initially by A. W. Pollard, R. B. McKerrow and W. W. Greg, aimed at determining the most authentic texts of Shakespeare's works, then producing authoritative editions of those works. Because the burden of authenticity had been relocated to Shakespeare's texts, the theater was now free to pursue other concerns. Once again, the timing could not have been better.

"IN THY BEST CONSIDERATION"

In important ways, the twentieth century belonged to *King Lear*. Freed from the obligation to recall a specific moment in the distant English past, the play—its splintered nationalism, its decentered authority and the resulting scramble for power, its representation of the generational impiety that tears apart bonds of family and state, its juxtaposition of nature's fury and human insignificance, its relentless portrait of human cruelty, and its stubborn insistence that our yearning for justice is the only salve against gods who amuse themselves with our suffering—had everything we needed to make it a cipher for what was on the minds of many people in many societies. Bound by the caprices of authority, blinded by propaganda, and often seeing death as the only escape from misery, those who struggled to survive in the gulags of the era could find the truth of their lives in Gloucester. Or naked, starving, and at the mercy of forces that seemed incognizant of their humanity, those "unaccommodated" beings who somehow lived to recall the charnel houses that sprang up in so many countries, yet offered no shelter, could find a kindred soul in Lear. And, tragically, for so many, the justice the king so vehemently pursues in the mock-trial scene, a trial that only really takes place in his anguished mind, typified the imaginary legal systems through which they were compelled to seek compensation in the darkness of sleepless nights. Perhaps more than any other of Shakespeare's plays, *Lear* became for the age "a mirror up to nature," to borrow a phrase from *Hamlet*. Accordingly, it quickly became among the most popular of Shakespeare's plays to be staged.

"SUCH UNCONSTANT STARTS ARE WE LIKE TO HAVE"

The twentieth century witnessed an extraordinary proliferation of important productions of *Lear*, both on stage and on film, the new medium that was profoundly well suited to Shakespeare. What follows are brief descriptions of those that have powerfully articulated the geist of its era.

The great Shakespeare critic A.C. Bradley set the stage for many *Lears* to come by freeing the play from the bondage of representing England's ancient past. But in cutting those chains, Bradley acknowledged that "*King Lear* is too huge for the stage," further observing: "there is something in its very essence which is at war with the senses, and demands a purely imaginative realization" (21). There would be no shortage of attempts at such realizations, and if in fact the play was too big for any stage, perhaps a movie camera could give it the space it needed.

Art rarely cooperates with arbitrary periodization, so perhaps it is only appropriate that the most important British theater director and producer of the first half of the twentieth century, Harley Granville-Barker (1877-1946), actually began his acting career at the age of fourteen in the previous century. In 1900, Granville-Barker joined the experimental Stage Society, and a decade or so later began a series of productions of Shakespeare's plays at the Savoy Theatre that would prove to be enormously influential. *Lear* was not among those productions, but Granville-Barker's significance in the performance history of the play would come a little later. Arguably, that significance would move indirectly from his stage to other stages by making an appearance on the page in the form of his *Prefaces to Shakespeare*, a series of studies focusing on issues of staging Shakespeare's plays that began to appear in 1927. In the specific case of *Lear*, Granville-Barker discussed the play at length in the first of these volumes, and much of what he said continues to impact productions of the play today. As Stanley Wells observes, "Barker's *Preface* of 1927, one of the most practically efficacious pieces of drama criticism ever written, is a landmark in the history of the reception of King Lear" (22).

I have suggested above that *Lear* would speak powerfully to twentieth century audiences. However, its ability to do so was complicated by a question textual scholars had begun to raise in earnest: Which *Lear*? Having taken over the craving for authenticity that had preoccupied Macready and his successors in the previous century, these scholars began to demonstrate in considerable detail that the play had come down to us in two substantially different versions: the First Quarto version of 1608 (Q1) and the First Folio version of 1623 (F1). This was not, of course, new information. As early as 1725, Alexander Pope had noted a number of differences between the two versions, including the fact that F1 was missing a number of substantial passages that appeared in Q1. One such section of missing text was Lear's mock trial of Gonoril and Regan (3.6.30-74). It is hard to conceive of a *Lear,* focused as the play is on the human longing for justice, that does not allow the King the consolation of demanding to "see their trial first", but F1 does not, in fact, offer him such comfort. Nevertheless, the seriousness of purpose displayed by early twentieth-century textual scholars, a seriousness inherited from the discipline's origins in Biblical studies, guaranteed that the differences between Q1 and F1 *Lear* would be taken seriously.

Thus, in precisely the same historical moment, both the atom and *King Lear* were being split, and the resulting fragmentation would have profound implications in each context. The kingdom had been divided yet again, and no one attempting to bring the play to the stage could ignore the new lines being drawn on the textual map. After 1681, there were two different versions of the *Lear*, one by Shakespeare, the other by Tate; anyone planning to mount a production of the play either had to choose between them or, subsequently, to choose how to conflate them. History was repeating itself, only now it was a matter of choosing between two Shakespeare plays – the 1608 Quarto and the 1623 Folio – or choosing how to conflate them. The decision that haunted Lear throughout the play seemed to haunt the performance history of the play itself. Or, as Granville-Barker would put things in the newly sophisticated language of textual scholarship, "a producer must ask himself whether these two versions do not come from different prompt-books, and whether the Folio does not, both in cuts and additions, sometimes represent Shakespeare's second thoughts" (25). Such second thoughts, as theorized by textual scholars who influenced Granville-Barker's thinking here, presumed that because the

F1 was printed after Q1, it reflected the play as Shakespeare himself chose to revise it upon seeing the earlier version staged. Regardless of whether this presumption can be substantiated (a topic of intense scholarly debate still) what matters is that Granville-Barker was persuaded that F1 was the superior of the two texts. Accordingly, he recommended that it be the basis of theatrical productions, though he also cautioned that directors should pick and choose readings from Q1 as well.

One of the first people to follow Granville-Barker's advice was Russian theatrical director and designer Theodore Komisarjevsky (1882-1954), who in 1936 staged a widely acclaimed production at the Memorial Theatre in Stratford-upon-Avon. Starring Randall Ayrton in the title role, the text upon which the performance was based suggests that Komisarjevsky rearranged several of the lines of the play and cut many others. As Ralph Berry notes, Komisarjevsky turned Lear's knights into "a Chorus commenting on the futility of the old king's aims. They repeated, in unison, the Fool's songs and sayings" (26). Though Komisarjevsky himself told the press before his first production at the Memorial Theater, "I am not in the least traditional" (27), he was not above relying on recently established traditions. Granville-Barker was clearly the source of one such tradition with regard to what a director could do with the two texts of *Lear*; A.C. Bradley may have been the source of another. Komizarjevski's Stratford production received a great deal of attention for its abstract, geometric set and imaginative use of lighting, and for placing the play altogether outside of time and beyond geography. It was, in other words, the realization of what Bradley had argued some three decades earlier.

In 1940, Granville-Barker would finally have the opportunity, as Wells observes, "to translate his *Preface* into theatrical practice and to show that it was possible to perform an almost complete text [of *Lear*], in Elizabethan costume, with great theatrical success when, in collaboration with Lewis Casson, he directed John Gielgud (1904-2000) as Lear at the Old Vic" (26). Born in the same year that Bradley unchained the play from Stonehenge, Gielgud was only thirty-five when he played the elderly king, and had first performed the role ten years earlier. In 1950, collaborating with the English actor and director, Anthony Quayle (1913-1989), Gielgud directed and starred in a critically acclaimed production of *Lear* at the Memorial Theatre in Stratford. That production, which did much to confirm Gielgud's reputation as one of the great English actors of his generation, also effectively demonstrated that Lamb's oft-cited indictment (that *Lear* "cannot be acted") had reached its statute of limitation. *Lear*'s day on stage had finally arrived, though in fact it had been there all along. Three years later, the English actor/theater manager Michael Redgrave (1908-85) brought another production to the Old Vic with himself in the lead. The influential theater critic Kenneth Tynan (1927-1980) praised Redgrave's performance even as he reminded readers of the play's checkered theatrical past: "Michael Redgrave has played King Lear and won...*Lear* is a labyrinthine citadel, all but impregnable, and it needed a Redgrave to assault it" (27).

"UNFRIENDED, NEW-ADOPTED TO OUR HATE"

Emboldened by the recent successes of Gielgud, Redgrave, Olivier, and others at staging a play that was for so long considered hostile to the theater, an increasing number of directors would try their luck, and some of the great productions of the century would follow soon after. There is tremendous critical consensus that one of the greatest of these productions is the one mounted by Peter Brook in 1962 for the Royal Shakespeare Company, and subsequently directed by him for the 1971 film version. Influenced by Jan Kott's bleak critical interpretation of *Lear*, the plays of Samuel Beckett, and, more generally, the Theatre of the Absurd, Brook declared "he wished to give his audiences 'no aesthetic shelter'. The house-lights were brought up mercilessly as the bleeding, blinded Gloucester crawled slowly off stage, with no help or words of comfort from the indifferent servants" (28). Gone was the Elizabethan costume of Granville-Barker's Old Vic staging, replaced by a cast dressed in furs and leathers, compelled to eke out survival in a primitive world and "gathered in ritualistic ceremony around the King's huge, boulder-like throne." Lear, played by Paul Scofield, "was a dangerous, tough king, with an inscrutable face, close-cropped grey hair and a terrifying voice" (29).

Like Macready more than a century earlier, Brook thrust the play back into the barbaric past, but not for the sake of making the production correspond "with the period, and with the circumstances of the text," as the 1838 staging had sought to do. Rather, Brook had something more contemporary in mind. In keeping with this vision, Brook chose sets that transformed the stage into a kind of stone-age junkyard, full of rusting metal, tattered, worn-out looking costumes, and beat-up furniture. Like the sets, Scofield's Lear wondered the stage, "a character stripped to its muscles and sinews, lacking ornament of any kind," according to Kevin Hagopian. "His world is clearly in austere yet meaningful order. Instantly, with his attempt to divide his kingdom equitably, that order starts to disintegrate. By the end of the play, with Lear descending deeper into emotional and physical disability, Brook's scene design choices, and his understanding of his protagonist, come together in a collision of dread and insight...Surreal, horrifying, deadly, Lear's world dissolves into a fractured series of glimpses of the inferno, splinters of a world gone mad" (30). By the end of that decade Brook would take the cast of the stage production to North Jutland in Denmark to film the play in a cold, winter landscape that was as unaccommodating and abstract as his stage had been. The result, according to Hagopian, was a film "that touched the minor chords of its age. Brook's Lear is the late 1960s everyman, toppled from sanity and sureness by the whirlwind of change" (31).

As was the case with Macready's Lear, which rendered so many of the previous efforts to commingle Shakespeare and Tate's versions obsolete, it can be argued that Brook's RSC production and subsequent film essentially erased the performance history of the play, forcing at least a generation of directors and actors who followed to negotiate with his/Scofield's Lear. One had to emulate it, build on it, or reject it; but there was no ignoring it. Thus Trevor Nunn's 1968 RSC production set the play in an ancient Bronze age kingdom, recalling the primitivism of Brook's set; but Nunn countered his effort to suggest decay perhaps by emphasizing just how far Lear would fall. Eric Porter's white-haired/-bearded king and the other characters appear onstage initially dressed in sumptuous gold robes. This was not Beckett's Lear. When Nunn returned to the play in 1976 to direct an RSC production starring Donald Sinden, the ancient past was gone, replaced by a late nineteenth-century kingdom.

Coming nearly three decades after Brook, perhaps Nicholas Hyntner's 1990 RSC production, with John Wood in the title role, sought in part to wipe the slate clean and restart the play from a vacuum. The minimalist set, consisting of a white open-sided box, "provided a painfully bright, white space for the action, isolating and alienating the characters within" (32). An empty white box brilliantly anticipates the absence that dominates so much of the linguistic, emotional, and spiritual content of the play once Cordelia informs her father that she has "nothing" to say. But might it also suggest the emptiness of a world rapidly becoming virtual—a world in which we, like the king who inadvertently turns his daughter into a prophet by being reduced to nothing, are moving inexorably toward—a divided kingdom consisting of and ruled by nothing more than 0s and 1s? Or should we "look up," as Edgar instructs Lear to do right before he dies? Maybe we should see the open-sided box of Hyntner's production as a space of possibility, an open invitation to re-start the history of *Lear* on stage, thereby doing all we really can do: domesticate the nothingness and the division in all our kingdoms by staging them again and again.

Notes:

1. See C.J. Sisson, "Shakespeare's quartos as prompt-copies, with some account of Cholomey's players, and a new Shakespeare allusion," Review of English Studies 18 (1942): 129-43.

2. From the "Dedicatory Epistle" to *The History of King Lear, Acted at the Duke's Theatre. Reviv'd with Alterations* (London: printed for E. Flesher, 1681)

3. *The Preface to Shakespeare: Together with selected notes on some of the plays* (1765).

4. *Dramatic Miscellanies* (Dublin, 1784), p. 212. Quoted in Barbara Freeman, "Performing the Bodies of King Lear." Studies in Philology (45).

5. Quoted in http://www.rsc.org.uk/lear/about/stage.html

6. *Memoirs of the life of David Garrick, Esq Interspersed with characters and anecdotes of his theatrical contemporaries. The whole forming a history of the stage, which includes a period of thirty-six years* (London, 1784), I: 49-50

7. Quoted in Freeman, "Performing."

8. Quoted in http://www.rsc.org.uk/lear/about/stage.html

10. *King Lear: A Tragedy in Five Acts*, By William Shakespeare, in *Cumberland's British Theatre*, Volume 6 (London: John Cumberland, 1830), p. 8. Quoted in *William Shakespeare's King Lear: A Sourcebook*, ed. Grage Ioppolo (London: Routledge, 2003), p. 78.

12. George C. D. Odell, *Annals of the New York Stage* 10 vols (New York: Columbia University Press, 1927-49), II: 588

13. Raymund FitzSimons, *Edmund Kean: Fire From Heaven* (London: Hamish Hamilton Ltd., 1976), p. 138.

14. James Rees, *The Life of Edwin Forrest. With Reminiscences and Personal Recollections* (Philadelphia: T.B. Peterson & Brothers, 1874), p. 168.

15. F. E. Halliday, *A Shakespeare Companion 1564-1964* (Baltimore, Penguin, 1964), pp. 265-66.

16. William Macready. *The Diaries of William Charles Macready 1833-1851*, ed. William Toynbee, 2 vols. (New York: G.P. Putnum's Sons, 1912), II: 229.

17. Odell, *Annals*, II: 195

18. Odell, *Annals*, II: 210-11

19. Wingate, Charles E.L. Wingate, *Shakespeare's Heroes on the Stage* 2 vols. (New York: Thomas Y. Crowell & Company, 1896), I: 93.

20. *Shakespearean Tragedy* (New York: Meridian Books/St. Martin's Press, 1960), 210.

21. *King Lear, A Tragedy in Five Acts, By William Shakespeare, as arranged for the stage by Henry Irving, and presented at The Lyceum Theatre, On November 10, 1892* (London: Nassau Steam Press, Ltd., 1892), p. 5.

22. Odell, *Annals*, II: 446

23. *Shakespearean Tragedy*, pp. 200, 201.

24. *The Oxford King Lear* (USA: Oxford University Press, 2002), p. 72.

25. *Prefaces to Shakespeare* (London: Sidwick & Jackson, Ltd, 1927), p. 229.

26. "Komisarjevsky at Stratford-upon-Avon," *Shakespeare Survey* 36 (1983): 73-84; p. 79.

27. Quoted in Berry, "Komisarjevsky," p. 73.

28. Wells, *Lear*, p. 73.

30. Quoted in http://www.rsc.org.uk/lear/about/stage.html

31. *Exploring Shakespeare/RSC*:
http://www.rsc.org.uk/explore/kinglear/2817_2814.htm

32. *Exploring Shakespeare/RSC*:
http://www.rsc.org.uk/explore/kinglear/2817_2814.htm

34. *New York Institute: Film Notes – King Lear*: http://www.albany.edu/writers-inst/fns98n11.html

35. *New York Institute: Film Notes – King Lear*: http://www.albany.edu/writers-inst/fns98n11.html

36. *Exploring Shakespeare/RSC*: www.rsc.org.uk/explore/kinglear/2817_2814.htm

As Performed

Bradley D. Ryner

In 2000, Michael Kahn, the Artistic Director of the Shakespeare Theatre Company, directed a production of *King Lear* that was highly original: without reducing the sweeping scope of Shakespeare's play to a domestic tragedy, Kahn placed a believably textured father-daughter relationship at the heart of the production.

Normally, the character of Cordelia is not the most memorable element of *King Lear*. The entire play hinges on her reluctance to speak, meaning she gets relatively few lines before disappearing for the majority of the play. The role was probably written for a third-string boy actor (the company's best two boys would have played Gonoril and Regan). How does one transform a role written for a young actor of modest talents into a more rounded and interesting character? For Kahn, the answer was to cast the deaf actress Monique Holt as a deaf Cordelia, who reads lips and communicates through sign language. In this production, the relationship between Cordelia and Lear was unusually nuanced because Lear's apparently genuine love for his favorite daughter had not extended to learning sign language in order to communicate with her directly.

THE ONSTAGE WORLD OF KAHN'S *Lear*

Because Kahn's production of *King Lear* stressed the significance of Cordelia's non-verbal communication, it seems appropriate to begin by looking at the production's own non-verbal signifying elements, such as setting, props, costumes, and the actors' physical appearances.

The bleak mood of the production was largely informed by Georgi Alexi-Meskhishvili's stage design, which suggested a post-industrial wasteland. The stage was littered with empty oil drums that served as chairs, tables, and hiding places for the characters. A large sheet of metal served as a backdrop, and one could easily imagine that the action was taking place inside a giant, rusty oil drum. The inorganic stage dressing fit with Kahn's idea that the protagonists "were all in purgatory" and must "go through a lot in order to emerge as real people, as humans with real human qualities" (1).

Most of the play's props seemed perfectly at home in this desolate world: a discarded tire in which to bind Gloucester and a leather blindfold to cover his empty eye sockets; wilted flowers for Lear to gather on the heath and a garland of dead weeds for him to wear in his madness. One memorable prop, however, stood out in sharp contrast to its surroundings. In the first act, Lear was presented with a giant, round birthday cake, decorated with a representation of England in lush green and electric blue frosting. It has become conventional to have a map of England onstage for the division of the kingdom scene. Some Lears have judiciously marked boundary lines on the map as they parceled out the land, and then angrily redrawn these boundaries to exclude Cordelia. Other Lears have furiously torn the map in two, flinging half to Gonoril and half to Regan. I found the cake's frosted map particularly effective, in part because it was such an obviously idealized vision of Lear's kingdom. It was very easy to feel sympathy for this childish, shortsighted Lear, who was unaware that by offering his daughters a slice of his fantasy world, he was simultaneously destroying it. Of course, a dream world made of confectioner's sugar and food coloring is ultimately no healthier a delusion than the nightmare world of metal and dead plants in which the protagonists of this production suffered.

The contrast between the starkly horrifying stuff of nightmares and the appealing but tawdry stuff of dreams was similarly evident in the production's costumes (also designed by Alexi-Meskhishvili). The male characters mostly wore vaguely pre-1945 military dress in blacks and grays. Lear and Gloucester both began the play in sleek, black formalwear and ended in tattered earth-toned rags. Gonoril and Regan, on the other hand, wore the garish trappings of 1950's and 1960's high fashion. They appeared mostly in cocktail dresses and high heels, accented with feathers and furs. Even when roused in the middle of the night to deal with Gloucester, Regan had taken the time to throw on an immense fur coat and stylish orange heels—though not the time to remove her beauty mask. Thus, the production established a simple gender division. The male characters were austere, at one with the inorganic, bleak world of the set. The female characters were glamorous, though their theatrical artifice was all too evident.

The Fool and Cordelia, however, failed to conform to this pattern. The Fool's costume was composed of rags and tatters, not unlike those that Lear and Gloucester wore by the end of the play, except that the Fool wore his with panache. Unlike Lear and Gloucester, who were forced to give up the sartorial markings of the conventional social order when they found themselves on the heath, the Fool had constructed himself outside this order from the beginning. He wore a bizarre skullcap with shining protuberances of hair or wire (it was impossible to tell which from a distance) jutting out from its top. The Fool's prosthetic hair seemed to parody Cordelia's actual hair, which was bleached white and spiked up in a punk hairstyle that was at least two decades more modern than the other characters. Her long jacket was

Tara Hicken as Gonoril
Courtesy of the Shakespeare Theatre Company

tailored to intimate the lines of a Jacobean doublet, but belonged to no actual historical period. Visually differentiated from the established order, the Fool and Cordelia were also exceptionally close in this production. Their closeness was underscored by the fact that the Fool, who appeared to be the only member of Lear's court who understood sign language, served as Cordelia's translator, so we heard the majority of her lines in his voice.

Clothes and hair were not the only markers that differentiated Cordelia from her sisters. Whereas Lear, Gonoril, and Regan were played by white actors, Holt was born in South Korea (2). Kahn reportedly wanted Cordelia to look "as if she was from a different family than [her] older avaricious sisters" (2). But how was the audience to know whether to read this difference metaphorically or literally? Should they have interpreted race as a metaphor for the differences in personality and temperament between Cordelia and the rest of her family? Or, should they have imagined that Cordelia was actually the product of a different marriage, or that she was a bastard, like Edmund? Contemplating these questions pulls us from the onstage world to the offstage world—the world of hypothetical narratives and real life biography.

The Offstage World of Kahn's *Lear*

Perhaps it is futile to speculate about what takes place offstage. After all, Cordelia, Lear, and the rest are fictional characters who have no independent lives offstage. When I saw this production, I assumed that Holt's race was being used metaphorically. Doing so seemed simpler than constructing an imaginary narrative that would account for Cordelia's biological difference from her sisters. However, it should be clear from what follows that such imaginary narratives are invaluable to actors, directors, and audience members trying to make sense of plays. Moreover, these imaginary narratives connect in profound ways to people's real life experiences.

In fact, Kahn only arrived at the idea of an imaginary deaf character because of his desire to cast a real-life deaf actor. Mary Vreeland, a deaf actor who had appeared in his production of *Mother Courage*, gave him a list of roles suited to deaf actors that included Cordelia (2). Using Lear's inability to understand sign language as a symbol for his failure to communicate with his daughter seemed perfect. As Kahn explains, "In the play's crucial first scene, people communicate by telling lies or use speech for

Ted van Griethuysen as Lear and Monique Holt as Cordelia
Courtesy of the Shakespeare Theatre Company

power or manipulation…The only daughter who tells the truth is banished. So I thought it might be interesting if indeed it was a person who didn't speak…" (2). Several very effective moments followed from this choice. Lear was able to chillingly silence Cordelia in the first act by grabbing her hands. In Act 4, the King of France's love for Cordelia was demonstrated by the fact that he had learned sign language. Lear himself, upon being reunited with Cordelia, attempted to invent signs by which to communicate with her. Clumsily signing to her, he exclaimed, "Do not laugh at me, / For as I am a man, I think this lady / To be my child, Cordelia" (4.7.66-68). At this point, Cordelia responded in a soft, unsteady voice with the irregular sound that results from not being able to hear one's own pronunciation, "And so, I am, I am" (4.7.68). This moment, in which each character tried to reach out to the other by using the other's mode of expression, was extremely moving.

Significantly, Holt approached Cordelia's deafness literally. As a result, she saw a problem that no one else seemed to notice: "Why would Cordelia sign if there were no one else to sign to?" wondered Holt, who pointed out that, "in real life, [she] would not sign to a non-signer" (3). To deal with this problem, Holt, Kahn, and the other actors created in imaginary backstory in which, "Lear had abandoned his responsibility for Cordelia by hiring teachers to instruct her in sign language, while remaining too distressed by her deafness to learn to sign himself." In this narrative, the Fool had secretly observed her lessons and learned how to communicate with her (Berson 48). Jessica Berson observes that this imaginary story is "a familiar one to those in the Deaf community" because "most hearing parents of deaf children never learn A[merican] S[ign] L[anguage]" (Berson 48). Thus, the imagined backstory, which is connected obliquely to Holt's lived experience, helps to frame the narrative within a set of real-world concerns.

The relationship between fictional and real-life narratives was also important to Ted van Griethuysen, who played Lear. Van Griethuysen is a student of Eli Siegel, whose theory of aesthetic realism involves seeing both the real world and works of art as structured by balanced oppositions (4). In van Griethuysen's words, "Lear is a certain relation of coolness and intensity...so am I. The way I'm cold and warm is different from the way Lear is cold and warm. But the opposites, the coldness and warmth, are universal" (4). To understand Lear's anger toward Cordelia, van Griethuysen remembered a time in his mid-twenties when he felt contempt for his mother. He said that aesthetic realism helped him to realize that this contempt stemmed from a more subtly pervasive contempt for "the whole world that was different from [himself]" (4). Recalling how difficult it was for him to learn to empathize with the outside world in his twenties, van Griethuysen extrapolated how devastating the lesson would have been for Lear in his eighties.

This fluid movement between the play and deeply personal real-world narratives must have been satisfying for Kahn, who staged the production in part because he wanted "to explore the issue of getting older and the issue of families" (1). He said that he was gratified to hear from audience members that the production "helped them understand their aged father, whom they'd just put in a nursing home" (1).

THE WORLD OF THE TEXT

As we have seen above, the director's, designer's, and actors' decisions about casting, characterization, sets, props, and costumes succeeded in creating an onstage world that connected meaningfully to the real lives of its cast and audience members. However, Shakespearean productions cannot generate meaning *ex nihilo*—as Lear knows, "Nothing can come of nothing" (1.1.87). Good productions, like this one, use the text as a framework: it serves a basis on which to build a new structure, but it also places limits on what shape that structure can take.

Obviously, Cordelia's deafness works within the framework of *King Lear* because one of its major thematic concerns is impediments to communication. Making the Fool her translator creates a new relationship between two characters that are never onstage at the same time in the text. Nonetheless, the affinity between the two is established in the text itself. They represent two opposed ways of speaking truth to Lear. Whereas Cordelia is laconic and reluctant to use rhetoric, the Fool employs highly wrought speeches filled with jests and wordplay. Both tell Lear what he does not want to hear, and Lear ignores them both. In the text, Lear's language conflates the two characters when he says of the dead Cordelia, "my poor fool is hanged" (5.3.306). During Shakespeare's time, "fool" was a term of endearment. Kahn's production literalized the association implicit in this line by bringing onstage the body of the Fool, who had apparently been hanged alongside Cordelia.

At one point, the production pushed the framework of the text almost to its breaking point. In the final scene, Lear, imagining that he hears the voice of his dead child, claims, "Her voice was ever soft, / Gentle, and low, an excellent thing in woman" (5.3.273-274). This line raised an unexpected set of questions in the context of Kahn's production. Why would Lear imagine hearing the voice of a daughter who almost never spoke? Moreover, was he imagining the soft, unsure voice that the audience had heard proclaiming "I am" in Act 4, or was he fantasizing about the voice he wished his daughter had? Although the text seemed to be pushing against the production choice at this moment, the resulting tension was highly effective, since it highlighted a tension already present in the text. On one hand, it is satisfying to see Lear, who failed to listen to his daughter early in the play, finally longing to hear her speak. On the other hand, he praises the qualities that diminish the forcefulness of her speech – its softness, gentleness, and lowness. Ultimately, I am forced to wonder if Lear ends by retreating into the same solipsistic fantasy world in which he began. In Kahn's production, these lines were even more troubling. Even if

Ted van Griethuysen as Lear and Monique Holt as Cordelia
Courtesy of the Shakespeare Theatre Company

Lear was not imagining away Cordelia's deafness, he was choosing to praise her vocal expression at the expense of her more fluent use of sign language. Thus, the final tableau felt like a sad falling off from their fourth act reunion. This scene, like the production in general, managed to work within the framework of the text to create a uniquely compelling new narrative.

Notes:

1. Horwitz, Jane. "'Lear' & Dear to the Heart." *The Washington Post* 5 Oct. 99: C05.
2. Kuchwara, Michael. "Playing Cordelia in 'Lear.' *Associated Press* 21 Sep. 1999. *Lexis-Nexis Academic*. 13 Apr. 2007.
3. Berson, Jessica. "Performing Deaf Identity: Toward a Continuum of Deaf Performance." *Bodies in Commotion*. Ed. Carrie Sandahl and Philip Auslander. Ann Arbor: University of Michigan Press, 2005.
4. Triplett, William. "Lear and Present Danger." *The Washington Post* 5 Sep. 99: G01

"Unaccommodated Man"

King Lear IN POPULAR CULTURE

Douglas Lanier, University of New Hampshire

OLD KING LEAR AND YOUTH CULTURE

The Mount Everest of the Shakespearean canon, *King Lear* would seem to offer adaptors a wealth of material with which to work: a plotline which in schematic form resembles a fairy tale of a foolish king; character relationships grounded in archetypal tensions between fathers and children; durable themes such as neglected love, political authoritarianism, downfall and redemption, and the vagaries of cosmic justice; memorable stage images like Lear raging at the storm or carrying his dead daughter; thrilling scenes of battle, madness, intrigue and pathos; and some of Shakespeare's most indelible speeches and lines. Yet, of Shakespeare's five most popular tragedies (*Romeo and Juliet, Hamlet, Othello, King Lear,* and *Macbeth*) *King Lear* has proved the least accommodating to adaptation in modern popular culture, and there are several reasons for this resistance. Contemporary popular culture is predominantly youth-oriented, so Shakespeare's focus on the travails of two old men runs against the prevailing grain. Indeed, the absolute power of Lear and Gloucester as aristocratic fathers and their capacity to tyrannize their children and underlings so completely (at first) is foreign to the fathers typical of current popular culture, whose attempts to exert authority are often portrayed as ineffectual or comic. Lear's ferocious misogyny toward his daughters, however indicative it may be of his complex psychology of infantile projection and child-like rage, makes him strikingly unsympathetic to modern audiences familiar with feminism. And perhaps most importantly, the overwhelming sense of loss and hopelessness that pervades the final scene of this play, Shakespeare's bleakest tragedy, is difficult to square with the predominantly affirmational nature of popular culture, its preference for happy endings or for edifying, reassuring lessons to be drawn from misfortune.

The play's resistance to pop culture conventions, however, has made *King Lear* suitable for avant-garde or confrontational adaptations. Samuel

Beckett's *Endgame* (1957) features myriad echoes of Shakespeare's play, and several commentators have remarked that Peter Brook's bleak film *King Lear* (1971) owes much to Beckett. Howard Barker's *Seven Lears* (1989) offers an unconventional prequel to *King Lear*, tracing Lear's life through the "seven ages of man" and situating Lear's mother at the center of his tormented psychology. Jean-Luc Godard's 1987 adaptation uses the play to meditate on the fate of art in a post-modern world dominated by American culture. In Godard's film, William Shakespeare Jr. the Fifth, a modern reporter, attempts to recover the words of his famous ancestor, lost after a Chernobyl-like disaster, by listening to the Shakespearean exchanges between an American gangster, Don Learo, and his daughter Cordelia. The relationship between politics and brutality is particularly strong in two British theatrical adaptations: Edward Bond's *Lear* (1971), in which Lear's cruel authoritarianism prompts rebellion from two of his daughters only in the end to lead to Cordelia's reestablishment of a tyrannical regime; and Adrian Mitchell's *The Tragedy of King Real* (1982, filmed as *King Real and the Hoodlums* in 1983), a rock musical which converts Shakespeare's tragedy into a nuclear holocaust morality play. Kristian Levring's superb Dogme film *The King is Alive* (2000) also partakes of this adaptational tradition. It offers a savage critique of Western middle-class privilege by portraying the gradual psychological breakdown of a group of tourists stranded in the Namibian desert. To stave off boredom and despair, the group decides to perform scenes from *King Lear* that, ironically, only magnify their escalating antagonisms and madness. Arguably, Ian Pollock's comic book version of *King Lear* (1984) is also affiliated with this avant-garde tradition, for though it uses an uncut version of Shakespeare's text, its expressionist illustrations and barren landscapes are more reminiscent of Beckett and Brook than conventional comic books.

Paul Mazursky's film *Harry and Tonto* (1974) illustrates nicely how adaptors often struggle to resolve the mismatch between Shakespeare's tragedy and the conventions of popular culture. Mazursky's film tells the tale of aging widower Harry Coombes and his cat Tonto who become homeless when Harry's New York apartment is demolished. Stripped of his belongings and acquaintances, Harry journeys to his children's homes and in the process, encounters an American underclass he has never before known. Mazursky pointedly mutes the unsympathetic, irascible qualities of

Shakespeare's father-king. Unlike Lear, Harry is quietly philosophical about his lot, though at the moment of his eviction he angrily launches into Lear's "reason not the need" (2.2.426) and "blow, winds, and crack your cheeks" (3.2.1) speeches. Grafting elements of *King Lear* onto the sixties' road movie, Mazursky's target for critique is the American bourgeois mainstream, exemplified by Harry's dysfunctional children. Like *King Lear*, *Harry and Tonto* ends with a poignant death, that of Harry's beloved pet and traveling companion Tonto, a surrogate for Cordelia and the Fool. However, in keeping with the affirmational tone of popular culture Mazursky softens Shakespeare's tragic ending: Harry will move in with an eccentric cat lady he has just met, perhaps to begin a romance. The film's final tableau shows Harry watching a boy build sand castles on a beach as the sun sets, an image of age and youth in tandem and of fragile renewal for an unfinished life.

GANGSTER EPICS, WESTERNS, AND FAMILY MELODRAMAS

Finding an apt analogy for Shakespeare's tyrannous patriarch-king in the post-dynastic modern world has posed a challenge for popular adaptations of *King Lear*, but the gangster and the Western genres offer solutions. Two recent British gangster films have reimagined Lear as an aging kingpin struggling to maintain his criminal empire. *Shiner* (dir. John Irvin, 2000) uses motifs from *Lear* in its exploration of petty boxing promoter Billy "Shiner" Simpson who, after losing a desperate gamble on a fight, gradually discovers the depths of distrust and fear he has bred among his children and followers. *My Kingdom* (dir. Don Boyd, 2001) is a more thoroughgoing adaptation of Shakespeare's play. In it, Sandeman, an authoritarian Merseyside, England mob boss, becomes consumed with rage, paranoia and revenge when his beloved wife Mandy is killed in a mugging. Disowning his loyal daughter Jo, he falls to the mercy of his daughters Tracy and Kath, both of whom resent their father's tyrannical control and lack of love. Tracy's brutally sadistic husband Jug corresponds to Cornwall, and Kath's son plays the Fool, acting as Sandeman's confidante as he confronts the consequences of his treatment of his daughters. Like *Harry and Tonto*, *My Kingdom* evidences some of pop culture's discomfort with Shakespeare's bleak ending. Though Sandeman sets up an elaborate revenge upon his daughters and survives the final carnage, at film's end, his remaining daughter Jo abandons him on the quayside, suggesting the Pyrrhic nature of his victory.

Because land empires are often at issue, the Western provides adaptations of *King Lear* with an epic scope. Two revisionist Westerns by noted directors, Edward Dmytryk's *Broken Lance* (1954) and Anthony Mann's *The Man from Laramie* (1955), have used elements from Shakespeare's tragedy, the former from the Lear plot (as imagined from the perspective of a faithful son, Cordelia's equivalent), the latter from the Gloucester plot (including his blindness and misplaced trust of his duplicitous child). As might be expected from this masculine genre, Lear's daughters become cattlemen's sons in both films. The TV film *King of Texas* (dir. Uli Edel, 2002) is a close adaptation of *Lear* as a Western. In this version Lear's children remain daughters and Lear dies in the end, cradling his devoted daughter Claudia after she has been shot. Interestingly, the film provides an explanation for Lear's irascible temperament, making him somewhat sympathetic: his emotional hardness

Spencer Tracy as Matt Devereaux in the 1954 film *Broken Lance* directed by Edward Dmytryk
Courtesy of Douglas Lanier

comes from his sacrifices to preserve his ranching empire, struggles which earlier led to the deaths of his wife and only son.

Popular adaptors often jettison the political dimensions of Shakespeare's tragedy, recrafting the narrative as a family melodrama in a range of settings:

- **Randolph Stow's novel To the Islands (1958)** - chronicles the decline of Stephen Heriot, master of a mission station for Aborginals in Northwest Australia
- **Angus Wilson's novel Late Call (1964)** - retired hotel housekeeper Sylvia Calvert is forced to live with her son and retreat into memory
- **David Lowell Rich's Rosie! (1967)** - (from Ruth Gordon's play, *A Very Rich Woman*) a matriarch is nearly driven insane by her money-hungry daughters but is saved by her granddaughter and her lawyer
- **John Boorman's film Where the Heart Is (1990)** - tensions arise between a property developer and children over a building scheduled for demolition; the children and the father become dispossessed and eventually reunite
- **Jon Robin Baitz's play The Substance of Fire (1991)** - a family struggles over the fate of a small publishing house
- **Nagle Jackson's play Taking Leave (2000)** - a Shakespeare professor and his family are forced to confront his descent into Alzheimer's disease

"O, HOW THIS MOTHER SWELLS UP TOWARD MY HEART!": FEMINIST REINTERPRETATIONS

Of these family melodramas, Jane Smiley's distinguished novel *A Thousand Acres* (1991, filmed 1997) is perhaps the best known (it won the Pulitzer Prize for fiction and the National Book Critics Circle Award). As in adaptations to the Western genre, a land empire, here a thousand-acre farm in rural Iowa, is at the heart of this family conflict. Ruled by a bullying patriarch, Larry Cook, the farm remains fertile, but the aquifer underneath the land is contaminated with pesticides and fertilizers, a metaphor for the poisoned feelings that run beneath the Cook family's superficially civil relationships with each other. Though the novel remains faithful to Shakespeare's narrative in its first half, Smiley's adaptation has been controversial for several reasons. First, the story is retold from the perspective of Ginny, the novel's Gonoril figure. Unlike Gonoril's presentation in *King Lear*, Smiley presents Ginny sympathetically; by contrast, the devotion of Caroline (Cordelia) to her father is misguided and condescending to her sisters. Second, Smiley reshapes Ginny's tale into a narrative of feminist awakening and redemption. As events unfold, Ginny comes to resent her father's power over the family and the effects it has wrought on her life. Most controversially, Smiley radically remotivates the antagonism between Gonoril and Lear. In her version, Ginny turns on Larry when repressed memories of Larry's sexual abuse of Ginny and her sister Rose resurface. Though Smiley delineates the tragic ruin of the Cook family and their farming empire, she offers hope amidst the ruin. Like her Shakespearean counterpart, Ginny is tempted to poison her sister but changes her mind in time to save Rose; she also leaves a cold, unfruitful marriage with her good-hearted but ineffectual husband Ty for a menial job, which offers her a measure of independence. Despite these parallels, Smiley publicly distances her work from *King Lear* comparisons.

Nevertheless, Smiley's novel is one of several popular adaptations that have addressed the problematic gender and sexual politics of *King Lear*. Gordon Bottomley's prequel *Lear's Wife* (1915), a Georgian verse drama, provides a proto-feminist critique of Shakespeare's play. Diana Paxson's *The Serpent's Tooth* (1991), a fantasy retelling of the Lear story from the perspective of Cordelia (here Cridilla), reimagines Lear's meek daughter as a warrior princess who returns after being exiled by her father to save and eventually to rule the kingdom. Elaine Feinstein's play *Lear's Daughters* (1987, for the Women's Theatre Group) is more explicitly feminist in its politics, anatomizing the psychologies of Cordelia, Regan, and Gonoril by imagining their family life before Shakespeare's play begins. In Feinstein's version, King Lear is largely an absent father, preoccupied with travel and philandering. After the aloof Queen's death, a nurse who tells the girls fairy stories about mythic fathers fulfills the parental role. An androgynous Fool serves as narrator and sardonic commentator, and the action occurs within a claustrophobic tower that symbolizes the economic privilege and patriarchal mythology shaping the girls' development. In 2000, Toronto's Necessary Angel Theatre (NAT) created *Hysterica*, a free adaptation of *Lear* with matriarch Mama Leda, a Greek businesswoman, as tyrant over her two sons; this adaptation was an offshoot of NAT's several cross-gendered productions of *King Lear*.

Indeed, several companies have experimented with cross-gendered recasting, including *The Lear Project* (1998) for Shakespeare & Co. in Massachusetts and Mabou Mines' *Lear* (1990) in New York City. Taking the prison episode that opens *King Lear* 5.3 as its starting point, Scottish playwright Joan Ure's *Something in it for Cordelia* (1979) recasts Lear and Cordelia as modern shabby aristocrats. The feminist Cordelia convinces her father to give his wealth to charity and take up residence in a Highland retreat, where the two sign autographs and sell produce to tourists. The sexual politics of the play have also been explored in two theatrical adaptations concerned with homosexual themes: Alison Lyssa's *Pinball* (1980, in which a lesbian mother fights for custody of her child) and Reginald Jackson's *House of Lear* (1994, in which Lear is a drag queen dying of AIDS).

Several other popular adaptations warrant mention, if only to suggest the extraordinary ingenuity of the adaptors. One is "Lear the Giant-King" (2000), a game scenario for the Dungeons & Dragons game published by Mike Selinker in *Dungeon Adventures*. (Selinker has also created Shakespeare-themed game scenarios for *Macbeth* and *The Tempest*.) Another is Scot LaHaie's recent *Lear Reloaded* (2007), which crosses *King Lear* with motifs drawn from the film series *The Matrix* (1999-2003). Both of these versions eschew the family melodrama genre, instead treating Shakespeare's narrative in terms of fantasy and science fiction. Though it would seem particularly uncongenial to revise *Lear* as a comedy, parodies have appeared in episodes of *Do Not Adjust Your Set* (1968) and *Saturday Night Live* (1990).

Music has not been an amenable form for adapting *King Lear* either. Despite the nineteenth century vogue for operatic adaptations of Shakespearean tragedies, major composers *bypassed King Lear*, though Hector Berlioz, Mily Balakirev, and Paul Dukas produced overtures based on the play. It was only in the twentieth century that major operas of *Lear* were produced, by Aribert Reimann in 1978, Darijan Bozic in 1986, and Aulis Sallinen in 2000.

"MY TEARS BEGIN TO TAKE HIS PART SO MUCH, / THEY'LL MAR MY COUNTERFEITING": RE-ENACTING *Lear*

Another strategy for adapting *King Lear* has been to explore parallels between actors performing *Lear* and the roles they play. Though this approach has been used for many other Shakespeare plays, particularly the major tragedies, it has been especially prominent for *King Lear* wherein the aging Lear becomes symbolic of the theater, faced as it has been throughout the twentieth century with dispossession by its own upstart children, film and television. Ronald Harwood's acclaimed play *The Dresser* (1980, filmed 1983) illustrates this sub-genre well. It chronicles the last days of Sir, an aging actor-manager struggling through a performance of *King Lear* in wartime Britain, and his faithful dresser Norman, a closeted gay man devoted to Sir's care. Like Lear, Sir has led a self-centered life, ignorant and abusive of those who truly love him. At once powerful and pathetic, self-dramatizing and self-pitying, he has become with age half-mad, half-senile as he faces death and cultural obsolescence, sustained by Norman who, unlike Lear's Fool, faithfully maintains Sir's illusions about himself. Tragedy comes when, after Sir's performance, he falls dead and Norman learns that Sir has said nothing about him in his unfinished memoir. Norman's final howl "What about me?" pathetically echoes that of Lear with the dead Cordelia, but it also voices the demands of modernity in the face of a tyrannical, outmoded cultural institution. Reportedly, Harwood modeled "Sir" on Donald Wolfit, a noted Shakespearean for whom he served as dresser. Other adaptations concerning theatrical institutions include:

• **Hy Kraft's Café Crown (1942)** - set in the Lower East Side's once-thriving Yiddish theater district, a flamboyant director hopes to improve *Lear* by giving Shakespeare's protagonist a wife and palatial apartment
• **Desmond Rayner's novel The Dawlish Season (1984)** - examines parallels between family production of *King Lear* and tensions in the Dawlish family
• **Marc van der Velden's children's play Cordelia (1996)** - imagines that Cordelia takes on the Fool's role in disguise after he had died
• **James Patrick Kelly's story "Itsy Bitsy Spider" (1997)** - portrays the performance of a scene from *Lear* between an aging Shakespearean and an android replacement for his deceased daughter
• **Fred Curchack and Shannon Kearns's multimedia play Lear's Shadow (2000)** - an aging actor becomes unhinged by memories of his dead lover as he watches a videotape of himself auditioning for *Lear*

• **Season 3 of the Canadian TV series Slings and Arrows (2006)** - chronicles the struggles of the resident company of the New Burbage Festival to perform *Lear*, with parallels between characters and actors

"THOU BEACON TO THIS UNDER GLOBE": CROSS-CULTURAL ADAPTATIONS OF *King Lear*

In contrast to *Lear*'s somewhat anemic afterlife in modern Anglo-American popular culture, *Lear* has been one of the favorite Shakespearean plays to adapt in several non-English speaking cultures, particularly in those where traditions of reverence and respect toward the elderly remain strong. For example, Yiddish adaptations of *King Lear*, particularly Jacob Gordin's *Der Yiddisher Koenig Lear* [*The Yiddish King Lear*, 1892] and *Mirele Efros* [*The Yiddish Queen Lear*, 1898], enjoyed considerable popularity, enough so that Harry Thomashefsky produced a film version of *The Yiddish King Lear* in 1935. Vestigial memory of that tradition lives on in popular culture, not only in Julia Pascal's play *The Yiddish Queen Lear* (1999, which portrays the efforts of a Jewish actress to establish a Yiddish theater in New York and the machinations of her daughters to depose her) but also in "Guess Who's Coming to Criticize Dinner" (1999), an episode of *The Simpsons* in which Krusty the Clown, the show's resident Jewish comic, performs his version of *King Lear* at a dinner theater. *The Kathakali King Lear* (1990), a multinational production by Annette Leday, David McRuvie, Kalamandalam Padmanabhan Nair, and K. Kumaran Nairthe, hybridized Shakespeare's tragedy with Kathakali, the traditional Southern Indian dance-drama form. This production was performed in the new Globe Theatre in London in its opening season in 1999. It might be fruitfully compared to the adaptation of Hindi director Amal Allana, *Maharaja Yashwant Rao* (1989), which reconceives Lear as an arrogant Rajput prince.

East Asian adaptations of *King Lear* have been equally robust. The affinities between Asian theatrical traditions and *King Lear* have long been recognized. John Gielgud's 1955 production of the play at Stratford-upon-Avon, for example, visually referenced the iconography of traditional Japanese Kabuki theater. When Singaporean director Ong Keng Sen wanted to create a pan-Asian play for the Perth Festival in 1997, he turned to *King Lear* because he regarded it as a fable of "universal significance" equally relevant to the six cultures he referenced. The result was *Lear*, a work in which Shakespeare's characters were inflected not only through traditional archetypes of Asian theater (e.g., the Old Man of Japanese Noh Theater, the Young Daughter of Thai dance-theater, and the older daughter of Chinese opera) but also through cultural stereotypes of modern Asia, such as the Fool, a girl in a jogging suit carrying a camera. Sen uses *King Lear* to provide not only an example of Asian interculturalism but also a portrait of

Kalamandalam Padmanabhan Nair as Lear, Kalamandalam MPS Namboodiri as Gonoril, and Kalamandalam Manoj Kumar as the Fool in "The Kathakali King Lear"
Photo: Donald Cooper

Asian conflicts between traditionalism and modernity. Several recent productions have offered imaginative transpositions of *King Lear* into Chinese operatic styles: Wang Lian and Wang Yongshi's *King Qi's Dream* (1995); Wu Hsing-kuo's tour-de-force one-man show *King Lear* (2000, a.k.a. *Lear Alone*), produced for the Contemporary Legend Theater; and Lu Jiang's *King Liguang* (dir. Yu Shengpu, 2002).

KOZINTSEV'S *Koral Lir* AND KUROSAWA'S *Ran*

Two non-English film adaptations of *King Lear*, Grigori Kozintsev's Russian adaptation *Korol Lir* (1969) and Akira Kurosawa's Japanese adaptation *Ran* ([*Chaos*], 1985), have been widely regarded as masterpieces of the cinematic adaptation of Shakespeare. Using Boris Pasternak's translation, Kozintsev favors a faithful period production of Shakespeare's tragedy, which stresses the play's political themes. Even so, the film reflects Russian cultural traditions in several respects: the yawning gap between the extravagance and heartlessness of the aristocrats and the abject poverty of the homeless peasants accords with Soviet critiques of bourgeois decadence, (and covertly critiques the corruption of the Soviet regime itself); the eccentricity and eerie appearance of Lear's Fool is reminiscent of the Russian artistic tradition of the *yurodivy*, the holy fool, a link also indicated by the predominance of Christian imagery throughout the film; and the pervasive fatalism of the film seems distinctively Slavic in its outlook.

In *Ran*, Kurosawa transposes *Lear*'s action to feudal Japan, where warlord Hidetora Ichimonji resolves to cede his royal authority to his eldest son Taro and divide his kingdom among his two younger sons, Jiro and Saburo, punctuating his decision with a parable of three arrows taken from Japanese medieval legend. When Saburo warns his father of his folly, Hidetora exiles him along with his own loyal servant Tango, setting in motion the patriarch's precipitous downfall. Rather than muting Shakespeare's misogyny, Kurosawa amplifies it, making Taro's scheming wife, the terrifyingly ruthless Lady Kaede, a catalyst for the betrayals by Hidetora's sons; Kyoami, Hidetora's Fool, is pointedly androgynous, neither fully male nor female. The film is renowned for its exceptional scenic beauty, particularly in the opening boar hunt and in the extraordinarily lavish battle scenes. Yet for its debt to samurai epics and Kabuki theater, *Ran* also weds *King Lear* to Buddhist philosophy, emphasizing the essential transience and precariousness of human existence, a point made visually by repeated shots of clouds passing in the sky. It is one of the few popular adaptations to engage the metaphysical questions so powerfully raised by Shakespeare's tragedy, questions articulated directly by Kyoami and Hideotara as they wander the landscape. The film ends with an unforgettable image: Tsurumaru, a man who Hidetora blinded and exiled as a child, awaits the arrival of his sister

Tatsuya Nakadai as Lord Hidetora Ichimonji and Shinnosuke "Peter" Ikehata as Kyoami in the 1985 film *Ran* directed by Akira Kurosawa
Courtesy of Douglas Lanier

Lady Sué, unaware that she has been killed. Edging toward a precipice without a guide, he stumbles on the brink, dropping a Buddhist scroll meant to protect and comfort him. As the sun sets behind him, Tsurumaru stands alone, his arms outstretched into the void, motionless lest he fall, a bleak yet beautiful metaphor for humankind's mortal circumstance. Kozintsev's and Kurosawa's films of *King Lear* point to the continuing vitality of Shakespeare's tragedy, the play's stature outside of Anglo-American popular culture as one of the great cross-cultural fables of the world.

Dramatis Personae

KING LEAR, King of Britain

GONORIL, Lear's eldest daughter
DUKE OF ALBANY, husband to Gonoril

REGAN, Lear's second daughter
DUKE OF CORNWALL, husband to Regan

CORDELIA, Lear's youngest daughter
KING OF FRANCE, suitor to Cordelia, later her husband
DUKE OF BURGUNDY, suitor to Cordelia

FOOL, servant to Lear

EARL OF KENT

EARL OF GLOUCESTER

EDGAR, son to Gloucester
EDMUND, bastard son to Gloucester

CURAN, a courtier

OSWALD, steward to Gonoril

OLD MAN, tenant to Gloucester

DOCTOR

CAPTAIN, employed by Edmund

GENTLEMAN, attendant on Cordelia

HERALD

SERVANTS TO CORNWALL

KNIGHTS OF LEAR'S TRAIN, Gentlemen, Officers, Messengers,
Soldiers, and Attendants

[King Lear

Act 1

0: Location: King Lear's Palace

0: Scene: In the production starring Laurence Olivier (1984), the set resembled Stone-henge. The set of Director Robin Philips's *King Lear* (Stratford, Ontario, 1979) was Victorian and the acting, prosaic. King Lear did not descend from a high throne to unfurl a ceremonial map; instead, Peter Ustinov begins by signing and stamping an order, as if he were a midlevel clerk in an import/export firm.

1: **more affected**: preferred

4: **equalities**: the division of the kingdom based on worth (perhaps connected to "equity")

6: **moiety**: portion

8: **breeding**: fathered; **charge**: expense, and perhaps a bawdy joke—the *dis*charge of semen

9: **brazed**: brazen, without shame

10: **conceive**: understand

12: **ere**: before

14: **issue**: 1) offspring, and 2) result; **proper**: upstanding, well-made

15: **a son by order of law**: a legitimate son, born within wedlock

16: **in my account**: in my eyes

17: **knave**: endearing term, akin to "rascal"; **something saucily**: under impolite circumstances, a reference to Edmund's bastardy

Act 1, Scene 1]

Enter [the Earl of] KENT, [the Earl of] GLOUCESTER,
and Bastard [EDMUND]

KENT

I thought the King had more affected the Duke of Albany than
Cornwall.

GLOUCESTER

It did always seem so to us but now in the division of the kingdoms
it appears not which of the Dukes he values most; for equalities are
so weighed, that curiosity in neither can make choice of either's   5
moiety.

KENT

Is not this your son, my lord?

GLOUCESTER

His breeding, sir, hath been at my charge. I have so often blushed
to acknowledge him that now I am brazed to it.

KENT

I cannot conceive you.   10

GLOUCESTER

Sir, this young fellow's mother could, whereupon she grew round-
wombed and had indeed, sir, a son for her cradle ere she had a
husband for her bed. Do you smell a fault?

KENT

I cannot wish the fault undone, the issue of it being so proper.

GLOUCESTER

But I have, sir, a son by order of law, some year elder than this,   15
who yet is no dearer in my account. Though this knave came
something saucily into the world before he was sent for, yet was

18: **fair**: attractive

19: **whoreson**: i.e., whore's son (bastard); used here affectionately, as in "knave"

24: **services**: duty

25: **sue**: beg your permission

26: **study deserving**: strive to merit

Set design for the 1959 production at the Shakespeare Memorial Theatre in Stratford-upon-Avon directed by Glen Byam Shaw

Rare Book and Special Collection Library, University of Illinois at Urbana-Champaign

29: **Attend**: accompany

31: **we**: i.e., the Royal "we", the King speaking on behalf of himself and his people; **darker**: secret, gloomy

33: **first**: primarily; the Folio prints "fast", meaning firm or resolute

his mother fair, there was good sport at his making, and the whoreson must be acknowledged. [*To EDMUND*] Do you know this noble gentleman, Edmund?   20

EDMUND
  No, my lord.

GLOUCESTER
  [*To EDMUND*] My Lord of Kent. Remember him hereafter as my honorable friend.

EDMUND
  [*To KENT*] My services to your lordship.

KENT
  I must love you, and sue to know you better.   25

EDMUND
  Sir, I shall study deserving.

GLOUCESTER
  [*To KENT*] He hath been out nine years, and away he shall again.
                                          Sound a sennet
  The King is coming.
                  *Enter one bearing a coronet, then [King] LEAR,
                  then the Dukes of ALBANY and CORNWALL; next
                  GONORIL, REGAN, CORDELIA, with followers*

LEAR
  Attend my lords of France and Burgundy, Gloucester.

GLOUCESTER
  I shall, my liege.   30
                                                              [Exit]

LEAR
  Meantime we will express our darker purposes.
  Give me the map there. Know that we have divided
  In three our kingdom, and 'tis our first intent

tracks 2–4

44–106
*Trevor Peacock as Lear, Penny Downie as Gonoril, Julia Ford as Cordelia
and Samantha Bond as Regan
Paul Scofield as Lear, Harriet Walter as Gonoril, Emilia Fox as Cordelia,
and Sara Kestelman as Regan*

34: Scene: **age**: John Philip Kemble (1757-1823), while initially favoring athleticism, eventually played Lear as aged and infirm; Henry Irving's Lear (1838-1905) played the King as "a scared, eccentric, lunatic shamble." In his book *On Acting* (1983), Laurence Olivier wrote: "Lear is easy. He's like all of us, really: he's just a stupid old fart."

35-40: **while we…now**: from the First Folio

36: **son**: i.e., son-in-law

38: **constant**: unwavering or long-planned

39: **several**: respective

3: **amorous sojourn**: courtship

45-46: **Since now…state**: from the First Folio

46: **Interest of**: management of

48-49: **doth with merit challenge**: rewards according to merit

56: **makes breath poor**: is dearer than life, outpaces expression

60-61: **champaigns riched…meads**: large tracts of rich, fertile land

62: **issue**: i.e., children (see line 14)

To shake all cares and business off our state,
Confirming them on younger years, while we   35
Unburdened crawl toward death. Our son of Cornwall,
And you, our no less loving son of Albany,
We have this hour a constant will to publish
Our daughters' several dowers, that future strife
May be prevented now. The two great princes,   40
France and Burgundy—
Great rivals in our youngest daughter's love—
Long in our court have made their amorous sojourn,
And here are to be answered. Tell me, my daughters,
Since now we will divest us both of rule,   45
Interest of territory, cares of state—
Which of you shall we say doth love us most,
That we our largest bounty may extend
Where merit doth most challenge it?
Gonoril, our eldest born, speak first.   50

GONORIL

Sir, I do love you more than words can wield the matter;
Dearer than eyesight, space, or liberty;
Beyond what can be valued, rich or rare;
No less than life; with grace, health, beauty, honor;
As much as child e'er loved, or father, friend;   55
A love that makes breath poor and speech unable.
Beyond all manner of so much I love you.

CORDELIA

[*Aside*] What shall Cordelia do? Love and be silent.

LEAR

[*To GONORIL*] Of all these bounds even from this line to this,
With shady forests and with champaigns riched,   60
With plenteous rivers and wide-skirted meads,
We make thee lady. To thine and Albany's issue
Be this perpetual.—What says our second daughter?
Our dearest Regan, wife to Cornwall, speak.

tracks 2–4

44–106
Trevor Peacock as Lear, Penny Downie as Gonoril, Julia Ford as Cordelia and Samantha Bond as Regan
Paul Scofield as Lear, Harriet Walter as Gonoril, Emilia Fox as Cordelia and Sara Kestelman as Regan

66: **mettle**: disposition
71: **square**: measure
72: **felicitate**: made happy (from "felicity")

73: Scene: **poor Cordelia**: In Kozintsev's 1969 film, Valentina Shendrikova's Cordelia is first seen quietly playing guitar. Granville-Barker (1877-1946) suggested one of two possibilities: that Cordelia is taken utterly by surprise when hearing Lear's plan to divide the kingdom and is thus choked into silence; or, that her failure to respond is the result of hours of deliberation.

76-77: "To thee and thine...our fair kingdom": the Ensemble in the 2000 Shakespeare Theatre Company production directed by Michael Kahn
Photo: Carol Rosegg

80-82: **to whose...interested**: from the First Folio
81: **vines**: vineyards; **milk**: fertility, hence, fertile lands
85-86: **Nothing? / Nothing.**: from the First Folio

REGAN
  Sir, I am made   65
  Of the self-same mettle that my sister is,
  And prize me at her worth. In my true heart
  I find she names my very deed of love—
  Only she came short, that I profess
  Myself an enemy to all other joys   70
  Which the most precious square of sense possesses,
  And find I am alone felicitate
  In your dear Highness' love.

CORDELIA
                        [*Aside*] Then poor Cordelia—
  And yet not so, since I am sure my love's
  More richer than my tongue.   75

LEAR
  [*To REGAN*] To thee and thine hereditary ever
  Remain this ample third of our fair kingdom,
  No less in space, validity, and pleasure
  Than that confirmed on Gonoril. [*To CORDELIA*] But now our joy,
  Although the last, not least in our dear love, to whose young love   80
  The vines of France and milk of Burgundy
  Strive to be interested; what can you say to win
  A third more opulent than your sisters? Speak.

CORDELIA
  Nothing, my lord.

KING LEAR
  Nothing?   85

CORDELIA
  Nothing.

KING LEAR
  How? Nothing can come of nothing. Speak again.

44–106
Trevor Peacock as Lear, Penny Downie as Gonoril, Julia Ford as Cordelia and Samantha Bond as Regan
Paul Scofield as Lear, Harriet Walter as Gonoril, Emilia Fox as Cordelia and Sara Kestelman as Regan

90: **bond**: natural obligation, duty

Ian McKellen as Lear, Romola Garai as Cordelia, and the Ensemble in the 2007 Royal Shakespeare Company production directed by Trevor Nunn
Photo: Donald Cooper

93: **bred me**: raised me
94: **fit**: appropriate
97: **Haply**: perhaps
98: **plight**: pledge of marriage

102-118: Scene: **But...sometime daughter**: In Peter Brook's 1971 film, Paul Scofield "chewed on his bitterness, ground out his plans with methodical anger"; William C. Macready (1773-1873) hurried on to other matters; Sir Lawrence Olivier (1907-1989) flung his crown to the ground in rage. The Italian actor Tommaso Salvini (1829-1915) drew Cordelia aside with great warmth and intimacy; the American actor, Edwin Forrest (1806-1872), feebly walked to Cordelia and caressed her, begging her to reconsider.

106: **dower**: a traditional gift given by the father of the bride (from "dowry")
108: **mysteries**: sacred rituals; **Hecate**: goddess of witches and the underworld; also mentioned in *Macbeth*: "Pale Hecate's offerings" (2.1.53)
109: **operation of the orbs**: influence of the planets and stars

CORDELIA

    Unhappy that I am, I cannot heave
    My heart into my mouth. I love your Majesty
    According to my bond, nor more nor less.   90

KING LEAR

    Go to, go to, mend your speech a little
    Lest it may mar your fortunes.

CORDELIA

                         Good my lord,
    You have begot me, bred me, loved me.
    I return those duties back as are right fit—
    Obey you, love you, and most honor you.   95
    Why have my sisters husbands if they say
    They love you all? Haply when I shall wed
    That lord whose hand must take my plight shall carry
    Half my love with him, half my care and duty.
    Sure, I shall never marry like my sisters,   100
    To love my father all.

LEAR

    But goes this with thy heart?

CORDELIA

    Ay, good my lord.

LEAR

    So young and so untender?

CORDELIA

    So young, my lord, and true.   105

LEAR

    Well, let it be so. Thy truth then be thy dower;
    For by the sacred radiance of the sun,
    The mysteries of Hecate and the night,
    By all the operation of the orbs
    From whom we do exist and cease to be,   110

111: "Here I disclaim all my paternal care": Kevin Kline as Lear, Kristen Bush as Cordelia, and the Ensemble in the 2007 Public Theater production directed by James Lapine

Photo: Michal Daniel

112: **Propinquity**: blood ties

114: **Scythian**: The Scythians were horse-riding nomads who inhabited Eurasia between the eighth century BCE and the second century CE. The reference here implies an uncivilized person.

115: **makes his generation messes**: i.e., makes his own children into food (messes) to be eaten; used similarly in *Othello*: "I will chop her into messes. Cuckold me!"(4.1.201)

118: **sometime daughter**: former daughter

119: **dragon**: a traditional sign, along with the lion, of kingship; a symbol of power

120: **set my rest**: rely on completely; the phrase comes from playing cards and refers to betting everything

121: **nursery**: care

123: **France**: i.e., the King of France; **Burgundy**: i.e., the Duke of Burgundy

126: **plainness**: the quality of being plain spoken or frank

128: **large effects**: outward signs

130: **With reservation**: reserving the right to be accompanied by

136: **crownet**: coronet (the Crown), which represents Cordelia's dowry

136–176

Anton Lesser as Kent and Trevor Peacock as Lear
David Burke as Kent and Paul Scofield as Lear

tracks 5-7

Here I disclaim all my paternal care,
Propinquity, and property of blood,
And as a stranger to my heart and me
Hold thee from this for ever. The barbarous Scythian,
Or he that makes his generation messes   115
To gorge his appetite, shall to my bosom
Be as well neighbored, pitied, and relieved
As thou, my sometime daughter.

KENT

                    Good my liege—

LEAR

Peace, Kent. Come not between the dragon and his wrath.
I loved her most, and thought to set my rest   120
On her kind nursery. [*To CORDELIA*] Hence, and avoid my sight!—
So be my grave my peace as here I give
Her father's heart from her. Call France. Who stirs?
Call Burgundy.
                              [Exit one or more]
                Cornwall and Albany,
With my two daughters' dowers digest this third.   125
Let pride, which she calls plainness, marry her.
I do invest you jointly in my power,
Pre-eminence, and all the large effects
That troop with majesty. Ourself by monthly course,
With reservation of an hundred knights   130
By you to be sustained, shall our abode
Make with you by due turns. Only we still retain
The name and all the additions to a king.
The sway, revenue, execution of the rest,
Beloved sons, be yours, which to confirm,   135
This crownet part betwixt you.

KENT

                    Royal Lear,
Whom I have ever honored as my king,
Loved as my father, as my master followed,
As my great patron thought on in my prayers—

tracks 5-7

136–176
Anton Lesser as Kent and Trevor Peacock as Lear
David Burke as Kent and Paul Scofield as Lear

Costume rendering for Lear by Susan Tsu from the 2004 Oregon Shakespeare Festival production directed by James Edmondson

Courtesy of the Oregon Shakespeare Festival

140: **bow is bent and drawn**: plan is already underway; **make from**: move out of the way of

141: **fall**: hit; **fork**: two-pronged head of an arrow

142: **unmannerly**: impolite, forthright

143: **mad**: unreasonable, angry

147: **in...consideration**: with much thought; **check**: hold back

150: **empty-hearted**: with empty or hollow words

151: **Reverbs no hollowness**: reverberates or echoes like something hollow; thus insincerely

152: **pawn**: worthless piece, to be used as the player (i.e., King Lear) decides

153: **wage**: wager, risk in battle

156: **blank**: white circle at the center of a target; **Apollo**: the ancient Greek and Roman god of light, healing, music, poetry, prophecy

158: **Vassal**: wretch; **recreant**: traitor

158: **Vassal, recreant!**: appears only in the First Quarto

LEAR

   The bow is bent and drawn; make from the shaft.   140

KENT

   Let it fall rather, though the fork invade
   The region of my heart. Be Kent unmannerly
   When Lear is mad. What wilt thou do, old man?
   Think'st thou that duty shall have dread to speak
   When power to flattery bows? To plainness honor's bound   145
   When majesty stoops to folly. Reverse thy doom,
   And in thy best consideration check
   This hideous rashness. Answer my life my judgment,
   Thy youngest daughter does not love thee least,
   Nor are those empty-hearted whose low sound   150
   Reverbs no hollowness.

LEAR

                  Kent, on thy life, no more!

KENT

   My life I never held but as a pawn
   To wage against thy enemies, nor fear to lose it,
   Thy safety being the motive.

LEAR

                  Out of my sight!

KENT

   See better, Lear, and let me still remain   155
   The true blank of thine eye.

LEAR

                  Now, by Apollo—

KENT

   Now, by Apollo, King, thou swear'st thy gods in vain.

LEAR [*Making to strike him*]

   Vassal, recreant!

tracks 5-7

136–176
Anton Lesser as Kent and Trevor Peacock as Lear
David Burke as Kent and Paul Scofield as Lear

158: **Dear sir, forbear**: from the First Folio

158-159: **kill thy physician...foul disease**: akin to "don't blame the doctor for diagnosing the illness from which you suffer"

160: **vent clamor**: cry out

165: **Our sentence**: i.e., the sentence passed down by a judge

172: **trunk**: body

173: **By Jupiter**: an oath, as in "By heaven and earth I swear"; Jupiter is the King of the gods

174: **This shall not be revoked**: Lear's threat is ironic because Jupiter is known, in Roman mythology, for changing his mind often.

175: **since**: if

176: Scene: **banishment is here**: When Sir John Gielgud (1904-2000) played Lear, Kent kissed the King's sword before taking his leave. Carnovsky's Lear (American Shakespeare Festival, 1965) was so upset by Kent's departure that he threw down his sword, but in Peter Brook's 1971 film, Paul Scofield's Lear "ground crisply on, seemingly as tough as ever."

177: **protection**: shelter

179: **large**: unrestrained; **approve**: confirm

ALBANY *and* CORDELIA
> Dear sir, forbear.

KENT
>   [*To LEAR*] Do, kill thy physician,
> And the fee bestow upon the foul disease.
> Revoke thy doom, or whilst I can vent clamor   160
> From my throat I'll tell thee thou dost evil.

LEAR
> Hear me, recreant; on thine allegiance hear me!
> Since thou hast sought to make us break our vow,
> Which we durst never yet, and with strayed pride
> To come between our sentence and our power,   165
> Which nor our nature nor our place can bear,
> Our potency made good take thy reward.
> Four days we do allot thee for provision
> To shield thee from diseases of the world,
> And on the fifth to turn thy hated back   170
> Upon our kingdom. If on the next day following
> Thy banished trunk be found in our dominions,
> The moment is thy death. Away! By Jupiter,
> This shall not be revoked.

KENT
> Why, fare thee well, King; since thus thou wilt appear,   175
> Friendship lives hence, and banishment is here.
> [*To CORDELIA*] The gods to their dear protection take thee, maid,
> That rightly thinks, and hast most justly said.
> [*To GONORIL and REGAN*] And your large speeches may your deeds
>   approve,
> That good effects may spring from words of love.   180
> Thus Kent, O princes, bids you all adieu;
> He'll shape his old course in a country new.
>   *[Exit]*
>   *Enter the [the King of] FRANCE and [the Duke of]*
>   *BURGUNDY, with GLOUCESTER*

GLOUCESTER
> Here's France and Burgundy, my noble lord.

185: **address**: address ourselves, here used in the plural form to denote Lear's status as king
186: **rivaled**: competed
187: **in present**: immediate

Costume rendering for Lear from the 1959 production at the Shakespeare Memorial Theatre in Stratford-upon-Avon directed by Glen Byam Shaw
Rare Book and Special Collection Library, University of Illinois at Urbana-Champaign

193: **little-seeming substance**: implying that Cordelia is not what she seems; **aught**: anything
194: **pieced**: added on
195: **fitly like**: properly please
197: **infirmities**: corrupt qualities
199: **strangered with**: isolated from us by
201: **Election...conditions**: i.e., No other choice is possible given the circumstances.
203: **great King**: in reference to the King of France
204: **make such a stray**: go so far away
205: **beseech**: I beseech

LEAR

My Lord of Burgundy,
We first address towards you, who with a king   185
Hath rivaled for our daughter. What in the least
Will you require in present dower with her
Or cease your quest of love?

BURGUNDY

                Most Royal Majesty,
I crave no more than what your Highness offered;
Nor will you tender less.

LEAR

              Right noble Burgundy,   190
When she was dear to us we did hold her so;
But now her price is fallen. Sir, there she stands.
If aught within that little-seeming substance,
Or all of it, with our displeasure pieced,
And nothing else, may fitly like your grace,   195
She's there, and she is yours.

BURGUNDY

              I know no answer.

LEAR

Sir, will you with those infirmities she owes,
Unfriended, new-adopted to our hate,
Covered with our curse and strangered with our oath,
Take her or leave her?

BURGUNDY

            Pardon me, royal sir.   200
Election makes not up on such conditions.

LEAR

Then leave her, sir; for by the power that made me,
I tell you all her wealth. [*To FRANCE*] For you, great King,
I would not from your love make such a stray
To match you where I hate, therefore beseech you   205

206: **avert your liking**: turn your love

209: **strange**: odd

210: **best object**: favorite; **argument**: central focus

211: **balm**: comfort

212: **trice**: instant

214: **folds**: levels, depth

216: **monsters it**: makes it monstrous; **fore-vouched**: previously affirmed

221: **want**: lack; **glib and oily**: smooth, insincere

222: **purpose not**: have no intention of doing

223: **acknow**: acknowledge

224: **blot**: stain

228: **still-soliciting**: always begging

231: "Better thou hadst not been born than not to have pleased me better":
Ian McKellen as Lear, Romola Garai as Cordelia, and Peter Hinton as Burgundy in
the 2007 Royal Shakespeare Company production directed by Trevor Nunn
Photo: Donald Cooper

230: **Go to, go to.**: from the First Folio

232: **tardiness**: reluctance to speak

233: **That**: what

To avert your liking a more worthier way
Than on a wretch whom nature is ashamed
Almost to acknowledge hers.

FRANCE
This is most strange, that she that even but now
Was your best object, the argument of your praise,   210
Balm of your age, most best, most dearest,
Should in this trice of time commit a thing
So monstrous to dismantle
So many folds of favor. Sure, her offense
Must be of such unnatural degree   215
That monsters it, or your fore-vouched affections
Fall'n into taint; which to believe of her,
Must be a faith that reason without miracle
Could never plant in me.

CORDELIA
[*To LEAR*] I yet beseech your Majesty,   220
If for I want that glib and oily art
To speak and purpose not—since what I well intend,
I'll do't before I speak—that you acknow
It is no vicious blot, murder, or foulness,
No unclean action or dishonored step   225
That hath deprived me of your grace and favor,
But even the want of that for which I am rich—
A still-soliciting eye, and such a tongue
As I am glad I have not, though not to have it
Hath lost me in your liking.

LEAR
                            Go to, go to.   230
Better thou hadst not been born than not to have pleased me better.

FRANCE
Is it no more but this—a tardiness in nature,
That often leaves the history unspoke
That it intends to do?—My Lord of Burgundy,
What say you to the lady? Love is not love   235

237: **have her**: marry her

Costume rendering for Burgundy by Susan Tsu from the 2004 Oregon Shakespeare
Festival production directed by James Edmondson

Courtesy of the Oregon Shakespeare Festival

241: **Nothing**: recalling Cordelia's remarks at 1.1.84 and 1.1.86
241: **I am firm.**: from the First Folio
251: **inflamed respect**: feverish love
254: **wat'rish**: irrigated by rivers, but also lacking strength, as in "watered down"
256: **though unkind**: though they have not acted like a family

When it is mingled with respects that stands
Aloof from the entire point. Will you have her?
She is herself a dower.

BURGUNDY

Royal Lear,
Give but that portion which yourself proposed,
And here I take Cordelia by the hand,   240
Duchess of Burgundy—

LEAR

Nothing. I have sworn. I am firm.

BURGUNDY

[*To CORDELIA*] I am sorry, then, you have so lost a father
That you must lose a husband.

CORDELIA

Peace be with Burgundy; since that respects
Of fortune are his love, I shall not be his wife.   245

FRANCE

Fairest Cordelia, that art most rich, being poor;
Most choice, forsaken; and most loved, despised.
Thee and thy virtues here I seize upon.
Be it lawful, I take up what's cast away.
Gods, gods! 'Tis strange that from their cold'st neglect   250
My love should kindle to inflamed respect.—
Thy dowerless daughter, King, thrown to my chance,
Is queen of us, of ours, and our fair France.
Not all the dukes in wat'rish Burgundy
Shall buy this unprized precious maid of me.—   255
Bid them farewell, Cordelia, though unkind.
Thou losest here, a better where to find.

LEAR

Thou hast her, France. Let her be thine, for we
Have no such daughter, nor shall ever see
That face of hers again. Therefore be gone,   260

261: **benison**: blessing

"King Lear: Cordelia's Farewell"
Painting by Edwin Austin Abbey, 1898

263: **jewels**: tears; **washed**: tearful
266: **as they are named**: for what they really are
267: **professèd bosoms**: public assertions of love
274: **Fortune**: the goddess of luck, mentioned in *Hamlet*: "In the secret parts of Fortune? O, most true—she is a strumpet" (2.2.224). See also 2.1.39, 2.2.155-56, 4.6.211, 5.3.6 and 5.3.173; **scanted**: neglected
275: **well...wanted**: rightly deserve to be treated the way you have treated others
276: **unfold**: bring to light; **pleated**: folded, hidden

279-299: Scene: **Sister...i' th' heat**: The least compassionate rendering of these sisters is found in the Orson Welles film (dir. Peter Brook, CBS-TV, 1953), which cut Gonoril and Regan's discussion about Lear's growing unruliness and their own need to defend themselves. As a result, their actions seemed far more malicious, if only because they no longer have clear motives for what they do.

279: **appertains**: concerns

Without our grace, our love, our benison.—
Come, noble Burgundy.

[Flourish.] Exeunt LEAR and BURGUNDY [then ALBANY,
CORNWALL, GLOUCESTER, EDMUND, and followers].

FRANCE
                              [To CORDELIA] Bid farewell to your sisters.

CORDELIA
Ye jewels of our father, with washed eyes
Cordelia leaves you. I know you what you are,
And like a sister am most loath to call   265
Your faults as they are named. Use well our father.
To your professèd bosoms I commit him.
But yet, alas, stood I within his grace
I would prefer him to a better place.
So farewell to you both.   270

GONORIL
Prescribe not us our duties.

REGAN
Let your study
Be to content your lord, who hath received you
At Fortune's alms. You have obedience scanted,
And well are worth the worst that you have wanted.   275

CORDELIA
Time shall unfold what pleated cunning hides.
Who cover faults, at last shame them derides.
Well may you prosper.

FRANCE
                              Come, my fair Cordelia.
                              Exeunt FRANCE and CORDELIA

GONORIL
Sister, it is not a little I have to say of what most nearly appertains
to us both. I think our father will hence tonight.   280

285: **gross**: obvious

Costume rendering for Regan from the 1959 production at the Shakespeare Memorial Theatre in Stratford-upon-Avon directed by Glen Byam Shaw
Rare Book and Special Collection Library, University of Illinois at Urbana-Champaign

289-290: **long-engrafted**: closely merged and longstanding

291: **choleric**: impatient, easily angered

292: **unconstant starts**: temper tantrums; **like**: likely

294: **compliment**: evidence or show

295: **hit**: concur; **authority**: power

297: **offend**: endangers

299: **i' th' heat**: immediately, as in "strike while the iron is hot"

REGAN
That's most certain, and with you. Next month with us.

GONORIL
You see how full of changes his age is. The observation we have
made of it hath not been little. He always loved our sister most,
and with what poor judgment he hath now cast her off appears
too gross.   285

REGAN
'Tis the infirmity of his age, yet he hath ever but slenderly known
himself.

GONORIL
The best and soundest of his time hath been but rash, then must
we look to receive from his age not alone the imperfection of long-
engrafted condition, but therewithal the unruly waywardness   290
that infirm and choleric years bring with them.

REGAN
Such unconstant starts are we like to have from him as this of
Kent's banishment.

GONORIL
There is further compliment of leave-taking between France and
him. Pray you, let's hit together. If our father carry authority with   295
such dispositions as he bears, this last surrender of his will but
offend us.

REGAN
We shall further think on't.

GONORIL
We must do something, and i' th' heat.

Exeunt

0: Location: The Earl of Gloucester's house

0: Scene: Missing Edmunds: Orson Welles' film (dir. Peter Brook, CBS-TV, 1953) cut Edmund altogether. Oswald plays the cheat, betrays Gloucester, plans Cordelia's murder, and offers himself to both Regan and Gonoril.

tracks 8-10

1–22
Simon Russell Beale as Edmund
Toby Stephens as Edmund

1: **Nature**: here deified. Edmund may have in mind any number of goddesses. In classical Greek literature, Nature was associated with the sexually active and lawless women of *The Bacchae*.
3: **Stand...custom**: submit to or accept a hurtful practice or habit
4. **curiosity of nations**: arbitrary social rankings
5: **moonshines**: months (from the lunar calendar)
6: **Lag of**: lagging behind
7: **dimensions**: physical attributes or proportions
9: **honest**: virtuous, chaste
10: **base, base bastardy**: The siring of bastards indicates base or low morality; Edmund argues that these characterizations are unfounded.
11: **lusty stealth**: secret lust
11-12: **Who...quality**: Whose conception is more fully realized and strong
14: **fops**: fools
16: **your land**: i.e., the land Edgar is meant to inherit as Gloucester's legitimate heir
19: **speed**: succeed
20: **invention thrive**: plot succeeds
23: **choler**: anger
24: **to-night**: last night; **subscribed his power**: limited his own power (by giving it away)
25: **exhibition**: his pension or allowance
26: **Upon the gad**: suddenly

Act 1, Scene 2]

EDMUND

    Thou, Nature, art my goddess. To thy law
    My services are bound. Wherefore should I
    Stand in the plague of custom and permit
    The curiosity of nations to deprive me
    For that I am some twelve or fourteen moonshines   5
    Lag of a brother? Why "bastard"? Wherefore "base,"
    When my dimensions are as well compact,
    My mind as generous, and my shape as true
    As honest madam's issue?
    Why brand they us with "base, base bastardy,"   10
    Who in the lusty stealth of nature take
    More composition and fierce quality
    Than doth within a stale, dull-eyed bed go
    To the creating a whole tribe of fops
    Got 'tween a sleep and wake? Well then,   15
    Legitimate Edgar, I must have your land.
    Our father's love is to the bastard Edmund
    As to the legitimate. Fine word,—legitimate!
    Well, my legitimate, if this letter speed
    And my invention thrive, Edmund the base   20
    Shall to the legitimate. I grow, I prosper.
    Now gods, stand up for bastards!

Enter GLOUCESTER
[EDMUND reads a letter]

GLOUCESTER

    Kent banished thus, and France in choler parted,
    And the King gone to-night, subscribed his power,
    Confined to exhibition—all this done   25
    Upon the gad?—Edmund, how now? What news?

31: **Nothing**: again, echoing Cordelia at 1.1.84 and 1.1.86

32: **terrible dispatch**: attempt to hide quickly

36: **o'er-read**: finished reading

37: **liking**: approval

42-43: **assay or taste**: an effort to test

Set design for the 1959 production at the Shakespeare Memorial Theatre in Stratford-upon-Avon directed by Glen Byam Shaw
Rare Book and Special Collection Library, University of Illinois at Urbana-Champaign

EDMUND
So please your lordship, none.

GLOUCESTER
Why so earnestly seek you to put up that letter?

EDMUND
I know no news, my lord.

GLOUCESTER
What paper were you reading?   30

EDMUND
Nothing, my lord.

GLOUCESTER
No? What needs then that terrible dispatch of it into your pocket?
The quality of nothing hath not such need to hide itself. Let's see.
Come, if it be nothing, I shall not need spectacles.

EDMUND
I beseech you, sir, pardon me. It is a letter from my brother that I   35
have not all o'er-read; and for so much as I have perused, I find it
not fit for your liking.

GLOUCESTER
Give me the letter, sir.

EDMUND
I shall offend either to detain or give it. The contents, as in part I
understand them, are to blame.   40

GLOUCESTER
Let's see, let's see.

EDMUND
I hope for my brother's justification he wrote this but as an assay
or taste of my virtue.

[He gives GLOUCESTER] the letter

44: Stage Direction: **_Reads_**: David Sabin as Gloucester and Andrew Long as Edmund in the 2000 Shakespeare Theatre Company production directed by Michael Kahn
Photo: Carol Rosegg

44: **policy and reverence of**: mandatory policy of revering
45: **the best of our times**: i.e., our youth
46: **relish**: enjoy; **idle and fond**: worthless and foolish
47: **who sways**: which rules
48: **suffered**: allowed
53: **breed it**: hatch this plot
55: **casement**: window; **closet**: small room, often used for reading and writing
56: **character**: handwriting
57: **matter**: contents
58: **fain**: happily
61: **sounded you**: discussed with you
62: **fit**: suitable
63: **perfect age**: i.e., prime of life; **declining**: getting old
65: **Abhorred**: abhorrent or hateful, but also a pun on whore
66: **brutish**: ill-mannered

GLOUCESTER

[Reads] *This policy and reverence of age makes the world bitter to*
the best of our times, keeps our fortunes from us till our oldness   45
cannot relish them. I begin to find an idle and fond bondage in the
oppression of aged tyranny, who sways not as it hath power but as
it is suffered. Come to me, that of this I may speak more. If our
father would sleep till I waked him, you should enjoy half his
revenue forever and live the beloved of your brother, Edgar.   50
Hum, conspiracy! "Slept till I waked him, you should enjoy half
his revenue,"—my son Edgar! Had he a hand to write this, a heart
and brain to breed it in? When came this to you? Who brought it?

EDMUND

It was not brought me, my lord, there's the cunning of it. I found
it thrown in at the casement of my closet.   55

GLOUCESTER

You know the character to be your brother's?

EDMUND

If the matter were good, my lord, I durst swear it were his; but in
respect of that, I would fain think it were not.

GLOUCESTER

It is his.

EDMUND

It is his hand, my lord, but I hope his heart is not in the contents.   60

GLOUCESTER

Hath he never heretofore sounded you in this business?

EDMUND

Never, my lord; but I have often heard him maintain it to be fit
that, sons at perfect age and fathers declining, his father should be
as ward to the son, and the son manage the revenue.

GLOUCESTER

O villain, villain—his very opinion in the letter! Abhorred villain,   65
unnatural, detested, brutish villain—worse than brutish! Go, sir,
seek him, ay, apprehend him. Abominable villain! Where is he?

70: **testimony**: evidence; **run a certain course**: proceed more judiciously; **where**: whereas

73: **pawn down**: stake

74: **feel**: get a sense of

77: **judge it meet**: think it appropriate

77-78: **hear us confer**: eavesdrop on us

78-79: **have your satisfaction**: be assured

82-83: **To his father...earth!**: appears only in the First Quarto

83: **wind me into him**: gain his confidence

84: **frame**: plan; **after...wisdom**: according to what you think is best

84-85: **I would...resolution**: i.e., I would give up everything I have to know the truth.

86: **presently**: immediately; **convey**: undertake

87: **acquaint you withal**: inform you of everything as soon as I can

88: **late**: recent

90: **sequent effects**: horrible consequences

91: **mutinies**: rebellions

EDMUND

I do not well know, my lord. If it shall please you to suspend
your indignation against my brother till you can derive from him
better testimony of this intent, you shall run a certain course;   70
where if you violently proceed against him, mistaking his
purpose, it would make a great gap in your own honor and shake
in pieces the heart of his obedience. I dare pawn down my life for
him that he hath wrote this to feel my affection to your honor, and
to no further pretense of danger.   75

GLOUCESTER

Think you so?

EDMUND

If your honor judge it meet, I will place you where you shall hear
us confer of this, and by an auricular assurance have your satisfaction, and that without any further delay than this very evening.

GLOUCESTER

He cannot be such a monster.   80

EDMUND

Nor is not, sure.

GLOUCESTER

To his father, that so tenderly and entirely loves him—heaven and
earth! Edmund, seek him out, wind me into him. I pray you,
frame your business after your own wisdom. I would unstate
myself to be in a due resolution.   85

EDMUND

I shall seek him, sir, presently, convey the business as I shall see
means, and acquaint you withal.

GLOUCESTER

These late eclipses in the sun and moon portend no good to us.
Though the wisdom of nature can reason it thus and thus, yet
nature finds itself scourged by the sequent effects. Love cools,   90
friendship falls off, brothers divide; in cities, mutinies, in countries,

92: **discords**: conflicts

93-97: **This villain...graves**: from the First Folio

94: **bias of nature**: the natural order of things

97: **it shall lose thee nothing**: i.e., You will be generously rewarded.

Costume rendering for Edmund from the 1959 production at the Shakespeare Memorial Theatre in Stratford-upon-Avon directed by Glen Byam Shaw

Rare Book and Special Collection Library, University of Illinois at Urbana-Champaign

100: **foppery**: foolishness

100-101: **sick in fortune**: plagued by bad luck

101: **surfeit...behavior**: result of our lavish lifestyles

101-102: **make guilty of**: blame

104: **treacherers**: traitors; **spherical predominance**: influence of the planets on the future based on the hour of one's birth (from astrology)

106: **divine thrusting on**: blaming the supernatural

107: **evasion**: unwillingness to confront the truth; **goatish**: lecherous

108-109: **My father...Dragon's tail**: i.e., My parents had sex and conceived me under the constellation Draco (not one of the signs of the Zodiac).

109-110: **Ursa Major**: the constellation of the Great Bear or Big Dipper—also not a standard sign of the zodiac

110: **Fut!**: an oath, short for 'sfoot or Christ's Foot

111: **maidenliest**: most virginal

113: **catastrophe of the comedy**: climax of a play

114: **Bedlam**: a reference to Bethlehem Hospital in London, a lunatic asylum

115: **divisions**: conflicts in the family and culture; **fa, sol, la, mi**: notes in the musical scale (from the First Folio)

discords, in palaces, treason, and the bond cracked between son
and father. This villain of mine comes under the prediction: there's
son against father. The King falls from bias of nature: there's father
against child. We have seen the best of our time. Machinations, hol-   95
lowness, treachery, and all ruinous disorders, follow us disquietly to
our graves. Find out this villain, Edmund; it shall lose thee nothing.
Do it carefully. And the noble and true-hearted Kent banished, his
offense honesty! Strange, strange.

[Exit]

EDMUND
   This is the excellent foppery of the world, that when we are sick   100
in fortune—often the surfeit of our own behavior—we make
guilty of our disasters the sun, the moon, and the stars, as if we
were villains by necessity, fools by heavenly compulsion, knaves,
thieves, and treacherers by spherical predominance, drunkards,
liars, and adulterers by an enforced obedience of planetary influ-   105
ence, and all that we are evil in by a divine thrusting on. An
admirable evasion of whoremaster man, to lay his goatish disposition to the charge of stars! My father compounded with my
mother under the Dragon's tail and my nativity was under Ursa
Major, so that it follows I am rough and lecherous. Fut! I should   110
have been that I am, had the maidenliest star of the firmament
twinkled on my bastardy. Edgar—

Enter EDGAR

And on's cue out he comes, like the catastrophe of the old comedy;
mine is villainous melancholy, with a sigh like Tom of Bedlam.—
O, these eclipses do portend these divisions! Fa, sol, la, mi.   115

EDGAR
   How now, brother Edmund, what serious contemplation are you in?

EDMUND
   I am thinking, brother, of a prediction I read this other day, what
should follow these eclipses.

EDGAR
   Do you busy yourself about that?

120: **promise**: guarantee; **succeed unhappily**: are the unlucky result of

120-126: **as of...astronomical?**: appears only in the First Quarto

121: **dearth**: famine

123: **needless diffidences**: unfounded distrust of others

124: **dissipation of cohorts**: military desertions

126: **sectary**: sectarian or religious dissenter; **sectary astronomical**: believer in astrology

129: **Spake**: speak

132: **countenance**: demeanor

135: **forbear his presence**: stay away from him; **qualified**: reduced

137: **with the mischief of your person**: in combination with your presence; **allay**: reduce or calm

EDMUND

I promise you, the effects he writ of succeed unhappily, as of 120
unnaturalness between the child and the parent, death, dearth,
dissolutions of ancient amities, divisions in state, menaces and
maledictions against king and nobles, needless diffidences, banishment of friends, dissipation of cohorts, nuptial breaches, and I
know not what. 125

EDGAR

How long have you been a sectary astronomical?

EDMUND

Come, come, when saw you my father last?

EDGAR

Why, the night gone by.

EDMUND

Spake you with him?

EDGAR

Two hours together. 130

EDMUND

Parted you in good terms? Found you no displeasure in him by
word or countenance?

EDGAR

None at all.

EDMUND

Bethink yourself wherein you may have offended him, and at my
entreaty forbear his presence till some little time hath qualified 135
the heat of his displeasure, which at this instant so rageth in him
that with the mischief of your person it would scarcely allay.

EDGAR

Some villain hath done me wrong.

139-143: **I pray you...brother?**: from the First Folio

139: **have a continent forbearance**: stay far away from

140: **till the speed of his rage goes slower**: i.e., until he calms down

141: **fitly**: at the right time

142: **stir abroad**: i.e., leave your house

142: "If you do stir abroad, go armed": Brian Avers as Edgar and Logan Marshall-Green as Edmund in the 2007 Public Theater production directed by James Lapine
Photo: Michal Daniel

144: **Brother** and **Go armed**: appear only in the First Quarto

145: **meaning**: intention

150: **credulous**: easily fooled

153: **practices ride easy**: plots go smoothly; **the business**: the way to proceed

155: **meet**: appropriate; **fashion fit**: rely on to further my plans

EDMUND

That's my fear, I pray you, have a continent forbearance till the
speed of his rage goes slower; and, as I say, retire with me to my   140
lodging, from whence I will fitly bring you to hear my lord speak.
Pray ye, go. There's my key. If you do stir abroad, go armed.

EDGAR

Armed, brother?

EDMUND

Brother. I advise you to the best. Go armed. I am no honest man
if there be any good meaning towards you. I have told you what I   145
have seen and heard but faintly, nothing like the image and horror of it. Pray you, away.

EDGAR

Shall I hear from you anon?

EDMUND

I do serve you in this business.

                                                    Exit EDGAR
A credulous father, and a brother noble,   150
Whose nature is so far from doing harms
That he suspects none; on whose foolish honesty
My practices ride easy. I see the business.
Let me, if not by birth, have lands by wit.
All with me's meet that I can fashion fit.   155

                                                    Exit

0: Location: The Duke of Albany's Palace

Set design for the 1959 production at the Shakespeare Memorial Theatre in
Stratford-upon-Avon directed by Glen Byam Shaw

Rare Book and Special Collection Library, University of Illinois at Urbana-Champaign

0: Scene: In the film adaptation of Peter Brook's 1962 RSC production, the knights
are very disrespectful; Gonoril's house looks like a tavern.

5: **gross crime**: unwarranted offense
6: **riotous**: ill-behaved; **upbraids**: reproaches
9: **come slack**: fall short
10: **answer**: explain or take responsibility for
13: **come to question**: be turned into a point of discussion
16-20: **Not to be...abused.**: appears only in the First Quarto
16: **Idle**: ridiculous
17: **manage those authorities**: exercise those royal powers
19-20: **used / With...abused**: reprimanded rather than flattered when they take
advantage of one's kindness

Act 1, Scene 3]

Enter GONORIL and Gentlemen [OSWALD]

GONORIL
Did my father strike my gentleman for chiding of his fool?

OSWALD
Yes, madam.

GONORIL
By day and night he wrongs me. Every hour
He flashes into one gross crime or other
That sets us all at odds. I'll not endure it.   5
His knights grow riotous, and himself upbraids us
On every trifle. When he returns from hunting
I will not speak with him. Say I am sick.
If you come slack of former services
You shall do well; the fault of it I'll answer.   10
                                        [Hunting horns within]

OSWALD
He's coming, madam; I hear him.

GONORIL
Put on what weary negligence you please,
You and your fellow servants. I'll have it come to question.
If he dislike it, let him to our sister,
Whose mind and mine I know in that are one,   15
Not to be overruled. Idle old man,
That still would manage those authorities
That he hath given away! Now, by my life,
Old fools are babes again, and must be used
With checks as flatteries, when they are seen abused.   20
Remember what I tell you.

23: **have colder looks**: be treated as strangers

25-26: **I would...speak**: appears only in the First Quarto

25: **occasions**: opportunities

26: **straight**: right away

OSWALD
  Well, madam.

GONORIL
  And let his knights have colder looks among you.
  What grows of it, no matter. Advise your fellows so.
  I would breed from hence occasions, and I shall,   25
  That I may speak. I'll write straight to my sister
  To hold my very course. Go prepare for dinner.

                                            Exeunt

0: Location: The Duke of Albany's Palace
2: **diffuse**: make unrecognizable
3: **May...issue**: will achieve the final result
4: **razed my likeness**: disguised myself
6: **come**: turn out that

Set design for the 1959 production at the Shakespeare Memorial Theatre in Stratford-upon-Avon directed by Glen Byam Shaw

Rare Book and Special Collection Library, University of Illinois at Urbana-Champaign

7: Scene: ***Enter LEAR [and servants from hunting]***: Orson Welles's (1915-1985) Lear occupied himself with a falcon which was perched on his arm; Edmund Kean's (1787-1833) Lear, fresh from the hunt, held a boar spear.

8: **not stay a jot**: not wait a moment
11: **What dost thou profess?**: i.e., What is your profession or calling?
13: **honest**: honorable; **converse**: associate
14: **fear judgment**: be devout, as in fearing God's final judgment
14-15: **cannot choose**: i.e., have no choice but to fight; **eat no fish**: Because Catholics eat fish on Fridays, this may suggest that Kent identifies as a Protestant; it could also refer to a manly meat-and-potatoes diet.

Act 1, Scene 4]

Enter KENT, [disguised]

KENT
If but as well I other accents borrow
That can my speech diffuse, my good intent
May carry through itself to that full issue
For which I razed my likeness. Now, banished Kent,
If thou canst serve where thou dost stand condemned,   5
So may it come thy master, whom thou lov'st,
Shall find thee full of labor.
          [Horns within.] Enter LEAR [and servants from hunting].

LEAR
Let me not stay a jot for dinner. Go get it ready.
                                [Exit one]

[To KENT] How now, what art thou?

KENT
A man, sir.   10

LEAR
What dost thou profess? What wouldst thou with us?

KENT
I do profess to be no less than I seem, to serve him truly that will
put me in trust, to love him that is honest, to converse with him that
is wise and says little, to fear judgment, to fight when I cannot
choose, and to eat no fish.   15

LEAR
What art thou?

KENT
A very honest-hearted fellow, and as poor as the King.

24: **countenance**: noble facial expression and bearing

29: **honest counsel**: a secret; **mar a curious tale**: ruin an elaborate story

30-31: "That which ordinary men are fit for I am qualified in; and the best of me is diligence": Michael Cerveris as Kent in the 2007 Public Theater production directed by James Lapine

Photo: Michal Daniel

LEAR

If thou be as poor for a subject as he is for a king, thou'rt poor
enough. What wouldst thou?

KENT

Service.   20

LEAR

Who wouldst thou serve?

KENT

You.

LEAR

Dost thou know me, fellow?

KENT

No, sir, but you have that in your countenance which I would fain call
master.   25

LEAR

What's that?

KENT

Authority.

LEAR

What services canst thou do?

KENT

I can keep honest counsel, ride, run, mar a curious tale in telling
it, and deliver a plain message bluntly. That which ordinary men   30
are fit for I am qualified in, and the best of me is diligence.

LEAR

How old art thou?

KENT

Not so young, sir, to love a woman for singing, nor so old to dote
on her for anything. I have years on my back forty-eight.

37: **knave**: jester

40: **clotpoll**: clodpole, an oafish person

45: **roundest**: most direct or blunt

48: **entertained**: treated

49: **abatement**: lessening

50: **dependants**: i.e., Gonoril's servants, including Oswald

LEAR

    Follow me. Thou shalt serve me, if I like thee no worse after   35
dinner. I will not part from thee yet.—Dinner, ho, dinner! Where's
my knave, my fool? Go you and call my fool hither.

[Exit one]
Enter Steward [OSWALD]

    You, you, sirrah, where's my daughter?

OSWALD

    So please you—

[Exit]

LEAR

    What says the fellow there? Call the clotpoll back.   40
[Exeunt SERVANT and KENT]
Where's my fool? Ho, I think the world's asleep.
[Enter KENT and a SERVANT]
How now, where's that mongrel?

SERVANT

    He says, my lord, your daughter is not well.

LEAR

    Why came not the slave back to me when I called him?

SERVANT

    Sir, he answered me in the roundest manner he would not.   45

LEAR

    A would not?

SERVANT

    My lord, I know not what the matter is, but to my judgment your
Highness is not entertained with that ceremonious affection as
you were wont. There's a great abatement of kindness appears as
well in the general dependants as in the Duke himself also, and   50
your daughter.

LEAR

    Ha, sayst thou so?

55: **rememberest**: reminds; **conception**: thought

56: **faint**: unenthusiastic

57: **jealous curiosity**: oversensitivity with regard to etiquette; **very pretense**: true intention

Costume rendering for Oswald from the 1959 production at the Shakespeare Memorial Theatre in Stratford-upon-Avon directed by Glen Byam Shaw
Rare Book and Special Collection Library, University of Illinois at Urbana-Champaign

67: **whoreson dog**: (a scathing insult)

70: **bandy looks**: exchange glances (as if Oswald sees himself as Lear's equal)

SERVANT

I beseech you pardon me, my lord, if I be mistaken, for my duty
cannot be silent when I think your Highness wronged.

LEAR

Thou but rememberest me of mine own conception. I have per-   55
ceived a most faint neglect of late, which I have rather blamed as
mine own jealous curiosity than as a very pretense and purport of
unkindness. I will look further into't. But where's this fool? I
have not seen him these two days.

SERVANT

Since my young lady's going into France, sir, the fool hath much   60
pined away.

LEAR

No more of that, I have noted it well. Go you and tell my daughter I would speak with her.

[Exit one]

Go you, call hither my fool.

[Exit one]
[Enter OSWALD, crossing the stage]

O you, sir, you, sir, come you hither. Who am I, sir?   65

OSWALD

My lady's father.

LEAR

My lady's father? My lord's knave, you whoreson dog, you slave,
you cur!

OSWALD

I am none of this, my lord; I beseech you pardon me.

LEAR

Do you bandy looks with me, you rascal?   70

[LEAR strikes him]

OSWALD

I'll not be struck, my lord—

72: **football**: low-class street game

74: **differences**: distinction in social rank

75: **If...again**: i.e., if you want to be knocked down again, you clumsy fool

76: **away...wisdom**: i.e., leave if you know what is good for you

77: Scene: ***Enter [Lear's] FOOL***: William C. Macready (1773-1873), seeking to soften the Fool's acerbic humor, cast a woman, Priscilla Horton (1818-1895), in the role. Granville-Barker (1877-1946) imagined the Fool to be agile and athletic, a gymnast; Alan Badel (1923-1982) as the Fool followed Orson Welles' Lear with dog-like loyalty.

78: **earnest of**: initial payment for

79: **coxcomb**: hat traditionally worn by fools

83-84: **Nay...shortly**: If you don't flatter those in power, you will be in trouble.

85: **banished...daughters**: lost two of his daughters

86: **done the third a blessing**: The fool implies that Cordelia is fortunate not to be associated with her sisters.

87: **nuncle**: mine uncle, an expression coined by the Fool for Lear

KENT

[*Tripping him*] Nor tripped neither, you base football player.

LEAR

[*To KENT*] I thank thee, fellow. Thou serv'st me, and I'll love thee.

KENT

[*To OSWALD*] Come, sir, arise, away. I'll teach you differences.
Away, away. If you will measure your lubber's length again, tarry;   75
but away if you have wisdom.

[Exit OSWALD]

LEAR

Now, my friendly knave, I thank thee.

Enter [Lear's] FOOL

There's earnest of thy service.

[He gives KENT money]

FOOL

Let me hire him, too. [*To KENT*] Here's my coxcomb.

LEAR

How now, my pretty knave, how dost thou?   80

FOOL

Sirrah, you were best take my coxcomb.

KENT

Why, fool?

FOOL

Why, for taking one's part that's out of favor. Nay, an thou canst
not smile as the wind sits, thou'lt catch cold shortly. There, take
my coxcomb. Why, this fellow hath banished two on's daughters   85
and done the third a blessing against his will. If thou follow him,
thou must needs wear my coxcomb. [*To LEAR*] How now, nuncle?
Would I had two coxcombs and two daughters.

LEAR

Why, my boy?

90: **If...myself**: i.e., If I gave away all of my property, I too would be a fool like you.

90-91: "There's mine; beg another off thy daughters": Kevin Kline as Lear and Philip Goodwin as the Fool in the 2007 Public Theater production directed by James Lapine
Photo: Michal Daniel

93: **Truth's...kennel**: i.e., Truth must be kept locked up.

94: **brach**: female hunting dog; **Lady...fire and stink**: idiomatic expression: A wet dog drying by the fire smells bad.

95: **pestilent gall**: painful truth

101: **thou owest**: you own

103: **trowest**: believe

104: **Set...throwest**: i.e., Do not bet everything on a single throw of the dice.

106: **in-a-door**: indoors

107-108: **more...a score**: A score is twenty, so more than two tens is a profit.

110-111: **like...for't**: i.e., you cannot expect good advice if you do not pay for it

FOOL

    If I gave them all my living I'd keep my coxcombs myself. There's   90
mine; beg another off thy daughters.

LEAR

    Take heed, sirrah—the whip.

FOOL

    Truth is a dog that must to kennel. He must be whipped out when
Lady the brach may stand by the fire and stink.

LEAR

    A pestilent gall to me!   95

FOOL

    [*To KENT*] Sirrah, I'll teach thee a speech.

LEAR

    Do.

FOOL

    Mark it, nuncle.
        [*Sings*]
        Have more than thou showest,
        Speak less than thou knowest,   100
        Lend less than thou owest,
        Ride more than thou goest,
        Learn more than thou trowest,
        Set less than thou throwest;
        Leave thy drink and thy whore,   105
        And keep in-a-door,
        And thou shalt have more
        Than two tens to a score.

LEAR

    This is nothing, fool.

FOOL

    Then, like the breath of an unfee'd lawyer, you gave me nothing   110
for't. Can you make no use of nothing, uncle?

113: **so...to**: i.e., nothing, because Lear has given away his land and cannot therefore collect money for it

115: **bitter**: satirical

118: Scene: **No, lad. Teach me**: The Fool is more than a mere entertainer; he uses word-play and song to remarkably philosophical ends. In director Joseph Papp's New York City production, 1974, the Fool (Tom Aldridge) was a pointedly caustic politician, rather than a court entertainer. When the King confessed that he had "done her [Cordelia] wrong", he said so not to his own conscience but as an admission to the Fool. In Adrian Noble's 1982 RSC production, Michael Gambon's Lear played opposite Antony Sher's Fool, the latter dressed as if he were a clown who had just tumbled out of a three-ring circus. In Richard Eyre's 1998 TV production, the Fool (Michael Bryant) scolded Lear for giving away his crown and promised to train the King in the art of courtly jesting.

119-133: **That lord...nuncle**: appears only in the First Quarto

125: **motley**: traditional dress of court jesters

126: **The other**: referring to Lear as one of two fools

LEAR
  Why no, boy. Nothing can be made out of nothing.

FOOL
  [*To KENT*] Prithee, tell him so much the rent of his land comes to.
  He will not believe a fool.

LEAR
  A bitter fool.   115

FOOL
  Dost know the difference, my boy, between a bitter fool and a
  sweet fool?

LEAR
  No, lad. Teach me.

FOOL
       [*Sings*]
       That lord that counseled thee
       To give away thy land,   120
       Come place him here by me;
       Do thou for him stand.
       The sweet and bitter fool
       Will presently appear,
       The one in motley here,   125
       The other found out there.

LEAR
  Dost thou call me fool, boy?

FOOL
  All thy other titles thou hast given away. That thou wast born with.

KENT
  [*To LEAR*] This is not altogether fool, my lord.

130: **lords...me**: i.e., important people at court compete with me for the title of "Fool"

131: a **monopoly out**: exclusive control of foolish wisdom

132: **snatching**: grasping for their part

135: **meat**: edible part

136: **clovest**: divided, a reference to Lear's recent division of the kingdom

137-138: **thou...dirt**: i.e., you carried the mule, rather than letting it carry you

142: **foppish**: foolish, like a fop, or courtier

144: **apish**: like an ape, i.e., primitive

145: Scene: **so full of songs**: Tommaso Salvini (1829-1915) reacted to the Fool's jibes with laughter, Sir John Gielgud (1904-2000) with fondness, William C. Macready (1773-1873) with curiosity, and Michael Redgrave (1908-1985) with rage.

146: **have used**: have been doing

147-148: **gavest...breeches**: invited them to punish you

151: **bo-peep**: a game played by mother and child, now commonly referred to as "peekaboo"

FOOL

No, faith; lords and great men will not let me. If I had a 130
monopoly out, they would have part on't, and ladies too, they will
not let me have all the fool to myself—they'll be snatching. Give
me an egg, nuncle, and I'll give thee two crowns.

LEAR

What two crowns shall they be?

FOOL

Why, after I have cut the egg in the middle and eat up the meat, 135
the two crowns of the egg. When thou clovest thy crown i' th'
middle and gavest away both parts, thou borest thy ass o' th'
back o'er the dirt. Thou hadst little wit in thy bald crown when
thou gavest thy golden one away. If I speak like myself in this, let
him be whipped that first finds it so. 140
    [*Sings*]
    Fools had ne'er less wit in a year,
    For wise men are grown foppish.
    They know not how their wits do wear,
    Their manners are so apish.

LEAR

When were you wont to be so full of songs, sirrah? 145

FOOL

I have used it, nuncle, ever since thou madest thy daughters thy
mother; for when thou gavest them the rod and puttest down
thine own breeches,
    [*Sings*]
    Then they for sudden joy did weep,
    And I for sorrow sung, 150
    That such a king should play bo-peep
    And go the fools among.
Prithee, nuncle, keep a schoolmaster that can teach thy fool to lie.
I would fain learn to lie.

LEAR

An you lie, sirrah, we'll have you whipped. 155

162: **one of the parings**: i.e., one of the two daughters who now control the kingdom

163: **frontlet**: cloth or bandage worn on the forehead (to smooth away wrinkles)

163: **What makes that frontlet on?**: Why are you wearing that frown on your forehead?

163: "What makes that frontlet on": Engraving by John Byam Shaw, ca. 1900

Courtesy of the Folger Shakespeare Library

166: **O without a figure**: a number with no value, literally a zero

171-172: **He...some**: he who gives everything away will regret it (proverbial)

173: **shelled peascod**: a peapod without the peas, an expression of meaninglessness

174: **all-licensed**: free to do whatever he wants

175: **retinue**: followers

177: **rank**: excessive

179: **safe redress**: sure resolution

180: **too late**: in the recent past

181: **put it on**: facilitate or encourage

183: **censure**: reprimand; **nor...sleep**: nor would we fail to punish

184: **in...weal**: out of concern for the commonwealth

185: **Might...offense**: could have a negative impact on you

186-197: **That...proceedings**: i.e., Measures that in previous times might have embarrassed you now seem necessary in these precarious times.

FOOL

I marvel what kin thou and thy daughters are. They'll have me
whipped for speaking true, thou wilt have me whipped for lying,
and sometime I am whipped for holding my peace. I had rather
be any kind of thing than a fool; and yet I would not be thee,
nuncle. Thou hast pared thy wit o' both sides and left nothing in   160
the middle.

Enter GONORIL

Here comes one of the parings.

LEAR

How now, daughter, what makes that frontlet on?
Methinks you are too much o' late i' th' frown.

FOOL

Thou wast a pretty fellow when thou hadst no need to care for her   165
frown. Now thou art an O without a figure. I am better than thou
art, now. I am a fool; thou art nothing. [*To* GONORIL] Yes, for-
sooth, I will hold my tongue; so your face bids me, though you say
nothing.

    [*Sings*]
    Mum, mum.   170
    He that keeps neither crust nor crumb,
    Weary of all, shall want some.
    That's a shelled peascod.

GONORIL

[*To LEAR*] Not only, sir, this your all-licensed fool,
But other of your insolent retinue   175
Do hourly carp and quarrel, breaking forth
In rank and not-to-be-endurèd riots.
Sir, I had thought by making this well known unto you
To have found a safe redress, but now grow fearful,
By what yourself too late have spoke and done,   180
That you protect this course, and put it on
By your allowance; which if you should, the fault
Would not scape censure, nor the redresses sleep
Which in the tender of a wholesome weal
Might in their working do you that offense,   185
That else were shame, that then necessity
Must call discreet proceedings.

189-190: hedge-sparrow...young: The cuckoo lays its eggs in the sparrow's nest; the sparrow feeds the young until the cuckoos are big enough to eat the sparrow. The Fool is inferring that Gonoril is an unnatural child who is at once consuming and ridding herself of her father.

191: darkling: in the dark

194: fraught: supplied

195: dispositions: inclinations or moods

197: May...horse?: i.e., Even a fool can see when things are so out of step that a daughter tells her father what to do.

Kalamandalam Padmanabhan Nair as Lear, Kalamandalam MPS Namboodiri as Gonoril, and Kalamandalam Manoj Kumar as the Fool in the 1999 Shakespeare's Globe production "Kathakali King Lear" directed by Annete Leday, adapted by David McRuvie

Photo: Donald Cooper

198: Jug: Steevens (1773) suggests a lost song; G.L. Kittredge (1940) suggests a nickname for Joan. Foakes (1997) suggests an evasive response. Orgel (2000) suggests a generic name for whore. "Jugge," a deep vessel for carrying liquids, dates to 1538.

201: notion: intellectual abilities

201-202: his...lethargied: i.e., his mental faculties have atrophied

205-208: Lear's shadow...obedient father: appears only in the First Quarto

205: Lear's shadow: a shadow of his former self, but also perhaps playing on the word "shade", meaning "ghost". Lear could be intimating that he is close to death.

205-206: marks of sovereignty: superficial indications of kingship, such as a crown or a sceptor

205-207: I would learn...I had daughters: All of the evidence would falsely indicate that I have loving and respectful daughters.

208: Which: whom

FOOL
[*To LEAR*] For, you trow, nuncle,
    [*Sings*]
    The hedge-sparrow fed the cuckoo so long
    That it had it head bit off by it young;   190
So out went the candle, and we were left darkling.

LEAR
[*To GONORIL*] Are you our daughter?

GONORIL
Come, sir, I would you would make use of that good wisdom,
Whereof I know you are fraught, and put away
These dispositions that of late transform you   195
From what you rightly are.

FOOL
May not an ass know when the cart draws the horse?
    [*Sings*]
    Whoop, Jug, I love thee!

LEAR
Doth any here know me? Why, this is not Lear.
Doth Lear walk thus, speak thus? Where are his eyes?   200
Either his notion weakens, or his discernings
Are lethargied. Sleeping or waking, ha?
Sure, 'tis not so.
Who is it that can tell me who I am?
Lear's shadow? I would learn that, for by the marks   205
Of sovereignty, knowledge, and reason
I should be false persuaded I had daughters.

FOOL
Which they will make an obedient father.

LEAR
[*To GONORIL*] Your name, fair gentlewoman?

210: **admiration**: phony sense of wonder or disbelief; **much of the savor**: consistent with

213: **reverend**: worthy of reverence

215: **disordered**: disorderly; **debauched**: depraved; **bold**: impudent

217: **Shows**: presents itself; **epicurism**: excessive, hedonistic behavior

222: **disquantity your train**: reduce the number of those who attend you

224: **besort**: be appropriate for

225: **That...you**: who are self-aware enough to serve you in an appropriate way

226: **train**: retinue

227: **Degenerate bastard**: ungrateful daughter who acts as if she were fathered by someone else

229: "You strike my people, and your disordered rabble / Make servants of their betters": Rosalind Cash as Gonoril in the 1973 Public Theater production directed by Edwin Sherin

Photo: George E. Joseph

231: **O sir, are you come?**: appears only in the First Quarto

233: **marble-hearted**: hard-hearted, unfeeling

GONORIL

                    Come, sir,
This admiration, sir, is much of the savor   210
Of other your new pranks. I do beseech you
To understand my purposes aright,
As you are old and reverend, should be wise.
Here do you keep a hundred knights and squires,
Men so disordered, so debauched and bold   215
That this our court, infected with their manners,
Shows like a riotous inn, epicurism
And lust make it more like to a tavern, or a brothel,
Than a great palace. The shame itself doth speak
For instant remedy. Be thou desired,   220
By her that else will take the thing she begs,
A little to disquantity your train,
And the remainder that shall still depend
To be such men as may besort your age,
That know themselves and you.

LEAR

                    Darkness and devils!   225
Saddle my horses, call my train together!—

                      [Exit one or more]

Degenerate bastard, I'll not trouble thee.
Yet have I left a daughter.

GONORIL

You strike my people, and your disordered rabble
Make servants of their betters.   230
                Enter Duke [of ALBANY]

LEAR

We that too late repents—O sir, are you come?
Is it your will that we—prepare my horses.

                      [Exit one or more]

Ingratitude, thou marble-hearted fiend,
More hideous when thou show'st thee in a child
Than the sea-monster—   235

249–264:
Laurence Olivier as Lear

235: **Pray sir, be patient.**: appears only in the First Quarto

236: **kite**: bird of prey

237: **rarest parts**: finest qualities

239-240: **support...name**: act in a way that does honor to their reputations

242-243: **That...place**: which, like a powerful tool, cut away my natural feelings of love (i.e., his fatherly love for Cordelia) from where they should be

244: **gall**: bitterness

248: **Of what hath moved you.**: from the First Folio

249-264: Scene: David Garrick's (1717-1779) curses took on the aura of holy prayer; Edmund Kean (1787-1833) threw himself on his knees, exhausted and breathless. Henry Irving (1838-1905) spoke his curses as if they had been torn from his heart.

254: **derogate**: corrupt

255: **teem**: give birth

256: **spleen**: anger and bad temper

257: **thwart disnatured torment**: stubborn, unnatural source of difficulty

259: **cadent**: cascading; **fret**: erode

260: **benefits**: joys of motherhood

263: **serpent's tooth**: fangs; see also 2.2.297 (**sharp-tooth'd**), 2.2.322-323 (**struck me...serpent-like**), 5.1.57-58 (**stung...adder**), 5.3.83 (**gilded serpent**)

264: **Go, go, my people!**: appears only in the First Quarto

ALBANY

Pray sir, be patient.   235

LEAR

[*To GONORIL*] Detested kite, thou liest.
My train are men of choice and rarest parts,
That all particulars of duty know,
And in the most exact regard support
The worships of their name. O most small fault,   240
How ugly didst thou in Cordelia show,
That, like an engine, wrenched my frame of nature
From the fixed place, drew from heart all love,
And added to the gall! O Lear, Lear, Lear!
Beat at this gate that let thy folly in,   245
And thy dear judgment out.—Go, go, my people!

ALBANY

My lord, I am guiltless as I am ignorant.
Of what hath moved you.

LEAR

It may be so, my lord. Hark, Nature, hear.
Dear goddess, hear. Suspend thy purpose if   250
Thou didst intend to make this creature fruitful.
Into her womb convey sterility.
Dry up in her the organs of increase,
And from her derogate body never spring
A babe to honor her. If she must teem,   255
Create her child of spleen, that it may live
And be a thwart disnatured torment to her.
Let it stamp wrinkles in her brow of youth,
With cadent tears fret channels in her cheeks,
Turn all her mother's pains and benefits   260
To laughter and contempt, that she may feel—
That she may feel
How sharper than a serpent's tooth it is
To have a thankless child.—Go, go, my people!
                    Exeunt LEAR, KENT, FOOL, and servants

Costume rendering for Lear's men by Susan Tsu from the 2004 Oregon Shakespeare Festival production directed by James Edmondson

Courtesy of the Oregon Shakespeare Festival

266: **Never...know**: do not bother trying to figure out
267: **disposition**: mood
268: **dotage**: senility
273: **hot tears**: womanly tears
274: **should make thee**: should be worthy of a king; **worst blasts and fogs**: terrible afflictions and plague-bearing fogs
275: **untented**: deep and infected
276: **fond**: ridiculous
277: **Beweep**: if you cry over
279: **temper clay**: mix with dirt (a threat to gouge out his eyes and stomp them into the ground)
279: **Yea...Whom**: appears only in the First Quarto
281: **comfortable**: comforting
283: **flay**: strip off the skin
284: **resume the shape**: take back the kingship
288: **To**: because of

ALBANY

Now, gods that we adore, whereof comes this?   265

GONORIL

Never afflict yourself to know the cause,
But let his disposition have that scope
That dotage gives it.

Enter LEAR and FOOL

LEAR

What, fifty of my followers at a clap?
Within a fortnight?

ALBANY

What is the matter, sir?   270

LEAR

I'll tell thee. [*To GONORIL*] Life and death! I am ashamed
That thou hast power to shake my manhood thus,
That these hot tears, that break from me perforce
And should make thee—worst blasts and fogs upon thee!
Untented woundings of a father's curse   275
Pierce every sense about thee! Old fond eyes,
Beweep this cause again I'll pluck you out
And cast you, with the waters that you make,
To temper clay. Yea,
Is't come to this? Yet have I left a daughter   280
Whom, I am sure, is kind and comfortable.
When she shall hear this of thee, with her nails
She'll flay thy wolvish visage. Thou shalt find
That I'll resume the shape which thou dost think
I have cast off forever; thou shalt, I warrant thee.   285

[Exit]

GONORIL

Do you mark that, my lord?

ALBANY

I cannot be so partial, Gonoril,
To the great love I bear you—

288: **Come, sir, no more.**: appears only in the First Quarto

293: **Should sure**: should certainly be sent

294: **halter**: leash for leading an animal to slaughter or hangman's noose

296-307: **This man...th' unfitness**: from the First Folio

296: **This...counsel**: Gonoril says this sarcastically

297: **politic**: wise (also said sarcastically)

298: **At point**: prepared for war; **dream**: imaginary grievance

299: **buzz**: rumor; **fancy**: whim

300: **enguard**: protect

301: **in mercy**: at his mercy

302: **fear too far**: exaggerate the risks

304: **Not...taken**: i.e., instead of living in fear of what could happen

307: **th' unfitness**: the impropriety of doing so

308-309: **What...madam**: appears only in the First Quarto

GONORIL

                        Come, sir, no more.—
You, sir, more knave than fool, after your master!

FOOL

Nuncle Lear, nuncle Lear, tarry, and take the fool with thee.   290
     [Sings]
     A fox when one has caught her,
     And such a daughter,
     Should sure to the slaughter,
     If my cap would buy a halter.
     So, the fool follows after.   295
                                [Exit]

GONORIL

This man hath had good counsel—a hundred knights?
'Tis politic and safe to let him keep
At point a hundred knights, yes, that on every dream,
Each buzz, each fancy, each complaint, dislike,
He may enguard his dotage with their powers   300
And hold our lives in mercy.—Oswald, I say!

ALBANY

Well, you may fear too far.

GONORIL

                  Safer than trust too far.
Let me still take away the harms I fear,
Not fear still to be taken. I know his heart.
What he hath uttered I have writ my sister.   305
If she sustain him and his hundred knights
When I have showed th' unfitness—
What, Oswald, ho!

                        [Enter OSWALD]

OSWALD

Here, madam.

GONORIL

What, have you writ this letter to my sister?   310

315: **compact**: further prove

317: **Milky gentleness**: motherly or effeminate manner

318: **under pardon**: if you will forgive me for saying so

319: **ataxed**: penalized

320: **harmful mildness**: dangerous gentleness

324: **the event**: i..e.,time will tell how things turn out

OSWALD
   Ay, madam.

GONORIL
   Take you some company, and away to horse.
   Inform her full of my particular fears,
   And thereto add such reasons of your own
   As may compact it more. Get you gone,   315
   And after, your retinue.

                                        [Exit OSWALD]

                           Now, my lord,
   This milky gentleness and course of yours,
   Though I dislike not, yet under pardon
   You're much more ataxed for want of wisdom
   Than praised for harmful mildness.   320

ALBANY
   How far your eyes may pierce I can not tell.
   Striving to better aught, we mar what's well.

GONORIL
   Nay, then—

ALBANY
   Well, well, the event.

                                        Exeunt

0: Location: Before Albany's Palace

Watercolor scene sketch from the promptbook for Charles Kean's 1858 production
Courtesy of the Folger Shakespeare Library

0: Scene: **Enter...and FOOL**: In Nahum Tate's 1687 adaptation, Shakespeare's Fool was cut altogether. Tate's version was so popular that Shakespeare's Fool was not restored to theatrical productions until 1838 (see "In Production," pages 2-9)

6–36:
Paul Scofield as Lear, David Burke as Kent, and Kenneth Branagh as the Fool
Laurence Olivier as Lear, Colin Blakely as Kent, and John Hurt as the Fool

2-3: **than...letter**: than what the letter compels her to ask you about
6: **kibes**: chapped or inflamed skin, especially on the heel, caused by exposure to the cold
8: **thy wit...slipshod**: i.e., you need not wear slippers to avoid kibes, since you have no brains
10: **Shalt**: thou shalt; **kindly**: befitting a family member
11: **crab**: crab apple

Act 1, Scene 5]

Enter LEAR, [KENT, disguised, and FOOL]

LEAR
[*To KENT*] Go you before to Gloucester with these letters.
Acquaint my daughter no further with anything you know than
comes from her demand out of the letter. If your diligence be not
speedy, I shall be there before you.

KENT
I will not sleep, my lord, till I have delivered your letter.   5

Exit

FOOL
If a man's brains were in his heels, were't not in danger of kibes?

LEAR
Ay, boy.

FOOL
Then, I prithee, be merry; thy wit shall ne'er go slipshod.

LEAR
Ha, ha, ha!

FOOL
Shalt see thy other daughter will use thee kindly, for though she's   10
as like this as a crab is like an apple, yet I can what I can tell.

LEAR
Why, what canst thou tell, my boy?

FOOL
She'll taste as like this as a crab doth to a crab. Thou canst not tell
why one's nose stands in the middle of his face?

tracks 13-15

6–36:
Paul Scofield as Lear, David Burke as Kent, and Kenneth Branagh as the Fool
Laurence Olivier as Lear, Colin Blakely as Kent, and John Hurt as the Fool

Costume rendering for Kent in disguise from the 1959 production at the Shakespeare
Memorial Theatre in Stratford-upon-Avon directed by Glen Byam Shaw

Rare Book and Special Collection Library, University of Illinois at Urbana-Champaign

16: **side's**: side of his; **that**: so that
18: **her**: i.e., Cordelia
23-24 **Why...case**: The Fool is suggesting that a snail is smarter than Lear because a
snail builds a house to protect itself, while the King has given his house away and
thus is vulnerable.
24: **horns**: 1) snails horns, but also 2) possibly a suggestion that Lear has been
cuckolded, betrayed sexually by his daughters. (A man whose wife strayed was
thought to grow horns on his forehead.)
25: **nature**: natural paternal love
26: **Thy...them**: i.e., Your servants, who work like mules for you, are getting the
horses ready. **seven stars**: the constellation known as the Pleiades

LEAR
No.   15

FOOL
Why, to keep his eyes on either side's nose, that what a man cannot smell out, a may spy into.

LEAR
I did her wrong.

FOOL
Canst tell how an oyster makes his shell?

LEAR
No.   20

FOOL
Nor I neither; but I can tell why a snail has a house.

LEAR
Why?

FOOL
Why, to put his head in, not to give it away to his daughter and
leave his horns without a case.

LEAR
I will forget my nature. So kind a father! Be my horses ready?   25

FOOL
Thy asses are gone about them. The reason why the seven stars
are no more than seven is a pretty reason.

LEAR
Because they are not eight?

FOOL
Yes, indeed. Thou wouldst make a good fool.

6–36:
Paul Scofield as Lear, David Burke as Kent, and Kenneth Branagh as the Fool
Laurence Olivier as Lear, Colin Blakely as Kent, and John Hurt as the Fool

30: **To...perforce**: Lear is contemplating 1) the possibility that Gonoril would use force to take back all that she has promised him, and 2) using his army to reclaim his throne.; **monster**: monstrous

36: **in temper**: mentally stable

41: **maid**: virgin; **things**: i.e., penises; **cut shorter**: castrated

LEAR

To take't again perforce—monster ingratitude!   30

FOOL

If thou wert my fool, nuncle, I'd have thee beaten for being old
before thy time.

LEAR

How's that?

FOOL

Thou shouldst not have been old before thou hadst been wise.

LEAR

O, let me not be mad, not mad, sweet heaven! I would not be mad.   35
Keep me in temper. I would not be mad.

[Enter SERVANT]

How now, are the horses ready?

SERVANT

Ready, my lord.

LEAR

[To FOOL] Come, boy.

Exeunt [LEAR and SERVANT]

FOOL

She that is a maid now, and laughs at my departure,   40
Shall not be a maid long, except things be cut shorter.

Exit

[King Lear

Act 2

0: Location: The Earl of Gloucester's house

Costume rendering for Curan from the 1959 production at the Shakespeare Memorial Theatre in Stratford-upon-Avon directed by Glen Byam Shaw

Rare Book and Special Collection Library, University of Illinois at Urbana-Champaign

1: **Save**: God save
6: **abroad**: during your travels
7: **ear-bussing arguments**: whispered topics
9: **towards 'twixt**: impending between

tracks 16-18

13–36:
Gerard Murphy as Edmund and David Tennant as Edgar
Toby Stephens as Edmund and Richard McCabe as Edgar

13: **The better, best**: all the better
14: **perforce**: inevitably

Act 2, Scene 1]

Enter Bastard [EDMUND] and CURAN, meeting

EDMUND
Save thee, Curan.

CURAN
And you, sir. I have been with your father, and given him notice
that the Duke of Cornwall and Regan his duchess will be here
with him tonight.

EDMUND
How comes that?   5

CURAN
Nay, I know not. You have heard of the news abroad?—I mean
the whispered ones, for they are yet but ear-bussing arguments.

EDMUND
Not. I pray you, what are they?

CURAN
Have you heard of no likely wars towards 'twixt the two Dukes
of Cornwall and Albany?   10

EDMUND
Not a word.

CURAN
You may do then in time. Fare you well, sir.

Exit

EDMUND
The duke be here tonight! The better, best.
This weaves itself perforce into my business.

Enter EDGAR [at a window above]

13–36:
Gerard Murphy as Edmund and David Tennant as Edgar
Toby Stephens as Edmund and Richard McCabe as Edgar

15: **take**: capture
16: **queasy**: question
17: **Which**: for which; **briefness**: quickness
20: **Intelligence**: report, information
23: **i' th' haste**: in great haste
26: **Advise you**: think about your situation; **on't**: of it
28: **In cunning** : i.e., I intend to act as if
29: **quit you**: defend yourself

29: "Now, quit you well": Andrew Long as Edmund and Cameron Folmar as Edgar in
the 2000 Shakespeare Theatre Company production directed by Michael Kahn
Photo: Carol Rosegg

31: **Fly**: run away
33-34: **beget...endeavor**: give the impression that I had fought fiercely
35: in **sport**: for fun, in jest
38: **wicked charms**: offers of money
39: **stand 's**: stand for his, act as if he were his; **auspicious mistress**: i.e., the goddess
Fortune. See also the following references to Fortune 1.1.274, 2.2.155-156, 4.6.211, 5.3.6,
and 5.3.173

My father hath set guard to take my brother;   15
And I have one thing of a queasy question
Which I must ask briefness. Wit and Fortune help!—
Brother, a word. Descend, brother, I say.

                                        [EDGAR climbs down]

My father watches. O sir, fly this place.
Intelligence is given where you are hid.   20
You have now the good advantage of the night.
Have you not spoken 'gainst the Duke of Cornwall aught?
He's coming hither now, in the night, i' th' haste,
And Regan with him. Have you nothing said
Upon his party against the Duke of Albany?   25
Advise you—

EDGAR
                    I am sure on't, not a word.

EDMUND
I hear my father coming. Pardon me.
In cunning I must draw my sword upon you.
Draw. Seem to defend yourself. Now, quit you well.
[Calling] Yield, come before my father. Light here, here!   30
[To EDGAR] Fly, brother, fly! *[Calling]* Torches, torches!
[To EDGAR] So, farewell.

                                        [Exit EDGAR]

Some blood drawn on me would beget opinion
Of my more fierce endeavor.

                            [EDMUND wounds his arm]
                    I have seen
Drunkards do more than this in sport. *[Calling]* Father, father!   35
Stop, stop! Ho, help!

                    Enter GLOUCESTER *[and others]*

GLOUCESTER
                    Now, Edmund, where is the villain?

EDMUND
Here stood he in the dark, his sharp sword out,
Warbling of wicked charms, conjuring the moon
To stand 's auspicious mistress.

44: **that**: when; **revengive gods**: revenging. In Greek mythology, the god of revenge was Nemesis.

45: **bend**: aim

44-45: "But I told him the revengive gods / 'Gainst parricides did all their thunders bend": Andrew Long as Edmund and David Sabin as Gloucester in the 2000 Shakespeare Theatre Company production directed by Michael Kahn

Photo: Carol Rosegg

46: **manifold**: many

47: **in fine**: in conclusion

48: **loathly opposite**: hatefully opposed

49: **fell motion**: deadly thrust

50: **preparèd**: drawn and ready; **home**: straight to the heart

51: **unprovided**: armorless

52: **best alarumed**: thoroughly alarmed and ready

53: **quarrel's rights**: justice on my side

54: **ghasted**: shocked, frightened (from "aghast")

55: [ ]: some words may be missing here in the Quarto

58: **dispatch**: dispensed with, taken care of

59: **My worthy arch and patron**: chief architect and supporter of my success

GLOUCESTER
                    But where is he?

EDMUND
  Look, sir, I bleed.

GLOUCESTER
                Where is the villain, Edmund?   40

EDMUND
  Fled this way, sir, when by no means he could—

GLOUCESTER
  Pursue him, ho! go after.
                                                [Exeunt others]
                    By no means what?

EDMUND
  Persuade me to the murder of your lordship,
  But that I told him the revengive gods
  'Gainst parricides did all their thunders bend,   45
  Spoke with how manifold and strong a bond
  The child was bound to the father. Sir, in fine,
  Seeing how loathly opposite I stood
  To his unnatural purpose, with fell motion,
  With his preparèd sword, he charges home   50
  My unprovided body, lanced mine arm;
  But when he saw my best alarumed spirits
  Bold in the quarrel's rights, roused to the encounter,
  Or whether ghasted by the noise I made,
  Or [   ] I know not,   55
  But suddenly he fled.

GLOUCESTER
                    Let him fly far.
  Not in this land shall he remain uncaught,
  And found, dispatch. The noble duke my master,
  My worthy arch and patron, comes tonight.
  By his authority I will proclaim it   60

62: **to the stake**: to the appropriate punishment

65: **pitched**: determined; **curst**: angry

66: **discover**: expose

67: **unpossessing bastard**: ineligible to inherit property (because of his illegitimacy)

68: **reposure**: bestowal

70: **faithed**: trusted, believed; **what**: that which

72: **very character**: actual handwritten testimony; **turn**: attribute

73: **suggestion**: instigation

74: **dullard**: idiot

76: **pregnant and potential spurs**: meaningful and potent motivations

77: **fastened villain**: hardened criminal

78: **got**: begot, fathered

80 **ports**: seaports and other exits

81: **picture**: description

84: **natural**: 1) natural love for one's father, and 2) a reference to illegitimacy, as in a child of nature whose birth is not legally sanctioned by marriage

85: **capable**: i.e., legally able to inherit property

That he which finds him shall deserve our thanks,
Bringing the murderous caitiff to the stake;
He that conceals him, death.

EDMUND
When I dissuaded him from his intent
And found him pitched to do it, with curst speech   65
I threatened to discover him. He replied,
"Thou unpossessing bastard, dost thou think
If I would stand against thee, could the reposure
Of any trust, virtue, or worth in thee
Make thy words faithed? No, what I should deny—   70
As this I would, ay, though thou didst produce
My very character—I'd turn it all
To thy suggestion, plot, and damned pretense,
And thou must make a dullard of the world
If they not thought the profits of my death   75
Were very pregnant and potential spurs
To make thee seek it."

GLOUCESTER
                              Strong and fastened villain!
Would he deny his letter? I never got him.
                                        [Trumpet within]

Hark, the duke's trumpets. I know not why he comes.
All ports I'll bar. The villain shall not scape.   80
The Duke must grant me that; besides, his picture
I will send far and near, that all the kingdom
May have the due note of him—and of my land,
Loyal and natural boy, I'll work the means
To make thee capable.   85
                    Enter the Duke of CORNWALL [and REGAN]

CORNWALL
How now, my noble friend? Since I came hither,
Which I can call but now, I have heard strange news.

REGAN
If it be true, all vengeance comes too short
Which can pursue the offender. How dost, my lord?

90: **cracked**: broken

Costume rendering for Regan by Susan Tsu from the 2004 Oregon Shakespeare
Festival production directed by James Edmondson

Courtesy of the Oregon Shakespeare Festival

97: **consort**: group
98: **though**: if; **ill affected**: disloyal
99: **put him on**: encouraged him to bring on
100: **the spoil and waste**: the squandering
106: **childlike**: dutiful
107: **betray his practice**: i.e., reveal Edgar's plot
108: **apprehend**: arrest

GLOUCESTER
O Madam, my old heart is cracked, is cracked.   90

REGAN
What, did my father's godson seek your life?
He whom my father named, your Edgar?

GLOUCESTER
Ay, lady, lady; shame would have it hid!

REGAN
Was he not companion with the riotous knights
That tend upon my father?   95

GLOUCESTER
I know not, madam. 'Tis too bad, too bad.

EDMUND
Yes, madam, he was of that consort.

REGAN
No marvel, then, though he were ill affected.
'Tis they have put him on the old man's death,
To have the spoil and waste of his revenues.   100
I have this present evening from my sister
Been well informed of them, and with such cautions
That if they come to sojourn at my house
I'll not be there.

CORNWALL
                    Nor I, assure thee, Regan.
Edmund, I heard that you have shown your father   105
A childlike office.

EDMUND
                    'Twas my duty, sir.

GLOUCESTER
[To CORNWALL] He did betray his practice, and received
This hurt you see striving to apprehend him.

111-112: **Make...please**: i.e., use my resources in whatever way you see fit to accomplish your goal

112: **For**: as for

117: **However else**: above everything else

120: **poise**: significance

123: **differences**: quarrels

125: **attend dispatch**: are waiting to be sent

128: **instant use**: immediate attention

CORNWALL
Is he pursued?

GLOUCESTER
                    Ay, my good lord.

CORNWALL
If he be taken, he shall never more   110
Be feared of doing harm. Make your own purpose
How in my strength you please. For you, Edmund,
Whose virtue and obedience doth this instant
So much commend itself, you shall be ours.
Natures of such deep trust we shall much need.   115
You we first seize on.

EDMUND
                    I shall serve you truly,
However else.

GLOUCESTER
            [*To CORNWALL*] For him I thank your grace.

CORNWALL
You know not why we came to visit you—

REGAN
Thus out-of-season threat'ning dark-eyed night—
Occasions, noble Gloucester, of some poise,   120
Wherein we must have use of your advice.
Our father he hath writ, so hath our sister,
Of differences which I best thought it fit
To answer from our home. The several messengers
From hence attend dispatch. Our good old friend,   125
Lay comforts to your bosom, and bestow
Your needful counsel to our business,
Which craves the instant use.

GLOUCESTER
                    I serve you, madam.
Your Graces are right welcome.

                                                    Exeunt

0: Location: Before Gloucester's house

1: **even**: evening; **Art**: are you not

4: **mire**: swamp

5: **love me**: honor and respect me (not a romantic question)

6: **I love thee not**: Kent deliberately misinterprets the phrase and answers in more romantic terms.

8: **pinfold**: a place where stray animals are kept; **If...pinfold**: if I had you clenched between my teeth; **care for**: be afraid of

10: **I know thee**: I am on to you

Act 2, Scene 2]

Enter KENT, [disguised, at one door,] and Steward
[OSWALD, at another door]

OSWALD
Good even to thee, friend. Art of the house?

KENT
Ay.

OSWALD
Where may we set our horses?

KENT
I' th' mire.

OSWALD
Prithee, if thou love me, tell me.   5

KENT
I love thee not.

OSWALD
Why then, I care not for thee.

KENT
If I had thee in Lipsbury pinfold I would make thee care for me.

OSWALD
Why dost thou use me thus? I know thee not.

KENT
Fellow, I know thee.   10

OSWALD
What dost thou know me for?

12: **broken meats**: scraps of food often handed out to the poor

13-14: **three-suited...knave**: the custodian of a house who is allotted three suits and a salary of one-hundred pounds but dresses like a lowly servant in dirty wool stockings

14: **lily-livered**: cowardly; **action-taking**: spending a lot of time in the courts filing frivolous lawsuits; **glass gazing**: narcissistic, as in one who constantly looks in the mirror

15: **superfinical**: finicky, insufferable; **one-trunk-inheriting**: owning so few possessions that they all fit in one suitcase

16: **bawd...service**: pimp who provides his clients with whatever they want; **composition**: combination

17: **pander**: pimp

18-19: **if thou...addition**: i.e., if you try to refute any of the things I have just said about you

24: **Draw**: draw your sword

25: **I'll make...moonshine**: i.e., I will give you so many wounds that you will soak up the moonlight the way a piece of toast soaks up brot.h

26: **cullionly barber-monger**: low-class person who loiters in barbershops

27: **have nothing**: want nothing

29: **Vanity the puppet's part**: an allusion the figure of Vanity in Renaissance morality plays, used here in reference to Gonoril's recent actions

30: **carbonado your shanks**: cut up your legs like meat for grilling

31: **come your ways**: come on

33 **neat**: ridiculous

KENT

A knave, a rascal, an eater of broken meats, a base, proud, shallow,
beggarly, three-suited, hundred-pound, filthy worsted-stocking
knave; a lily-livered, action-taking knave; a whoreson, glass-gazing,
superfinical rogue; one-trunk-inheriting slave; one that wouldst be a   15
bawd in way of good service, and art nothing but the composition of
a knave, beggar, coward, pander, and the son and heir of a mongrel
bitch, one whom I will beat into clamorous whining if thou deny the
least syllable of the addition.

OSWALD

Why, what a monstrous fellow art thou, thus to rail on one   20
that's neither known of thee nor knows thee!

KENT

What a brazen-faced varlet art thou, to deny thou knowest me! Is
it two days ago since I beat thee and tripped up thy heels before
the King? Draw, you rogue; for though it be night, yet the moon
shines. [*Draws his sword*] I'll make a sop of the moonshine o' you.   25
Draw, you whoreson, cullionly barber-monger, draw!

OSWALD

Away. I have nothing to do with thee.

KENT

Draw, you rascal. You bring letters against the King, and take
Vanity the puppet's part against the royalty of her father. Draw,
you rogue, or I'll so carbonado your shanks—draw, you rascal,   30
come your ways!

OSWALD

Help, ho, murder, help!

KENT

Strike, you slave! Stand, rogue! Stand, you neat slave, strike!

OSWALD

Help, ho, murder, help!

Enter EDMUND with his rapier drawn, [then] GLOUCESTER,
[then the] Duke [of CORNWALL] and Duchess [REGAN]

35: **matter**: problem

36: **With you**: i.e., my problem is with you; **goodman boy**: an expression of contempt directed at Edmund; **flesh you**: cut you

42: **difference**: 1) quarrel, and 2) reason for fighting

43: **scarce in breath**: winded

45: **disclaims**: disowns; **a tailor made thee**: an insult suggesting that there is nothing to him but the clothes he is wearing

EDMUND
[*Parting them*] How now, what's the matter?   35

KENT
With you, goodman boy. An you please come, I'll flesh you. Come
on, young master.

GLOUCESTER
Weapons? Arms? What's the matter here?

CORNWALL
Keep peace, upon your lives. He dies that strikes again. What's
the matter?   40

REGAN
The messengers from our sister and the King.

CORNWALL
[*To KENT and OSWALD*] What's your difference? Speak.

OSWALD
I am scarce in breath, my lord.

KENT
No marvel, you have so bestirred your valor, you cowardly rascal.
Nature disclaims in thee; a tailor made thee.   45

CORNWALL
Thou art a strange fellow—a tailor make a man?

KENT
Ay, a tailor, sir. A stone-cutter or painter could not have made him
so ill though he had been but two hours at the trade.

CORNWALL
Speak yet; how grew your quarrel?

OSWALD
This ancient ruffian, sir, whose life I have spared at suit of his   50
gray beard—

52: **Z**: often interchangeable with S in spelling, hence, an unnecessary letter of the alphabet; **unbolted**: crude, unsophisticated

54: **daub**: plaster; **jakes**: bathroom

55: **wagtail**: a bird like a peacock that wags its tail feathers

60: **rogues**: villains

61: **cords**: family ties or allegiances that keep the peace

62: **too entrench'd to unloose**: too tightly knotted to be undone; **smooth**: flatter

63: **rebel**: go against reason

65: **Renege, affirm**: disagree one minute, agree the next

65-66: **turn...masters**: The kingfisher, whose magical powers included charming the winds and waves, would supposedly turn its beak into the wind if suspended by a rope. Oswald responds similarly to whatever his master tells him; he is like a puppet with no will of his own.

66: **gale and vary**: change in the direction of the wind

67: **following**: flattering and fawning

68: **epileptic visage**: face trembling with fear

69: **Smile you**: do you smile at

70: **Sarum plain**: a plain near Stonehenge; see note for 1.1.0:Scene

71: **Camelot**: ;egendary capitol of Arthur's Britain. Kent presents himself as a man of chivalry, and sees Oswald as a man without honor.

70-71: **Goose...Camelot**: If allowed to, Kent would send Oswald on his way, cackling like a goose.

KENT

Thou whoreson Z, thou unnecessary letter—[*To CORNWALL*] my
lord, if you'll give me leave I will tread this unbolted villain into
mortar, and daub the wall of a jakes with him. [*To OSWALD*]
Spare my gray beard, you wagtail?   55

CORNWALL

Peace, sir. You beastly knave, have you no reverence?

KENT

Yes, sir, but anger has a privilege.

CORNWALL

Why art thou angry?

KENT

That such a slave as this should wear a sword,
That wears no honesty. Such smiling rogues   60
As these, like rats, oft bite those cords in twain
Which are too entrenched to unloose, smooth every passion
That in the natures of their lords rebel,
Bring oil to fire, snow to their colder moods,
Renege, affirm, and turn their halcyon beaks   65
With every gale and vary of their masters,
Knowing naught, like dogs, but following.
[*To OSWALD*] A plague upon your epileptic visage!
Smile you my speeches as I were a fool?
Goose, if I had you upon Sarum Plain   70
I'd send you cackling home to Camelot.

CORNWALL

Why, art thou mad, old fellow?

GLOUCESTER

                        [*To KENT*] How fell you out?
Say that.

KENT

No contraries hold more antipathy
Than I and such a knave.   75

76: **likes**: pleases

82: **affect**: imitate the style of

83-84: **constrains...nature**: pushes plain-speaking, or the absence of flattery, to the point that it becomes a form of deception

84: **He cannot flatter, he.**: a sarcastic reference to Kent as a man who makes grand claims about his hatred for flattering speech

86: **An...plain**: i.e., if people tolerate his bluntness, great; if not, he is just justifying himself by claiming to speak only the truth.

89: **silly-ducking observants**: constantly bowing, ridiculously fawning , obsequious courtiers

90: **That...nicely**: those courtiers who go out of their way to perform their duties as flattering courtiers

91-94: **Sir...front**: Kent here is imitating the words and mannerisms of a fawning courtier

92: **allowance**: approval; **aspect**: 1) countenance, and 2) astrological position

93: **influence**: astrological power

94: **Phoebus' front**: the forehead of the sun

CORNWALL

                  Why dost thou call him knave?   75
What's his offense?

KENT

             His countenance likes me not.

CORNWALL

No more perchance does mine, or his, or hers.

KENT

Sir, 'tis my occupation to be plain:
I have seen better faces in my time
Than stands on any shoulder that I see   80
Before me at this instant.

CORNWALL

                 This is a fellow,
Who, having been praised for bluntness, doth affect
A saucy roughness, and constrains the garb
Quite from his nature. He cannot flatter, he.
He must be plain, he must speak truth.   85
An they will take't, so; if not, he's plain.
These kind of knaves I know, which in this plainness
Harbor more craft and more corrupter ends
Than twenty silly-ducking observants
That stretch their duties nicely.   90

KENT

Sir, in good sooth, or in sincere verity,
Under the allowance of your grand aspect,
Whose influence, like the wreath of radiant fire
In flickering Phoebus' front—

CORNWALL

                     What mean'st thou by this?

95: **dialect**: normal manner of speaking; **discommend**: criticize

96-98: **He that...to't**: i.e., He who strategically used plain speech to make you suspicious of plain speakers, was in fact nothing but a plain rascal. I refuse to play that role even though it would make me happy, if, in doing so, it displeased you.

100: **late**: recently

101: **upon his misconstruction**: as a result of the King's misinterpretation of me

103: **When...displeasure**: i.e., when he (Kent), conspiring with the King and his men, and seeking to ingratiate himself with the King, who is angry with me

104: **being down**: already in a disadvantaged position; **railed**: insulted

104-105: **And put...him**: and acted so passionately that it made him look good in the King's eyes

106: **For him...self-subdued**: for attacking me even though I chose not to defend myself

107: **And...exploit**: and he was so thrilled by his first success at carrying out this act of bravery (said ironically)

109: **Ajax**: In Homer's *Illiad*, the warrior Ajax was tripped by the clever Ulysses in the funeral games for Achilles' armor. He is depicted as a dullard in Shakespeare's *Troilus and Cressida*. **stocks**: device used for punishment that locked either hands or feet, or sometimes both, in place. Stocks were often placed in a public setting for further social rebuke.

108-109: **None...fool**: One never encounters such rogues and cowards who do not try to be more boastful than Ajax.

110: **reverend**: revered because of age

115: **grace**: sovereignty

KENT

To go out of my dialect, which you discommend so much. I know,   95
sir, I am no flatterer. He that beguiled you in a plain accent was a
plain knave, which for my part I will not be, though I should win
your displeasure to entreat me to't.

CORNWALL

[*To OSWALD*] What's the offense you gave him?

OSWALD

I never gave him any.
It pleased the King his master very late   100
To strike at me upon his misconstruction,
When he, conjunct, and flattering his displeasure,
Tripped me behind; being down, insulted, railed,
And put upon him such a deal of man
That worthied him, got praises of the King   105
For him attempting who was self-subdued,
And in the fleshment of this dread exploit
Drew on me here again.

KENT

None of these rogues and cowards
But Ajax is their fool.

CORNWALL

[*Calling*] Bring forth the stocks, ho!
                                        [*Exeunt some servants*]
You stubborn, ancient knave, you reverend braggart,   110
We'll teach you.

KENT

Sir, I am too old to learn.
Call not your stocks for me. I serve the King,
On whose employments I was sent to you.
You shall do small respect, show too bold malice
Against the grace and person of my master,   115
Stocking his messenger.

120: **being**: because you are

121: **nature**: character

122: **away**: along

123-128: **Let me...punish'd with**: appears only in the First Quarto

125: **check**: correct; **low correction**: punishment unworthy of Kent's rank

126: **contemnèd**: 1) condemned, and 2) despised

127: **pilf'rings**: thefts

130: **I'll answer that**: I will answer for that (i.e., I will answer to the King for punishing him.)

133: **For following...his legs**: appears only in the First Quarto

133: Stage Direction: *[They put KENT in the stocks.]*: appears only in the First Quarto

134: Stage Direction: *Manet*: Latin for "He (or she) remains," *manet* is used as a stage direction preceding the names of characters who are to remain on stage for the ensuing action while others leave.

CORNWALL
>   [*Calling*] Fetch forth the stocks!—
> As I have life and honor, there shall he sit till noon.

REGAN
> Till noon? Till night, my lord, and all night too.

KENT
> Why, madam, if I were your father's dog
> You could not use me so.

REGAN
>   Sir, being his knave, I will.   120
>   *Stocks brought out*

CORNWALL
> This is a fellow of the selfsame nature
> Our sister speaks of.—Come, bring away the stocks.

GLOUCESTER
> Let me beseech your grace not to do so.
> His fault is much, and the good King his master
> Will check him for't. Your purposed low correction   125
> Is such as basest and contemnèd wretches
> For pilf'rings and most common trespasses
> Are punish'd with. The King must take it ill
> That he's so slightly valued in his messenger,
> Should have him thus restrained.

CORNWALL
>   I'll answer that.   130

REGAN
> My sister may receive it much more worse
> To have her gentleman abused, assaulted,
> For following her affairs. Put in his legs.
>   *[They put KENT in the stocks.]*
> Come, my good lord, away.
>   *[Exeunt. Manet GLOUCESTER and KENT.]*

137: **rubbed**: hindered; **entreat**: intercede

138: **watched**: kept the watch at night instead of sleeping

140: **A good...heels**: Even good men suffer major setbacks sometimes. Literally, the phrase means "to become so poor that one's feet come through the holes in their threadbare stockings".

141: **Give you**: may God give you

143: **Approve...say**: prove the proverb true

146: **Approach, thou beacon**: sun, spread your light (i.e., rise)

147: **comfortable**: comforting

148-149 **Nothing...misery**: i.e., How much more dear miracles are when one is miserable.

151: **obscurèd**: Kent is in disguise and thus, obscured.

153: **remedies**: i.e., cures for what ails the kingdom; **overwatched**: exhausted from not sleeping

154: **Take vantage , heavy eyes**: take advantage of your tiredness

155: **shameful lodging**: i.e., the stocks in which he has been placed

155-156 **Fortune...wheel**: Since Kent is at the bottom of the wheel of Fortune, he's hoping it will turn for him while he sleeps (see also 1.1.274, 2.1.39, 4.6.211, 5.3.6 and 5.3.173).

156: Stage Direction: *Sleeps*: Most editions introduce a new scene division here. This edition does not because Kent remains on stage throughout and the location, before Gloucester's house, remains unchanged.

156: Stage Direction: *Enter Edgar*: In Joseph Papp's 1974 New York City production, Edgar (played by Rene Auberjonois, later of *Deep Space Nine* and *Boston Legal*), was easy-going, open, and, like Cordeila, a little naïve. However, by the time he put on his Poor Tom disguise, he had learned just how profoundly he was deceived. His brother, Edmund, was a lot like Iago in *Othello*: playful and confident, but never jovial.

157: **proclaimed**: declared a wanted man

158: **happy**: luckily or fortunately found

160: **That**: in which

GLOUCESTER

I am sorry for thee, friend. 'Tis the Duke's pleasure,   135
Whose disposition, all the world well knows,
Will not be rubbed nor stopped. I'll entreat for thee.

KENT

Pray you, do not, sir. I have watched and traveled hard.
Some time I shall sleep out; the rest I'll whistle.
A good man's fortune may grow out at heels.   140
Give you good morrow.

GLOUCESTER

The duke's to blame in this; 'twill be ill took.

Exit

KENT

Good King, that must approve the common say,
Thou out of heaven's benediction com'st
To the warm sun.   145
[He takes out a letter]

Approach, thou beacon to this under globe,
That by thy comfortable beams I may
Peruse this letter. Nothing almost sees miracles
But misery. I know 'tis from Cordelia,
Who hath most fortunately been informed   150
Of my obscurèd course, and shall find time
For this enormous state, seeking to give
Losses their remedies. All weary and overwatched,
Take vantage, heavy eyes, not to behold
This shameful lodging. Fortune, good night;   155
Smile; once more; turn thy wheel.

Sleeps
[Enter EDGAR]

EDGAR

I heard myself proclaimed,
And by the happy hollow of a tree
Escaped the hunt. No port is free, no place
That guard and most unusual vigilance   160

161: **attend my taking**: wait to capture me

162: **bethought**: determined

164: **penury**: poverty

165: **grime**: cover

166: **elf**: tangle (elves were thought to mess up one's hair during sleep)

167: **presented**: uncovered, fully displayed; **outface**: confront

169: **proof**: example

170: **Bedlam beggars**: beggars from Bedlam, a lunatic asylum in London

171: **strike**: stick; **numbed and mortified**: cold and deadened

173: **object**: spectacle; **low**: lowly

174: **pelting**: paltry

175: **lunatic bans**: insane curses

176: **Enforce their charity**: persuade them to give me something; **Tuelygod**: meaning unknown, but the term may suggest the meaningless babble of Edgar's adopted persona as a beggar

176: **Poor...Tom!**: Edgar seems to be practicing his new identity as a beggar. Beggars were known as "poor Toms".

177: **That's...am**: As poor Tom I can make a life for myself. My life as Edgar has ceased to be.

177: Stage Direction: **_Exit_**: Most editions introduce a new scene division here. Again, this edition does not because Kent remains on stage throughout, and the location, before Gloucester's house, remains unchanged.

178: **they**: i.e., Regan and Cornwall

181: **remove**: move to a different location

182: **shame**: i.e., being in the stocks

Does not attend my taking. While I may scape
I will preserve myself, and am bethought
To take the basest and most poorest shape
That ever penury in contempt of man
Brought near to beast. My face I'll grime with filth,   165
Blanket my loins, elf all my hair with knots,
And with presented nakedness outface
The wind and persecution of the sky.
The country gives me proof and precedent
Of Bedlam beggars who with roaring voices   170
Strike in their numbed and mortified bare arms
Pins, wooden pricks, nails, sprigs of rosemary,
And with this horrible object from low farms,
Poor pelting villages, sheep-cotes and mills,
Sometime with lunatic bans, sometime with prayers   175
Enforce their charity. "Poor Tuelygod, Poor Tom!"
That's something yet. Edgar I nothing am.

Exit
Enter [King] LEAR, [FOOL, and a KNIGHT]

LEAR
  'Tis strange that they should so depart from home
  And not send back my messenger.

KNIGHT
                    As I learned,
  The night before there was no purpose in them   180
  Of his remove.

KENT
            [*Waking*] Hail to thee, noble master.

LEAR
  How! Mak'st thou this shame thy pastime?

KENT
                    No, my lord.

183: **cruel garters**: a joke: garters cover legs, hence the stocks are garters

183: "Ha, ha, look, he wears cruel garters!": Henry Woronicz as Kent and Floyd King as the Fool in the 2000 Shakespeare Theatre Company production directed by Michael Kahn

Photo: Carol Rosegg

185: **over-lusty at legs**: 1) prone to running, or 2) sexually hyperactive

186: **nether-stocks**: stockings

188: **To**: as to

190: **No, no...they have**: appears only in the First Quarto

192: **By Juno, I swear ay**: from the First Folio

192: **Juno**: wife of Jupiter (Kent may be laying the blame with Regan more than with Cornwall.)

FOOL
Ha, ha, look, he wears cruel garters! Horses are tied by the heads,
dogs and bears by th' neck, monkeys by th' loins, and men by th'
legs. When a man's over-lusty at legs, then he wears wooden   185
nether-stocks.

LEAR
[*To KENT*] What's he that hath so much thy place mistook
To set thee here?

KENT
                    It is both he and she:
Your son and daughter.

LEAR
                    No.

KENT
                         Yes.

LEAR
                              No, I say.

KENT
I say, yea.

LEAR
        No, no, they would not.

KENT
                              Yes, they have.   190

LEAR
By Jupiter, I swear, no.

KENT
By Juno, I swear ay.

194: **upon respect**: in spite of my officers, who deserve to be obeyed; **outrage**: insult to the King

195: **Resolve**: inform; **modest**: moderate

198: **commend**: deliver

199-200: **from...kneeling**: from the kneeling position (an indication of my duty)

200: **reeking post**: mail carrier who is hot, sweaty and smelling from his journey

201: **Stewed**: soaked in sweat

203: **spite of intermission**: without concern for interrupting me

205: **meiny**: servants

211: **Displayed so saucily**: behaved in such an impudent manner

212: **Having...wit**: being more manly or fierce than sensible

214: **trespass**: uncivil behavior

216-224: **Winter's not...a year**: from the First Folio

216: **Winter's...way**: if the geese are still flying south, then harsh winter weather is still on its way; i.e., things could still get worse

218: **blind**: indifferent to their fathers' needs

219: **bags**: bags of money

222: **turns the key**: unlocks the door

223: **dolors**: 1) pains, but also 2) a pun on "dollars", a foreign coin at the time

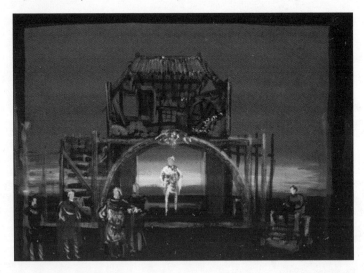

Set design for the 1959 production at the Shakespeare Memorial Theatre in Stratford-upon-Avon directed by Glen Byam Shaw

Rare Book and Special Collection Library, University of Illinois at Urbana-Champaign

LEAR
                    They durst not do't,
They would not, could not do't. 'Tis worse than murder,
To do upon respect such violent outrage.
Resolve me, with all modest haste which way   195
Thou may'st deserve or they propose this usage,
Coming from us.

KENT
                    My lord, when at their home
I did commend your Highness' letters to them,
Ere I was risen from the place that showed
My duty kneeling, came there a reeking post   200
Stewed in his haste, half breathless, panting forth
From Gonoril, his mistress, salutations,
Delivered letters spite of intermission,
Which presently they read, on whose contents
They summoned up their meiny, straight took horse,   205
Commanded me to follow and attend
The leisure of their answer, gave me cold looks;
And meeting here the other messenger,
Whose welcome I perceived, had poisoned mine—
Being the very fellow that of late   210
Displayed so saucily against your Highness—
Having more man than wit about me, drew.
He raised the house with loud and coward cries.
Your son and daughter found this trespass worth
This shame which here it suffers.   215

FOOL
Winter's not gone yet if the wild geese fly that way.
        [Sings]
        Fathers that wear rags
        Do make their children blind,
        But fathers that bear bags
        Shall see their children kind.   220
        Fortune, that arrant whore,
        Ne'er turns the key to th' poor.
But for all this thou shalt have as many dolors for thy daughters
as thou canst tell in a year.

225-226 **O, how...*passio***: Based on ancient Greek medical traditions, it was thought in the Renaissance that the womb moved around in the body. When a woman remained a virgin too long, the womb was thought to move upward in the body, thus making breathing difficult. Lear feels as if he is suffocating.

226 ***Hysterica passio***: Literally, hysterical passion or passion of the womb. Lear is afraid that he will go mad from grief and that he is reacting in an unmanly way be being so emotional (see 1.4.271-274 for an expression of Lear's fear of feminine emotion).

227: **Thy element's below**: The womb belongs lower in the body, where it will not interfere with one's breathing.

230: **How...King**: why does Lear risk

231: **An**: if

234-235 **We'll...winter**: If an ant knows not to work in the winter, then a wise man knows not to work on behalf of someone who is down on his luck.

235-237 **All that...stinking**: A person who has fallen on hard times may be easily avoided by those who can smell (detect) his misfortune.

244: **pack**: depart

LEAR
O, how this mother swells up toward my heart!   225
Hysterica passio, down, thou climbing sorrow;
Thy element's below.—Where is this daughter?

KENT
With the Earl, sir, here within.

LEAR
                            Follow me not; stay there.

                                                    [Exit]

KNIGHT
[*To KENT*] Made you no more offense than what you speak of?

KENT
No. How chance the King comes with so small a train?   230

FOOL
An thou hadst been set in the stocks for that question, thou hadst
well deserved it.

KENT
Why, fool?

FOOL
We'll set thee to school to an ant, to teach thee there's no laboring
in the winter. All that follow their noses are led by their eyes but   235
blind men, and there's not a nose among a hundred but can smell
him that's stinking. Let go thy hold when a great wheel runs
down a hill, lest it break thy neck with following it; but the great
one that goes up the hill, let him draw thee after. When a wise
man gives thee better counsel, give me mine again. I would have   240
none but knaves follow it, since a fool gives it.
          [*Sings*]
          That sir that serves and seeks for gain
          And follows but for form,
          Will pack when it begins to rain,
          And leave thee in the storm,   245

246: "But I will tarry, the fool will stay": Henry Woronicz as Kent and Floyd King as the Fool in the 2000 Shakespeare Theatre Company production directed by Michael Kahn

Photo: Carol Rosegg

248: **The knave...away**: a servant who leaves his master is a fool

249: **pardie**: from the French, "*par Dieu*," for "by God"

254: **images**: signs; **flying off**: desertion

261-262: **Well...man?**: from the First Folio

But I will tarry, the fool will stay,
And let the wise man fly.
The knave turns fool that runs away,
The fool no knave, pardie.

KENT

Where learnt you this, fool?   250

FOOL

Not in the stocks, fool.

Enter LEAR and GLOUCESTER

LEAR

Deny to speak with me? They're sick, they're weary?
They have traveled hard tonight?—mere insolence,
Ay, the images of revolt and flying off.
Fetch me a better answer.

GLOUCESTER

                                    My dear lord,   255
You know the fiery quality of the Duke,
How unremoveable and fixed he is
In his own course.

LEAR

                          Vengeance, death, plague, confusion!
What "fiery quality"? Why, Gloucester, Gloucester, I'd
Speak with the Duke of Cornwall and his wife.   260

GLOUCESTER

Well, my good lord, I have informed them so.

LEAR

"Informed them"! Dost thou understand me, man?

GLOUCESTER

Ay, my good lord.

265: **tends**: waits for

266: **Are...blood**: from the First Folio

266: **My breath and blood**: by my very life (an oath)

269-270: **Infirmity...bound**: i.e., Illness compels us to neglect those duties we would be obligated to perform if we were well.

272: **forbear**: hold off my condemnation

273: **am fallen out**: now disapprove of; **headier**: impetuous

274: **to take**: to have initially assumed

275: **sound man**: those who are in good health; **Death...state**: a common oath, relevant here given the status of Lear's kingship

277: **remotion**: removal from the King's sight

278: **practice**: deception; **Give...forth**: Release my servant from the stocks.

282: **cry sleep to death**: make so much noise that sleep will become extinct

284: **cockney**: a woman from London who does not know how to cook eels

285: **paste**: pie crust; **coxcombs**: heads

286: **wantons**: 1) playful creatures, but also 2) a sexual reference because eels are phallic. The fool is making an analogy between a cockney wife's unsuccessful efforts to persuade eels to lie still so she can bake them in a pie and Lear's comparably unsuccessful effort to keep his emotions under control.

286-287: **'Twas...hay**: A man who butters hay in order to give his horses a treat is foolish because horses do not like greasy hay (i.e., good intentions cannot compensate for ignorance). This expression is another analogy aimed at depicting the foolishness of Lear's "womanly" emotions and tender-heartedness.

LEAR
      The King would speak with Cornwall; the dear father
      Would with his daughter speak, commands, tends service.   265
      Are they "informed" of this? My breath and blood—
      "Fiery?" The "fiery" Duke?—tell the hot Duke that Lear—
      No, but not yet. Maybe he is not well.
      Infirmity doth still neglect all office
      Whereto our health is bound. We are not ourselves   270
      When nature, being oppressed, commands the mind
      To suffer with the body. I'll forbear,
      And am fallen out with my more headier will,
      To take the indisposed and sickly fit
      For the sound man.—Death on my state,   275
      Wherefore should he sit here? This act persuades me
      That this remotion of the Duke and her
      Is practice only. Give me my servant forth.
      Go tell the Duke and 's wife I'll speak with them,
      Now, presently. Bid them come forth and hear me,   280
      Or at their chamber door I'll beat the drum
      Till it cry sleep to death.

GLOUCESTER
                              I would have all well
      Betwixt you.
                                                              [Exit]

LEAR
                        O me, my heart, my heart!

FOOL
      Cry to it, nuncle, as the cockney did to the eels when she put 'em
      i' th' paste alive. She rapped 'em o' th' coxcombs with a stick,   285
      and cried "Down, wantons, down!" 'Twas her brother that, in
      pure kindness to his horse, buttered his hay.
                        Enter [Duke of] CORNWALL and REGAN,
                                [GLOUCESTER, and others]

LEAR
      Good morrow to you both.

293-294: **I would...adultress**: i.e., I would refuse to honor your mother's tomb because an adulteress is buried there.

296: **naught**: evil

297: **Sharp-tooth'd**: as a serpent (see also 1.4.263, 2.2.322-323, 5.1.57-58 and 5.3.83); **here**: in his heart

299: **quality**: disposition

300-302: **I have...duty**: i.e., I must believe that she is better at fulfilling her obligations to you than you are at evaluating her.

302-307: **Say, how...all blame**: from the First Folio

Costume rendering for Gloucester from the 1959 production at the Shakespeare Memorial Theatre in Stratford-upon-Avon directed by Glen Byam Shaw
Rare Book and Special Collection Library, University of Illinois at Urbana-Champaign

CORNWALL
  Hail to your Grace!

[KENT here set at liberty]

REGAN
  I am glad to see your Highness.   290

LEAR
  Regan, I think you are. I know what reason
  I have to think so. If thou shouldst not be glad
  I would divorce me from thy mother's shrine,
  Sepulch'ring an adultress. [*To KENT*] Yea, are you free?
  Some other time for that.—Belovèd Regan,   295
  Thy sister is naught. O, Regan, she hath tied
  Sharp-tooth'd unkindness like a vulture here.
  I can scarce speak to thee. Thou'lt not believe
  Of how deplored a quality—O, Regan!

REGAN
  I pray you, sir, take patience. I have hope.   300
  You less know how to value her desert
  Than she to slack her duty.

LEAR
                      Say, how is that?

REGAN
  I cannot think my sister in the least
  Would fail her obligation. If, sir, perchance
  She have restrained the riots of your followers,   305
  'Tis on such ground and to such wholesome end
  As clears her from all blame.

LEAR
  My curses on her.

309-310: **Nature...confine**: you have one foot in the grave

311: **By...state**: by someone who is astute enough to understand your present condition

315: **becomes the house**: is appropriate behavior for the royal family (said sarcastically)

318: **raiment**: clothing

319: **unsightly**: distasteful, unendurable

321: **abated**: deprived

322: **black**: disparagingly

322-323: **struck me...serpent-like**: see also 1.4.263, 2.2.297, 5.1.57-58, 5.2.83

325: **ungrateful top**: ungrateful head

326: **taking**: infectious

326: **Fie, fie, sir.**: appears only in the First Quarto

329: **fen-sucked fogs**: infectious vapors from marshes (it was thought that the sun sucked up poisonous gasses from marshes)

330: **blast her pride**: destroy her vanity by causing blisters to form on her (appears only in the First Quarto)

REGAN

                   O sir, you are old.
Nature in you stands on the very verge
Of her confine. You should be ruled and led   310
By some discretion that discerns your state
Better than you yourself. Therefore I pray you
That to our sister you do make return;
Say you have wronged her, sir.

LEAR

                       Ask her forgiveness?
Do you but mark how this becomes the house?   315
[*Kneeling*] "Dear daughter, I confess that I am old.
Age is unnecessary. On my knees I beg
That you'll vouchsafe me raiment, bed, and food."

REGAN

Good sir, no more. These are unsightly tricks.
Return you to my sister.

LEAR

              [*Rising*] No, Regan.   320
She hath abated me of half my train,
Looked black upon me, struck me with her tongue
Most serpent-like upon the very heart.
All the stored vengeances of heaven fall
On her ungrateful top! Strike her young bones,   325
You taking airs, with lameness!

CORNWALL

                  Fie, fie, sir.

LEAR

You nimble lightnings, dart your blinding flames
Into her scornful eyes. Infect her beauty,
You fen-sucked fogs drawn by the pow'rful sun
To fall and blast her pride.   330

333: **tender-hefted**: gentle, sensitive

337: **bandy**: exchange; **scant my sizes**: reduce my monetary allotments

339: **oppose the bolt**: lock the door

340: **The offices...childhood**: those duties and obligations that are natural between parent and child

341: **effects**: standard practices

343: **to th' purpose**: get to the point

345: **approves**: confirms

347: **easy-borrowed**: easily assumed

348: **fickle grace**: unpredictable favor

349: **varlet**: worthless person

REGAN

      O, the blest gods!   330
 So will you wish on me when the rash mood—

LEAR

 No, Regan. Thou shalt never have my curse.
 Thy tender-hefted nature shall not give
 Thee o'er to harshness. Her eyes are fierce, but thine
 Do comfort and not burn. 'Tis not in thee   335
 To grudge my pleasures, to cut off my train,
 To bandy hasty words, to scant my sizes,
 And, in conclusion, to oppose the bolt
 Against my coming in. Thou better know'st
 The offices of nature, bond of childhood,   340
 Effects of courtesy, dues of gratitude.
 Thy half of the kingdom hast thou not forgot,
 Wherein I thee endowed.

REGAN

      Good sir, to th' purpose.

LEAR

 Who put my man i' th' stocks?

            [Trumpet within]

CORNWALL

      What trumpet's that?
      Enter Steward [OSWALD]

REGAN

 I know't, my sister's. This approves her letters 345
 That she would soon be here. *[To OSWALD]* Is your lady come?

LEAR

 This is a slave, whose easy-borrowed pride
 Dwells in the fickle grace of her a follows.

         [He strikes OSWALD]

 Out, varlet, from my sight!

353: **Allow**: approve

358: **indiscretion**: lack of good judgment

359: **sides**: i.e., the sides of his chest, which can hardly contain his bursting sorrow

362: **much less advancement**: to be treated much more harshly

363: **seem so**: act accordingly

363: "I pray you, father, being weak, seem so": Angela Pierce as Gonoril and Laura Odeh as Regan in the 2007 Public Theater production directed by James Lapine
Photo: Michal Daniel

365: **sojourn**: stay with

367: **from**: away from

368: **entertainment**: appropriate care

CORNWALL

What means your grace?

Enter GONORIL

GONORIL

Who struck my servant? Regan, I have good hope   350
Thou didst not know on't.

LEAR

Who comes here? O heavens,
If you do love old men, if your sweet sway
Allow obedience, if yourselves are old,
Make it your cause! Send down and take my part.
[*To GONORIL*] Art not ashamed to look upon this beard?   355
O Regan, wilt thou take her by the hand?

GONORIL

Why not by the hand, sir? How have I offended?
All's not offense that indiscretion finds
And dotage terms so.

LEAR

O sides, you are too tough!
Will you yet hold?—How came my man i' th' stocks?   360

CORNWALL

I set him there, sir; but his own disorders
Deserved much less advancement.

LEAR

You? Did you?

REGAN

I pray you, father, being weak, seem so.
If till the expiration of your month
You will return and sojourn with my sister,   365
Dismissing half your train, come then to me.
I am now from home, and out of that provision
Which shall be needful for your entertainment.

370: **abjure**: do without

372: **wage**: do battle

373: **Necessity's sharp pinch**: hunger's discomfort

374: **hot-blood**: youthful and spirited; **in France**: (referring to the King of France)

376: **knee**: kneel down before

378: **sumpter**: packhorse (a beast of burden)

386: **embossèd carbuncle**: swollen tumor

388: **call**: summon

389: **thunder-bearer**: i.e., Jove (Jupiter, in Roman mythology), the god of the sky and thunder (see also 1.1.173)

390: **high-judging**: judging from on high

394: **look not for you**: was not expecting you

395: **Give ear**: listen

396: **For...passion**: for those who rationally interpret your temper tantrums

LEAR

    Return to her, and fifty men dismissed?

    No, rather I abjure all roofs, and choose   370

    To be a comrade with the wolf and owl,

    To wage against the enmity of the air

    Necessity's sharp pinch. Return with her?

    Why, the hot-blood in France that dowerless took

    Our youngest born—I could as well be brought   375

    To knee his throne and, squire-like, pension beg

    To keep base life afoot. Return with her?

    Persuade me rather to be slave and sumpter

    To this detested groom.

GONORIL

                         At your choice, sir.

LEAR

    Now I prithee, daughter, do not make me mad.   380

    I will not trouble thee, my child. Farewell.

    We'll no more meet, no more see one another.

    But yet thou art my flesh, my blood, my daughter –

    Or rather a disease that lies within my flesh,

    Which I must needs call mine. Thou art a boil,   385

    A plague-sore, an embossèd carbuncle

    In my corrupted blood. But I'll not chide thee.

    Let shame come when it will, I do not call it.

    I do not bid the thunder-bearer shoot,

    Nor tell tales of thee to high-judging Jove.   390

    Mend when thou canst; be better at thy leisure.

    I can be patient, I can stay with Regan,

    I and my hundred knights.

REGAN

                   Not altogether so, sir.

    I look not for you yet, nor am provided

    For your fit welcome. Give ear, sir, to my sister;   395

    For those that mingle reason with your passion

    Must be content to think you are old, and so—

    But she knows what she does.

399: **avouch**: vouch for

401: **sith that**: since; **charge**: expense

407: **slack**: neglect

408: **control**: discipline

410: **five-and-twenty**: appears only in the First Quarto (see also lines 416 and 423)

411: **place or notice**: residence or hospitality

413: **depositaries**: trustees of royal power

414: **kept a reservation**: reserved the right

416: **five-and-twenty**: appears only in the First Quarto (see also lines 410 and 423)

LEAR

Is this well spoken now?

REGAN

I dare avouch it, sir. What, fifty followers?
Is it not well? What should you need of more,   400
Yea, or so many, sith that both charge and danger
Speaks 'gainst so great a number? How in a house
Should many people under two commands
Hold amity? 'Tis hard, almost impossible.

GONORIL

Why might not you, my lord, receive attendance   405
From those that she calls servants, or from mine?

REGAN

Why not, my lord? If then they chanced to slack you,
We could control them. If you will come to me—
For now I spy a danger—I entreat you
To bring but five-and-twenty; to no more   410
Will I give place or notice.

LEAR

I gave you all.

REGAN

And in good time you gave it.

LEAR

Made you my guardians, my depositaries,
But kept a reservation to be followed
With such a number. What, must I come to you   415
With five-and-twenty, Regan? Said you so?

REGAN

And speak't again, my lord. No more with me.

418: **well favored**: attractive

420: **Stands...praise**: is, by comparison, deserving of praise

423: **five-and-twenty**: appears only in the First Quarto (see also lines 410 and 416)

424: **follow**: wait on you

426: **reason not**: do not interpret rationally

427-428: **Our...superfluous**: Even the most impoverished among us have some small thing beyond what they absolutely need to survive.

437-438: **fool me...tamely**: do not make me so foolish as to tolerate this calmly

439: **woman's weapons**: tears

441: "I will have such revenges on you both": Ted van Griethuysen as Lear and Jennifer Harmon as Regan in the 2000 Shakespeare Theatre Company production directed by Michael Kahn

Photo: Carol Rosegg

LEAR
    Those wicked creatures yet do seem well favored
    When others are more wicked. Not being the worst
    Stands in some rank of praise. [*To GONORIL*] I'll go with thee.   420
    Thy fifty yet doth double five-and-twenty,
    And thou art twice her love.

GONORIL
                          Hear me, my lord
    What need you five-and-twenty, ten, or five,
    To follow in a house where twice so many
    Have a command to tend you?

REGAN
                    What needs one?   425

LEAR
    O, reason not the need! Our basest beggars
    Are in the poorest thing superfluous.
    Allow not nature more than nature needs,
    Man's life's as cheap as beast's. Thou art a lady.
    If only to go warm were gorgeous,   430
    Why, nature needs not what thou, gorgeous, wearest,
    Which scarcely keeps thee warm. But for true need—
    You heavens, give me that patience, patience I need.
    You see me here, you gods, a poor old fellow,
    As full of grief as age, wretchèd in both.   435
    If it be you that stir these daughters' hearts
    Against their father, fool me not so much
    To bear it tamely. Touch me with noble anger.
    O, let not women's weapons, water-drops,
    Stain my man's cheeks! No, you unnatural hags,   440
    I will have such revenges on you both
    That all the world shall—I will do such things—
    What they are, yet I know not; but they shall be
    The terrors of the earth. You think I'll weep.
    No, I'll not weep.   445
                         [Storm within]

447: **flaws**: pieces

448: **Or ere**: before

451: **bestowed**: accommodated; **blame**: fault

452: **Hath**: that he has; **put...rest**: 1)made himself homeless, 2) lost his sense of security; **taste**: suffer the consequences of

453: **For his particular**: with regard for him individually

457: **high**: extreme

457-458: **Whither...horse**: from the First Folio

458: **calls to horse**: call for his horse

459: **give him way**: let him go where he pleases; **He leads himself**: he follows his own stubborn path

I have full cause of weeping, but this heart
Shall break into a hundred thousand flaws
Or ere I'll weep.—O fool, I shall go mad!
          Exeunt LEAR, GLOUCESTER, KENT, [KNIGHT] and FOOL

CORNWALL
    Let us withdraw. 'Twill be a storm.

REGAN
    This house is little. The old man and his people   450
    Cannot be well bestowed.

GONORIL
                    'Tis his own blame;
    Hath put himself from rest, and must needs taste his folly.

REGAN
    For his particular I'll receive him gladly,
    But not one follower.

GONORIL
    So am I purposed. Where is my Lord of Gloucester?   455

CORNWALL
    Followed the old man forth.
                                    Enter GLOUCESTER
                    He is returned.

GLOUCESTER
    The king is in high rage.

CORNWALL
                    Whither is he going?

GLOUCESTER
    He calls to horse, and will I know not whither.

REGAN
    'Tis good to give him way. He leads himself.

460: entreat...means: do not ask him under any circumstances

462: rustle: blow

467-468: being...abused: predisposed to take bad advice

GONORIL
[*To GLOUCESTER*] My lord, entreat him by no means to stay.   460

GLOUCESTER
Alack, the night comes on, and the bleak winds
Do sorely rustle. For many miles a bout
There's not a bush.

REGAN
                              O, sir, to willful men
The injuries that they themselves procure
Must be their schoolmasters. Shut up your doors.   465
He is attended with a desperate train,
And what they may incense him to, being apt
To have his ear abused, wisdom bids fear.

CORNWALL
Shut up your doors, my lord. 'Tis a wild night.
My Regan counsels well. Come out o' th' storm.   470
                                                      Exeunt

[King Lear

Act 3

0: **Location**: a clearing in Gloucestershire

3: **fretful element**: agitated earth

5: **main**: mainland

6-14: **tears his...take all**: appears only in the First Quarto

7: **eyeless rage**: rage that is blind (to Lear's royal status)

8: **make nothing of**: toss about disrespectfully

11: **cub-drawn bear**: mother bear who is weak and weary from starving herself to feed her cubs; **couch**: crouch, hide inside the den

13: **keep their fur dry**: i.e., remain inside; **unbonneted**: hatless, uncovered

14: **bids what will take all**: goes all in (from gambling, signalling desperate defiance, when a gambler defiantly bets everything on one last hand)

15-16: **outjest...injuries**: rid the body of illness with humor

Act 3, Scene 1]

KENT
What's here, besides foul weather?

FIRST GENTLEMAN
                                    One minded like the weather,
Most unquietly.

KENT
                    I know you. Where's the king?

FIRST GENTLEMAN
Contending with the fretful element;
Bids the winds blow the earth into the sea
Or swell the curlèd water 'bove the main,   5
That things might change or cease; tears his white hair,
Which the impetuous blasts, with eyeless rage,
Catch in their fury, and make nothing of;
Strives in his little world of man to outstorm
The to-and-fro-conflicting wind and rain.   10
This night, wherein the cub-drawn bear would couch,
The lion and the belly-pinchèd wolf
Keep their fur dry, unbonneted he runs,
And bids what will take all.

KENT
                        But who is with him?

FIRST GENTLEMAN
None but the Fool, who labors to outjest   15
His heart-struck injuries.

Costume rendering for Kent from the 1959 production at the Shakespeare
Memorial Theatre in Stratford-upon-Avon directed by Glen Byam Shaw

Rare Book and Special Collection Library, University of Illinois at Urbana-Champaign

17-18: **And dare...you**: and risk, on the basis of what kind of person I know you to
be, to entrust you with a secret mission

20: **mutual cunning**: seeming goodwill on both sides

21-28: **Who have...furnishings**: from the First Folio

21-22: **as who...high**: as all who have achieved greatness do

22: **no less**: nothing more than servants

23: **speculations**: secret agents

24: **Intelligent of**: providing information pertinent to

25: **snuffs and packings**: resentments and plots

26-27: **Or the...King**: or the harsh restrictions the two of them have imposed on Lear

28: **furnishings**: outward shows

29-41: **But true...to you**: appears only in the First Quarto

29: **power**: army

30: **scattered**: fragmented, divided

31: **wise in**: capitalizing upon; **feet**: footholds

32: **at point**: prepared for battle

33: **open banner**: unfurled flag (here implying true intentions)

34: **credit**: trustworthiness; **so far**: so far as

35: **make your speed**: make haste, go quickly

36: **just**: accurate

38: **plain**: complain

39: **of blood and breeding**: of noble birth

40: **assurance**: confidence

41: **office**: assignment

44: **out-wall**: outer wall; i.e., external appearance

46: **fear not but**: be assured that

47: **fellow**: i.e., Kent

KENT
>   Sir, I do know you,
And dare, upon the warrant of my art
Commend a dear thing to you. There is division,
Although as yet the face of it be covered
With mutual cunning, 'twixt Albany and Cornwall;   20
Who have—as who have not that their great stars
Throned and set high—servants, who seem no less,
Which are to France the spies and speculations
Intelligent of our state. What hath been seen,
Either in snuffs and packings of the Dukes,   25
Or the hard rein which both of them have borne
Against the old kind King; or something deeper,
Whereof perchance these are but furnishings—
But true it is. From France there comes a power
Into this scattered kingdom, who already,   30
Wise in our negligence, have secret feet
In some of our best ports, and are at point
To show their open banner. Now to you:
If on my credit you dare build so far
To make your speed to Dover, you shall find   35
Some that will thank you, making just report
Of how unnatural and bemadding sorrow
The King hath cause to plain.
I am a gentleman of blood and breeding,
And, from some knowledge and assurance offer   40
This office to you.

FIRST GENTLEMAN
I will talk further with you.

KENT
>   No, do not.
For confirmation that I am much more
Than my out-wall, open this purse, and take
What it contains. If you shall see Cordelia—   45
As fear not but you shall—show her this ring
And she will tell you who your fellow is,
That yet you do not know. Fie on this storm!
I will go seek the King.

50: **to effect**: in their consequences

50-51: **Few words...yet**: I have but a few words to say, but they are of greater consequence than all I have said so far.

52: **in which...that**: in which effort, I'll go my way and you'll go yours

53: **lights on him**: comes upon him

FIRST GENTLEMAN

                    Give me your hand.
Have you no more to say?

KENT

                    Few words, but to effect,   50
More than all yet: that, when we have found the King—
In which endeavor I'll this way, you that—
He that first lights on him holla the other.

                                [Exeunt]

0: Location: a clearing in Gloucestershire

0: Scene: Edmund Kean (1787-1833) experimented with a wind machine, but the noise was such that audiences had difficulty hearing his lines. The productions of his son, Charles Kean (1811-1868), included masses of black clouds drifting across the sky, glimpses of moonlight, howling winds, thunderclaps, and even rain pattering on the stage. Laurence Olivier (1907-1989) "moved like a tall ship driven before the storm," while in Peter Brook's 1971 film, Paul Scofield seemed detached, as if speaking from another world.

tracks 19-21

1–24:
Donald Wolfit as Lear and Job Stewart as the Fool
Paul Scofield as Lear and Kenneth Branagh as the Fool

1: **Blow, wind, and crack your cheeks**: Maps in Shakespeare's day often depicted Aeolus, god of the wind, with puffed cheeks, blowing ships upon the sea.
2: **cataracts**: heavy downpours; **hurricanoes**: waterspouts
3: **drenched**: drowned; **steeples**: churches; **cocks**: weathervanes
4: **thought-executing fires**: lightning that acts with the quickness of thought
5: **Vaunt-couriers**: forerunners
8: **Crack nature's mould**: break apart the mold from which all life is made;
all germens spill: damage all the seeds
10: **court holy water**: courtly flattery
14: **Nor**: neither
15: **tax**: accuse
17: **subscription**: allegiance
20: **ministers**: agents
21: **pernicious**: evil
22: **high-engendered battles**: regiments of troops created in heaven

[Storm.] Enter LEAR and FOOL.

LEAR
    Blow, wind, and crack your cheeks! Rage, blow,
    You cataracts and hurricanoes, spout
    Till you have drenched the steeples, drowned the cocks!
    You sulphurous and thought-executing fires,
    Vaunt-couriers to oak-cleaving thunderbolts,   5
    Singe my white head; and thou all-shaking thunder,
    Smite flat the thick rotundity of the world,
    Crack nature's mould, all germens spill at once
    That make ingrateful man.

FOOL
    O nuncle, court holy water in a dry house is better than this   10
    rainwater out o' door. Good nuncle, in, and ask thy daughter's
    blessing. Here's a night pities neither wise man nor fool.

LEAR
    Rumble thy bellyful; spit, fire; spout, rain.
    Nor rain, wind, thunder, fire are my daughters.
    I tax not you, you elements, with unkindness.   15
    I never gave you kingdom, called you children.
    You owe me no subscription. Why then, let fall
    Your horrible pleasure. Here I stand your slave,
    A poor, infirm, weak and despised old man,
    But yet I call you servile ministers,   20
    That have with two pernicious daughters joined
    Your high-engendered battles 'gainst a head
    So old and white as this. O, ho, 'tis foul!

1–24:
Donald Wolfit as Lear and Job Stewart as the Fool
Paul Scofield as Lear and Kenneth Branagh as the Fool

Alan Howard as Lear and Alan Dobie as the Fool in the 1997 production at the
Old Vic directed by Peter Hall

Photo: Donald Cooper

24: **head piece**: 1) helmet, and 2) a head for common sense
25: **codpiece**: an ornamental covering for the male genitals worn over the pants
(here, a house for the penis)
25-26: **The codpiece...any**: the man who busies himself finding a woman in which
to put his genitals before he has found a place to live
27: **The head...louse**: will wind up, as many penniless married, couples do, in
lice-infested poverty
29-30: **The man...make**: the man who foolishly prioritizes the baser things in life
over matters of the heart
31-32: **Shall have...wake**: will suffer sadness and sleeplessness
33: **made mouths in a glass**: made faces in a mirror
37: **Marry**: an oath, contracted form of "by the Virgin Mary"; **grace**: royal grace
40: **Gallow**: frighten or terrify; **wanderers of the dark**: wild beasts of the night
41: **keep**: remain inside
46: **pother**: hubbub; i.e., the noise of the storm

FOOL

He that has a house to put his head in has a good head piece.
    [*Sings*]
        The codpiece that will house   25
        Before the head has any,
        The head and he shall louse,
        So beggars marry many.
        The man that makes his toe
        What he his heart should make   30
        Shall have a corn cry woe,
        And turn his sleep to wake—
For there was never yet fair woman but she made mouths in a glass.

LEAR

No, I will be the pattern of all patience.
                              [He sits.] Enter KENT, [disguised].
I will say nothing.   35

KENT

Who's there?

FOOL

Marry, here's grace and a codpiece—that's a wise man and a fool.

KENT

[*To LEAR*] Alas, sir, sit you here? Things that love night
Love not such nights as these. The wrathful skies
Gallow the very wanderers of the dark   40
And makes them keep their caves. Since I was man
Such sheets of fire, such bursts of horrid thunder,
Such groans of roaring wind and rain I ne'er
Remember to have heard. Man's nature cannot carry
The affliction nor the force.

LEAR

                              Let the great gods,   45
That keep this dreadful pother o'er our heads,
Find out their enemies now. Tremble, thou wretch
That hast within thee undivulgèd crimes

50: **simular**: phony
51: **caitiff**: wretch
52: **convenient seeming**: opportune deception
53: **practiced on**: plotted against
54: **Close...centers**: O, you secret and repressed feelings of guilt, tear open those hiding places that conceal you.
55: **And cry...grace**: And pray for mercy; **summoners**: officers who served offenders with warrants to appear before ecclesiastical courts
62: **Which**: the occupants of which; **demanding**: inquiring
64: **scanted**: withheld, meager

"King Lear and the Fool in the Storm"; Painting ca. 1851
William Dyce (1806-1864)

68-69: **The art...precious**: Poverty (necessity) performs the work of alchemy, transforming worthless objects into precious ones. (Lear is mocking the alchemists' practice by ascribing such skills to himself. Like these practitioners, Lear and the Fool's need for shelter have transformed straw into a bed, a hovel into a palace.)
72-75: **He that...day**: part of a popular song sung by Feste in *Twelfth Night* (5.1)

Unwhipped of justice; hide thee, thou bloody hand,
Thou perjured and thou simular man of virtue   50
That art incestuous; caitiff, in pieces shake,
That under covert and convenient seeming
Hast practiced on man's life;
Close pent-up guilts, rive your concealèd centers
And cry these dreadful summoners grace.   55
I am a man more sinned against than sinning.

KENT
Alack, bare-headed?
Gracious my lord, hard by here is a hovel.
Some friendship will it lend you 'gainst the tempest.
Repose you there whilst I to this hard house—   60
More hard than is the stone whereof 'tis raised,
Which even but now, demanding after you,
Denied me to come in—return, and force
Their scanted courtesy.

LEAR
My wit begins to turn.   65
[To FOOL] Come on, my boy. How dost, my boy? Art cold?
I am cold myself.—Where is this straw, my fellow?
The art of our necessities is strange,
That can make vile things precious. Come, your hovel—
Poor fool and knave, I have one part of my heart   70
That sorrows yet for thee.

FOOL
    [Sings]
    He that has and a little tiny wit,
    With heigh-ho, the wind and the rain,
    Must make content with his fortunes fit,
    For the rain it raineth every day.   75

LEAR
True, my good boy. [To KENT] Come, bring us to this hovel.
                              Exit LEAR and KENT

77-92: This is...his time: from the First Folio

77: brave: excellent

77: This is...courtesan: this night is so stormy it could cool down the lust of a courtesan (prostitute)

78: When...matter: when priests do not practice what they preach

79: mar: dilute

80: When...tailors: when aristocrats try to teach their tailors about fashions

81: No heretics...suitors: when heretics are no longer burned at the stake for violating religious truths; instead, practitioners of lechery, the new heresy, are punished, not by burning but by contracting venereal disease

82: realm of Albion: Kingdom of England. "Albion" is from the Latin *albus*, meaning "white", an allusion to the white cliffs of Dover.

84: right: just

86: When slanders...tongues: when tongues cease to speak slanders

87: cutpurses: pickpockets

88: tell: count

90: who: whoever

91: That going...feet: that walking will be accomplished by use of the feet (an anti-climatic, rather pessimistic conclusion suggesting that in the end, nothing will have changed because none of the reforms mentioned before will ever come to pass)

92: Merlin: the legendary wizard at the court of King Arthur, who lived and ruled after the time of Lear's reign

FOOL
  This is a brave night to cool a courtesan. I'll speak a prophecy ere I go:
      When priests are more in word than matter;
      When brewers mar their malt with water;
      When nobles are their tailors' tutors,   80
      No heretics burned, but wenches' suitors,
      Then shall the realm of Albion
      Come to great confusion.
      When every case in law is right;
      No squire in debt nor no poor knight;   85
      When slanders do not live in tongues,
      Nor cutpurses come not to throngs;
      When usurers tell their gold i' th' field,
      And bawds and whores do churches build,
      Then comes the time, who lives to see't,   90
      That going shall be used with feet.
  This prophecy Merlin shall make; for I live before his time.
                                            Exit

0: Location: Gloucester's house

Set design for the 1959 production at the Shakespeare Memorial Theatre in Stratford-upon-Avon directed by Glen Byam Shaw

Rare Book and Special Collection Library, University of Illinois at Urbana-Champaign

3: **pity**: take mercy on
6: **entreat**: intervene or speak on his behalf
10: **closet**: private chamber
11: **revenged home**: revenged thoroughly
12: **power**: armed force; **incline to**: side with
13: **privily**: privately
17: **toward**: impending
18: **courtesy**: i.e., compassion for Lear; **forbid thee**: forbidden (to be shown by) thee
20-21: **This seems...all**: My betrayal of my father is something he has brought on himself. As such, it will surely put me in line to become the Earl of Gloucester and to receive all of Gloucester's wealth.

Act 3, Scene 3]

Enter GLOUCESTER and the Bastard [EDMUND], with lights

GLOUCESTER
Alack, alack, Edmund, I like not this
Unnatural dealing. When I desired their leave
That I might pity him, they took from me
The use of mine own house, charged me on pain
Of their displeasure neither to speak of him,   5
Entreat for him, nor any way sustain him.

EDMUND
Most savage and unnatural!

GLOUCESTER
Go to, say you nothing. There's a division betwixt the dukes, and
a worse matter than that. I have received a letter this night—'tis
dangerous to be spoken—I have locked the letter in my closet.   10
These injuries the King now bears will be revenged home. There's
part of a power already landed. We must incline to the King. I will
seek him and privily relieve him. Go you and maintain talk with
the Duke, that my charity be not of him perceived. If he ask for
me, I am ill and gone to bed. Though I die for't—as no less is   15
threatened me—the King my old master must be relieved. There
is some strange thing toward. Edmund, pray you be careful.

Exit

EDMUND
This courtesy, forbid thee, shall the Duke
Instantly know, and of that letter too.
This seems a fair deserving, and must draw me   20
That which my father loses: no less than all.
The younger rises when the old do fall.

Exit

0: Location: A clearing before a hovel

Watercolor scene sketch from the promptbook for Charles Kean's 1858 production
Courtesy of the Folger Shakespeare Library

2: **tyranny**: harshness

3: **nature**: human nature

4: **Will't...heart?**: By taking shelter from the storm, Lear will be free to focus on what his daughters have done to him, and it will break his heart (see lines 3.4.11–14).

8: **fixed**: lodged

11: **i' th' mouth**: head on; **free**: i.e., free of anxiety

12: **The body's delicate**: i.e., The body's needs become more pressing.

15: **as**: as if

16: **sure**: fully

Act 3, Scene 4]

Storm. Enter LEAR, KENT [disguised] and FOOL.

KENT
Here is the place, my lord. Good my lord, enter.
The tyranny of the open night's too rough
For nature to endure.

[Storm still]

LEAR
Let me alone.

KENT
Good my lord, enter here.

LEAR
Will't break my heart?

KENT
I had rather break mine own. Good my lord, enter. 5

LEAR
Thou think'st 'tis much that this contentious storm
Invades us to the skin. So 'tis to thee;
But where the greater malady is fixed,
The lesser is scarce felt. Thou'dst shun a bear,
But if thy flight lay toward the roaring sea 10
Thou'dst meet the bear i' th' mouth. When the mind's free,
The body's delicate. This tempest in my mind
Doth from my senses take all feeling else
Save what beats there: filial ingratitude.
Is it not as this mouth should tear this hand 15
For lifting food to't? But I will punish sure.
No, I will weep no more.—In such a night
To shut me out? Pour on, I will endure.

20: **frank**: generous

24: **will not give me leave to ponder**: keeps me from thinking

25: **things**: things such as my daughter's ingratitude

30: **unfed sides**: bodies so thin from hunger that their ribs are visible

31: **looped and windowed raggedness**: ragged clothes full of holes like windows and loopholes

32-33: **I have...this**: When I was King, I did not concern myself enough with the welfare of the impoverished subjects in my kingdom

33: **Take physic, pomp**: fix this problem, you pompous fools who care so little for others; **pomp**: 1) pompous fools, and also 2) a reference to himself, the formerly pompous, meaning "stately" or "splendid"

35: **shake...them**: share the wealth of the kingdom with the poor

37: **Fathom and half**: a nautical cry exclaimed by sailors when measuring the depth of water; here, a playful reference to the heavy rains (from the First Folio)

37–69:
David Tennant as Edgar, John Rogan as the Fool, Anton Lesser as Kent, and Trevor Peacock as Lear
Richard McCabe as Edgar, Kenneth Branagh as the Fool, David Burke as Kent, and Paul Scofield as Lear

In such a night as this! O Regan, Gonoril,
Your old kind father, whose frank heart gave you all—   20
O, that way madness lies. Let me shun that.
No more of that.

KENT
                Good my lord, enter here.

LEAR
Prithee, go in thyself. Seek thy own ease.
This tempest will not give me leave to ponder
On things would hurt me more; but I'll go in.   25
[To FOOL] In, boy; go first. *[Kneeling]* You houseless poverty—
Nay, get thee in. I'll pray, and then I'll sleep.
                                   [Exit FOOL]

Poor naked wretches, whereso'er you are,
That bide the pelting of this pitiless night,
How shall your houseless heads and unfed sides,   30
Your looped and windowed raggedness, defend you
From seasons such as these? O, I have ta'en
Too little care of this. Take physic, pomp,
Expose thyself to feel what wretches feel,
That thou may'st shake the superflux to them   35
And show the heavens more just.
                                   [Enter FOOL]

EDGAR
Fathom and half! Fathom and half! Poor Tom!

FOOL
Come not in here, nuncle; here's a spirit. Help me, help me!

KENT
Give me thy hand. Who's there?

FOOL
A spirit, a spirit. He says his name's Poor Tom.   40

tracks 22-24

37–69:
David Tennant as Edgar, John Rogan as the Fool, Anton Lesser as Kent,
and Trevor Peacock as Lear
Richard McCabe as Edgar, Kenneth Branagh as the Fool, David Burke as Kent,
and Paul Scofield as Lear

45-46: "Hast thou given all to thy two daughters, / And art thou come to this?":
James Earl Jones as Lear, Rene Auberjonois as Edgar, and Tom Aldredge as Fool in
the 1973 Public Theater production directed by Edwin Sherin
Photo: George E. Joseph

49-50: **has laid...potage**: According to Poor Tom, these are all the things that the
devil has done to tempt him to commit suicide and damn him to hell: stowed knives
under his pillow while he was asleep, placed a hangman's noose in his church pew,
and set rat poison next to his soup.
50-52: **made him...traitor**: Here the devil tempts him to sin by encouraging him to
commit flashy, prideful acts such as, in this case, trying to ride a horse over bridges
that are only four inches wide in order to chase his own shadow.
52: **five wits**: a reference either to the five senses, or to the Renaissance notion of the
five mental faculties: common wit, imagination, fantasy, estimation, and memory
53: **star-blasting and taking**: afflictions caused by stars and evil spirits
54-55: **There could...there**: Edgar is swatting at head lice and other insects as if they
were devils.
56: **pass**: wretched situation (Lear is projecting his own troubles onto Poor Tom)
58: **reserved a blanket**: kept a piece of cloth to cover himself; **shamed**: naked
59: **pendulous**: 1) thick, heavy, fog-like, and 2) hanging, suspended

KENT

What art thou that dost grumble there in the straw?
Come forth.

[Enter EDGAR as a Bedlam beggar]

EDGAR

Away, the foul fiend follows me. Through the sharp hawthorn
blows the cold wind. Go to thy cold bed and warm thee.

LEAR

Hast thou given all to thy two daughters,   45
And art thou come to this?

EDGAR

Who gives any thing to Poor Tom, whom the foul fiend hath led
through fire and through flame, through ford and whirlpool, o'er
bog and quagmire; that has laid knives under his pillow and halters
in his pew, set ratsbane by his potage, made him proud of heart to   50
ride on a bay trotting-horse over four-inched bridges, to course his
own shadow for a traitor. Bless thy five wits, Tom's a-cold! Bless
thee from whirlwinds, star-blasting and taking. Do Poor Tom some
charity, whom the foul fiend vexes. There could I have him, now,
and there, and there again, and there.   55

[Storm still]

LEAR

What, has his daughters brought him to this pass?
[To EDGAR] Couldst thou save nothing? Didst thou give them all?

FOOL

Nay, he reserved a blanket, else we had been all shamed.

LEAR

[To EDGAR] Now all the plagues that in the pendulous air
Hang fated o'er men's faults fall on thy daughters!   60

KENT

He hath no daughters, sir.

tracks 22-24

37–69:
David Tennant as Edgar, John Rogan as the Fool, Anton Lesser as Kent, and Trevor Peacock as Lear
Richard McCabe as Edgar, Kenneth Branagh as the Fool, David Burke as Kent, and Paul Scofield as Lear

65: should have thus...flesh: should mutilate themselves by sticking pins into their flesh, as Edgar has done
67: pelican: greedy, parasitic (young pelicans were thought to kill their parents and then feed on their mother's blood)
68: Pillicock: similar in sound to pelican, this word appears in nursery rhymes of the time and may have been a euphemism for penis

69: "This cold night...fools and madmen": Christopher Benjamin as Kent, Michael Maloney as Edgar, Nigel Hawthorne as Lear, and Hiroyuki Sanada as the Fool in the 1999 Royal Shakespeare Company production directed by Yukio Ninagawa
Photo: Donald Cooper

71: commit...spouse: i.e., do not commit adultery. Edgar is mimicking the Ten Commandments in this speech.
75: gloves: gloves given by one's mistress as a token of her love
80: light of ear: attentive for useful gossip; **bloody of hand:** murderous
81-82: creaking...silks: referring to noises made by lovers who sneak around to be with each other
83: placket: opening in a woman's skirt or petticoat
85: Heigh no...boy: random fragments of lyrics from songs

LEAR

    Death, traitor! Nothing could have subdued nature
    To such a lowness but his unkind daughters.
    [*To EDGAR*] Is it the fashion that discarded fathers
    Should have thus little mercy on their flesh?   65
    Judicious punishment. 'Twas this flesh begot
    Those pelican daughters.

EDGAR

    Pillicock sat on pillicock's hill; a lo, lo, lo.

FOOL

    This cold night will turn us all to fools and madmen.

EDGAR

    Take heed o' th' foul fiend; obey thy parents; keep thy word   70
    justly; swear not; commit not with man's sworn spouse; set not
    thy sweet heart on proud array. Tom's a-cold.

LEAR

    What hast thou been?

EDGAR

    A servingman, proud in heart and mind, that curled my hair,
    wore gloves in my cap, served the lust of my mistress' heart, and   75
    did the act of darkness with her; swore as many oaths as I spake
    words, and broke them in the sweet face of heaven; one that slept
    in the contriving of lust, and waked to do it. Wine loved I deeply,
    dice dearly, and in woman out-paramoured the Turk. False of
    heart, light of ear, bloody of hand; hog in sloth, fox in stealth, wolf   80
    in greediness, dog in madness, lion in prey. Let not the creaking of
    shoes nor the rustlings of silks betray thy poor heart to women.
    Keep thy foot out of brothel, thy hand out of placket, thy pen from
    lenders' books, and defy the foul fiend. Still through the hawthorn
    blows the cold wind. Heigh no nonny. Dolphin, my boy, my boy!   85
    Cease, let him trot by.

                                                  [Storm still]

89-90: Thou owest...perfume: Out here, naked to the elements, one is freed from debts to animals who provide materials for making elegant clothes worn at court.
90: the cat no perfume: Musky perfume was derived from the anal glands of the civet cat, a small African or Asian mammal that looks like a cat.
90-91: Here's three...itself: Lear is contrasting Kent, the Fool, and himself, all still dressed in the fineries of the royal court, with Edgar, who is nearly naked and thus close to nature.
91: Unaccommodated: animal-like, stripped of the trappings of society such as clothes

93: Scene: Off, off, you lendings!: Lear begins to take off his clothes here.

94: This is...swim in: the weather is much too nasty to act as if one is about to go for a swim
95: wild field: uncultivated land, like Edgar, who is uncivilized
96: on 's: of his
97: *Flibbertigibbet*: the name of a devil in English folklore who is mentioned in Samuel Harsnett's *Declaration of Egregious Popish Impostures* (1603)

97: "This is the foul fiend": Ted van Griethuysen as Lear, Henry Woronicz as Kent, Floyd King as the Fool, and Cameron Folmar as Edgar in the 2000 Shakespeare Theatre Company production directed by Michael Kahn
Photo: Carol Rosegg

97-98: He...cock: He roams the earth from sundown to sunup (the first crowing of the cock)
98: web and the pin: cataract of the eye; **squinies**: squints
99: white wheat: wheat that is ready to be harvested
101: footed thrice the wold: walked around the earth three times
105: aroint thee: begone

LEAR

Why, thou wert better in thy grave than to answer with thy
uncovered body this extremity of the skies. Is man no more but
this? Consider him well. Thou owest the worm no silk, the beast
no hide, the sheep no wool, the cat no perfume. Ha, here's three   90
on 's are sophisticated; thou art the thing itself. Unaccommodated
man is no more but such a poor, bare, forked animal as thou art.
Off, off, you lendings! Come on, be true.

FOOL

Prithee, nuncle, be content. This is a naughty night to swim in. Now
a little fire in a wild field were like an old lecher's heart—a small   95
spark, all the rest on 's body cold. Look, here comes a walking fire.

                     Enter GLOUCESTER [with a torch]

EDGAR

This is the foul fiend, *Flibbertigibbet*. He begins at curfew, and
walks till the first cock. He gives the web and the pin, squinies the
eye, and makes the harelip; mildews the white wheat, and hurts
the poor creature of earth.   100
      [*Sings*]
      Swithin footed thrice the wold,
      A met the night mare and her nine foal;
      Bid her alight
      And her troth plight,
      And aroint thee, witch, aroint thee!   105

KENT

[*To LEAR*] How fares your Grace?

LEAR

                         What's he?

KENT

[*To GLOUCESTER*] Who's there? What is't you seek?

GLOUCESTER

What are you there? Your names?

110: **wall-newt**: lizard; **water**: frog or water newt

112: **ditch-dog**: a dead dog in a ditch; **green mantle**: pond scum

112: **standing**: stagnant

113: **tithing to tithing**: from one hospital ward to another (see note 1.2.114);
stock-punished: placed in the stocks

116: **deer**: creatures

118: **Smolking**: a familiar demon that appears in Harsnett's *Declaration*
(see note 3.4.97)

120: **The Prince of Darkness**: i.e., the devil

121: **Modo, Mahu**: both are names for the Devil in Harsnett's *Declaration*
(see note 3.4.97)

122-23: **Our flesh...it**: 1) children are now so sinful that they hate their parents,
or 2) life has become so utterly wretched that people regret being born

124: **suffer**: allow me

125: **hard**: merciless

EDGAR
    Poor Tom, that eats the swimming frog, the toad, the tadpole, the
    wall-newt and the water; that in the fury of his heart, when the foul   110
    fiend rages, eats cow-dung for salads, swallows the old rat and the
    ditch-dog, drinks the green mantle of the standing pool; who is
    whipped from tithing to tithing, and stock-punished, and impris-
    oned; who hath had three suits to his back, six shirts to his body,
        Horse to ride, and weapon to wear.   115
        But mice and rats and such small deer
        Have been Tom's food for seven long year—
    Beware my follower. Peace, Smolking; peace, thou fiend!

GLOUCESTER
    [*To LEAR*] What, hath your grace no better company?

EDGAR
    The Prince of Darkness is a gentleman;   120
    Modo he's called, and Mahu—

GLOUCESTER
    [*To LEAR*] Our flesh and blood is grown so vile, my lord,
    That it doth hate what gets it.

EDGAR
                Poor Tom's a-cold.

GLOUCESTER
    [*To LEAR*] Go in with me. My duty cannot suffer
    To obey in all your daughters' hard commands.   125
    Though their injunction be to bar my doors
    And let this tyrannous night take hold upon you,
    Yet have I ventured to come seek you out
    And bring you where both food and fire is ready.

LEAR
    First let me talk with this philosopher.   130
    [*To EDGAR*] What is the cause of thunder?

133: **Theban**: Perhaps a reference to Crates of Thebes (ca. 368–288 BCE), a Hellenistic philosopher; here, used generally to refer someone who has studied philosophy

134: **study**: area of expertise

135: **prevent**: thwart

138: **His wits…unsettle**: he is going insane

143: **outlawed…blood**: disowned; a fugitive from the law

147: **cry your mercy**: I beg your pardon

148: "Tom's a-cold": Simon Russell Beale as Edgar in the 1993 Royal Shakespeare Company production directed by Adrian Noble

Photo: Donald Cooper

KENT
                              My good lord,
   Take his offer; go into the house.

LEAR
   I'll talk a word with this most learnèd Theban.
   [*To EDGAR*] What is your study?

EDGAR
   How to prevent the fiend, and to kill vermin.   135

LEAR
   Let me ask you one word in private.

                                        [They converse apart]

KENT
   [*To GLOUCESTER*] Importune him once more to go, my lord.
   His wits begin to unsettle.

GLOUCESTER
                        Canst thou blame him?

                                              [Storm still]
   His daughters seek his death. O, that good Kent,
   He said it would be thus, poor banished man!   140
   Thou sayst the King grows mad; I'll tell thee, friend,
   I am almost mad myself. I had a son,
   Now outlawed from my blood; a sought my life
   But lately, very late. I loved him, friend;
   No father his son dearer. True to tell thee,   145
   The grief hath crazed my wits. What a night's this!
   [*To LEAR*] I do beseech your grace—

LEAR
                              O, cry your mercy.
   [*To EDGAR*] Noble philosopher, your company.

EDGAR
                              Tom's a-cold.

152: **soothe**: humor

153: **Take him you on**: he can go ahead with you

155: **Athenian**: philosopher, perhaps Lear is thinking of Socrates (ca. 470–399 BCE)

156: **Child Roland...come**: line perhaps from a ballad of medieval origin, now lost

157: **Fie, fo, and fum**: similar to what appears in the English fairy tale, Jack and the Beanstalk

GLOUCESTER
In, fellow, there in t' hovel; keep thee warm.

LEAR
Come, let's in all.

KENT
        This way, my lord.

LEAR
                    With him!   150
I will keep still with my philosopher.

KENT
[*To GLOUCESTER*] Good my lord, soothe him; let him take the fellow.

GLOUCESTER
Take him you on.

KENT
[*To EDGAR*] Sirrah, come on. Go along with us.

LEAR
[*To EDGAR*] Come, good Athenian.

GLOUCESTER
                  No words, no words. Hush.   155

EDGAR
    Child Roland to the dark tower come,
    His word was still "Fie, fo, and fum;
    I smell the blood of a British man."

                                    Exeunt

0: Location: Gloucester's house

Watercolor scene sketch from the promptbook for Charles Kean's 1858 production
Courtesy of the Folger Shakespeare Library

2: **censured**: judged; **nature**: familial devotion

3: **something fears**: somewhat frightens

5: **his**: i.e., his father's

5-6: **but a...himself**: rather it was brought on by self-esteem generated by the Earl of Gloucester's reprehensible badness

7: **that...just**: that I must betray my own father to be deemed loyal and honest

8-9: **which approves...of France**: which proves he is a spy working for France

10: **detector**: discoverer

15: **for our apprehension**: for us to arrest him

Act 3, Scene 5]

CORNWALL
  I will have my revenge ere I depart the house.

EDMUND
  How, my lord, I may be censured, that nature thus gives way to
  loyalty, something fears me to think of.

CORNWALL
  I now perceive, it was not altogether your brother's evil disposition made him seek his death, but a provoking merit set a-work   5
  by a reprovable badness in himself.

EDMUND
  How malicious is my fortune that I must repent to be just! This is
  the letter which he spoke of, which approves him an intelligent
  party to the advantages of France. O heavens, that his treason
  were not, or not I the detector!   10

CORNWALL
  Go with me to the duchess.

EDMUND
  If the matter of this paper be certain, you have mighty business in
  hand.

CORNWALL
  True or false, it hath made thee Earl of Gloucester. Seek out
  where thy father is, that he may be ready for our apprehension.   15

16: **him**: i.e., Gloucester; **comforting**: giving aid and comfort to

16-17: **it will...fully**: it will make him even more suspicious

18: **sore...blood**: painful between my loyalty to you (Cornwall) and to my family

EDMUND

[*Aside*] If I find him comforting the King, it will stuff his suspicion
more fully. [*To CORNWALL*] I will persever in my course of loyalty,
though the conflict be sore between that and my blood.

CORNWALL

I will lay trust upon thee, and thou shalt find a dearer father in
my love.   20

Exeunt

0: Location: inside a building on Gloucester's estate

1-2: **piece out the comfort**: make it more comfortable

3: **impatience**: unwillingness to endure anything else

5: **Frateretto**: another devil identified by Harsnett (see note 3.4.97); **Nero**: brutal Roman emperor who ruled from 54-68 CE; **Nero is an angler**: Rome burned during Nero's reign, and he blamed the Christians, whose symbol was the fish. Nero tortured some, crucified others. Edgar may be saying that Nero was selecting or fishing for Christians.

6: **innocent**: simpleton

7-8: "Whether a madman be a gentleman": Engraving by John Byam Shaw, ca. 1900
Courtesy of the Folger Shakespeare Library

8: **yeoman**: property owner of lower status than a gentleman

10-11: **he's a...him**: it drives a father to madness when he sees his son advance to a higher status before he does (from the First Folio)

12-13: **To have...them**: Lear fantasizes that Gonoril and Regan will someday be painfully tortured, either by their enemies or in hell; inserting red-hot pokers into an advesary's anus was a common form of torture

14-49: **The foul fiend...let her 'scape**: appears only in the First Quarto

15-16: **tameness...health**: wolves cannot be tamed, and horses are very vulnerable to disease

Act 3, Scene 6]

Enter GLOUCESTER and KENT[, disguised]

GLOUCESTER
Here is better than the open air; take it thankfully. I will piece out
the comfort with what addition I can. I will not be long from you.

KENT
All the power of his wits have given way to his impatience; the
gods discern your kindness!

[Exit GLOUCESTER]
[Enter LEAR, EDGAR as a Bedlam beggar, and FOOL]

EDGAR
Frateretto calls me, and tells me Nero is an angler in the lake of   5
darkness. Pray, innocent; and beware the foul fiend.

FOOL
[*To LEAR*] Prithee, nuncle, tell me whether a madman be a gentleman or a yeoman.

LEAR
A king, a king!

FOOL
No, he's a yeoman that has a gentleman to his son; for he's a mad   10
yeoman that sees his son a gentleman before him.

LEAR
To have a thousand with red burning spits
Come hissing in upon them!

EDGAR
The foul fiend bites my back.

FOOL
[*To LEAR*] He's mad that trusts in the tameness of a wolf, a   15

17: **arraign them straight**: immediately put his daughters on trial

18: **justicer**: judge, justice; Lear implies that Edgar is to serve as the judge in the trial

19: **sapient**: learned, all-knowing

20: **he**: i.e., Lear, who by this point, has had mental breakdown; **want'st thou...madam?**: are you in need of more spectators at your trial, your Majesty?

21: **burn**: brook; **Come...me**: the first line of a well-known ballad by William Birche (1558)

22: **Her...leak**: she is a promiscuous woman, or she's menstruating

25: **Poor Tom...nightingale**: Edgar asserts that Poor Tom has been possessed by a demon disguised as a bird.

26: **Hoppedance**: Harsnett's *Declaration* (see note 3.4.97) refers to a devil named Hoberdidance; **white herring**: herring that have not been smoked (as opposed to the black angel, a demon darkened by the fires of hell)

26-27: **croak not**: telling his growling, hungry stomach to be quiet

30: **the evidence**: the witnesses (who will testify against his daughters)

30: "I'll see their trial first. Bring in the evidence": Pal Aron as Edgar, Leo Wringer as the Fool, Louis Hilyer as Kent, and Corin Redgrave as Lear in the 2005 Royal Shakespeare Company production directed by Bill Alexander

Photo: Donald Cooper

31: **robèd man**: referring to Edgar, who is dressed in his blanket

32: **yokefellow in equity**: legal partner

33: **Bench**: be seated on the bench; **o' th' commission**: the person hired to be the judge

36-39: **Sleepest...harm**: perhaps an Elizabethan nursery rhyme

horse's health, a boy's love, or a whore's oath.

LEAR

It shall be done. I will arraign them straight.
[*To EDGAR*] Come, sit thou here, most learnèd justicer.
[To FOOL] Thou sapient sir, sit here.—No, you she-foxes –

EDGAR

Look where he stands and glares. Want'st thou eyes at troll-madam?   20
[*Sings*]
Come o'er the burn, Bessy, to me.

FOOL

[*Sings*]
Her boat hath a leak,
And she must not speak
Why she dares not come over to thee.

EDGAR

The foul fiend haunts Poor Tom in the voice of a nightingale.   25
Hoppedance cries in Tom's belly for two white herring. Croak
not, black angel: I have no food for thee.

KENT

[*To LEAR*] How do you, sir? Stand you not so amazed.
Will you lie down and rest upon the cushions?

LEAR

I'll see their trial first. Bring in the evidence.   30
[*To EDGAR*] Thou robèd man of justice, take thy place;
[*To FOOL*] And thou, his yokefellow of equity,
Bench by his side. [*To KENT*] You are o' th' commission,
Sit you too.

EDGAR

Let us deal justly.   35
[*Sings*]
Sleepest or wakest thou, jolly shepherd?
Thy sheep be in the corn,

38-39: **And for...harm**: should you utter but one scream from your small mouth, your sheep shall return from the field safely

40: **Purr, the cat**: Purr is identified as a devil in Harsnett's *Declaration* (see note 3.4.97).

41-74: Scene: Garrick (1717-1779) played Lear as distracted and alienated; William C. Macready (1773-1873) wrestled to hold onto sanity; and Edmund Kean (1787-1833) maintained a dream-like state . Tommaso Salvini (1829-1915) played the role as if Lear had become completely unhinged while John Gielgud (1904-2000) doddered and twitched.

45: **joint-stool**: low stool; **Cry you...joint-stool**: i.e., I beg your pardon for not noticing you.

46: **another**: i.e., Regan

46: **warped looks**: twisted or evil countenance

47: **store**: stored materials; **on**: of

49: **let her 'scape**: permitted Regan to leave the courtroom

54: **They'll mar my counterfeiting**: i.e., His tears will wash off the dirt he has rubbed on his face as part of his disguise.

And for one blast of thy minikin mouth
Thy sheep shall take no harm.
Purr, the cat is gray.   40

LEAR
Arraign her first. 'Tis Gonoril. I here take my oath before this
honorable assembly she kicked the poor King her father.

FOOL
Come hither, mistress. Is your name Gonoril?

LEAR
She cannot deny it.

FOOL
Cry you mercy, I took you for a joint-stool.   45

LEAR
And here's another, whose warped looks proclaim
What store her heart is made on. Stop her there.
Arms, arms, sword, fire, corruption in the place!
False justicer, why hast thou let her 'scape?

EDGAR
Bless thy five wits.   50

KENT
[*To LEAR*] O pity! Sir, where is the patience now
That thou so oft have boasted to retain?

EDGAR
[*Aside*] My tears begin to take his part so much
They'll mar my counterfeiting.

LEAR
                                   The little dogs and all,
Tray, Blanch, and Sweetheart—see, they bark at me.   55

56: throw his head at them: bark back, i.e., threaten the dogs so that they'll be quiet

57: or black: either black

60: brach: a type of dog, probably a bloodhound or other kind of hunting dog

61: Bobtail tike or trundle-tail: a mixed-species dog with a docked tail or a curly tail

64: hatch: the lower half of a Dutch door

65: wakes: parish festivals

66: horn: container used by beggars as a cup for both drinking and panhandling

67: anatomize: dissect

69: entertain...hundred: hire you to be one of my hundred knights

70-71: Persian attire: rich, handmade robes from Persia

73: curtains: bed curtains; Lear, hallucinating from madness, thinks he is in a proper bed

75: And I'll go to bed at noon: from the First Folio

79: upon: against

EDGAR

    Tom will throw his head at them.—Avaunt, you curs!
    Be thy mouth or black or white,
    Tooth that poisons if it bite,
    Mastiff, greyhound, mongrel grim,
    Hound or spaniel, brach or him,   60
    Bobtail tike or trundle-tail,
    Tom will make them weep and wail;
    For with throwing thus my head,
    Dogs leap the hatch, and all are fled.
    Loudla, doodla! Come, march to wakes and fairs   65
    And market towns. Poor Tom, thy horn is dry.

LEAR

    Then let them anatomize Regan; see what breeds about her heart.
    Is there any cause in nature that makes this hardness? [*To*
    EDGAR] You, sir, I entertain you for one of my hundred, only I do
    not like the fashion of your garments. You'll say they are Persian   70
    attire, but let them be changed.

KENT

    Now, good my lord, lie here and rest awhile.

LEAR

    Make no noise, make no noise. Draw the curtains. So, so, so. We'll
    go to supper i' th' morning. So, so, so.
                         [He sleeps.] Enter GLOUCESTER.

FOOL

    And I'll go to bed at noon.   75

GLOUCESTER

    [*To KENT*] Come hither, friend. Where is the King my master?

KENT

    Here, sir, but trouble him not; his wits are gone.

GLOUCESTER

    Good friend, I prithee take him in thy arms.
    I have o'erheard a plot of death upon him.

80: **litter**: portable bed

83: **dally**: delay

86-87: **to some...conduct**: to safety quickly take you

87-91: **Oppressèd nature...stay behind**: appears only in the First Quarto

88: **balmed...sinews**: soothed, healed your damaged nerves

89: **convenience**: circumstances

90: **Stand...cure**: will be hard to cure

92: **our woes**: similar problems

92-105: **When we...Lurk, lurk.**: appears only in the First Quarto

93: **We scarcely...foes**: we almost stop thinking about our own miseries

94: **Who alone suffers**: He who suffers alone

95: **free...shows**: carefree ways and happy times

96-97: **But then...fellowship**: Whereas the mind can overcome great suffering when one has companionship

98: **portable**: bearable

100: **He...fathered**: he has been treated as badly by his children as I have by my father

101-102: **Mark...thee**: Pay attention to what is said about important people or events, then keep your identity hidden until those who have slandered you, when convinced of innocence, invite you to return and restore you to favor

104: **What...King!**: whatever else may happen tonight, let us hope the king escapes to safety

105: **Lurk**: Stay out of sight

There is a litter ready. Lay him in't   80
And drive towards Dover, friend, where thou shalt meet
Both welcome and protection. Take up thy master.
If thou shouldst dally half an hour, his life,
With thine and all that offer to defend him,
Stand in assurèd loss. Take up, take up,   85
And follow me, that will to some provision
Give thee quick conduct.

KENT

                    [*To LEAR*] Oppressèd nature sleeps.
This rest might yet have balmed thy broken sinews
Which, if convenience will not allow,
Stand in hard cure. [*To FOOL*] Come, help to bear thy master.   90
Thou must not stay behind.

GLOUCESTER
                    Come, come, away.
                                        Exeunt. [Manet EDGAR.]

EDGAR
When we our betters see bearing our woes,
We scarcely think our miseries our foes.
Who alone suffers, suffers most i' th' mind,
Leaving free things and happy shows behind.   95
But then the mind much sufferance doth o'erskip
When grief hath mates, and bearing fellowship.
How light and portable my pain seems now,
When that which makes me bend, makes the King bow.
He childed as I fathered. Tom, away.   100
Mark the high noises, and thyself bewray
When false opinion, whose wrong thoughts defiles thee,
In thy just proof repeals and reconciles thee.
What will hap more tonight, safe scape the King!
Lurk, lurk.   105

                                        Exit

0: Location: Gloucester's house

Set design for the 1959 production at the Shakespeare Memorial Theatre in Stratford-upon-Avon directed by Glen Byam Shaw

Rare Book and Special Collection Library, University of Illinois at Urbana-Champaign

1: **Post speedily**: hurry
6: **sister**: i.e., sister-in-law, Gonoril
7: **bound**: obliged, obligated
8: **Duke**: i.e., the Duke of Albany
9: **festinate**: hasty
9: **are bound**: are committed
10: **posts**: messengers; **intelligence**: information
14: **his**: i.e., Lear's
15: **questants after him**: searchers for Lear
16: **the lord's dependants**: servants belonging to Gloucester

Enter CORNWALL and REGAN, GONORIL and
Bastard [EDMUND, and SERVANTS]

CORNWALL
[*To GONORIL*] Post speedily to my lord your husband.Show him
this letter. The army of France is landed. [*To SERVANTS*] Seek
out the villain Gloucester.

[Exeunt some]

REGAN
Hang him instantly.

GONORIL
Pluck out his eyes.   5

CORNWALL
Leave him to my displeasure.—Edmund, keep you our sister company. The revenges we are bound to take upon your traitorous
father are not fit for your beholding. Advise the Duke where you
are going, to a most festinate preparation; we are bound to the like.
Our posts shall be swift, and intelligence betwixt us.—Farewell,   10
dear sister. Farewell, my lord of Gloucester.

Enter Steward [OSWALD]

How now, where's the King?

OSWALD
My lord of Gloucester hath conveyed him hence.
Some five- or six-and-thirty of his knights,
Hot questants after him, met him at gate,   15
Who, with some other of the lord's dependants,
Are gone with him towards Dover, where they boast
To have well-armèd friends.

CORNWALL
Get horses for your mistress.

[Exit OSWALD]

21: **Pinion him**: bind his hands

22: **pass upon his life**: sentence him to death

23: **form of justice**: a proper trial

24: **do a curtsy**: do a courtesy to, yield to

26: **corky**: dried and withered from age

31: Stage Direction: *[REGAN plucks his beard]*: Ellen Holly as Regan, Paul Sorvino as Gloucester, and the Ensemble in the 1973 Public Theater production directed by Edwin Sherin

Photo: George E. Joseph

32: Stage Direction: **Plucks**: pulls out at the root

GONORIL
                    Farewell, sweet lord, and sister.

CORNWALL
    Edmund, farewell.
                                Exeunt GONORIL and Bastard [EDMUND]
            [*To Servants*] Go seek the traitor Gloucester.   20
    Pinion him like a thief; bring him before us.
                                        [*Exeunt other SERVANTS*]
    Though well we may not pass upon his life
    Without the form of justice, yet our power
    Shall do a curtsy to our wrath, which men
    May blame but not control. Who's there—the traitor?   25
                            Enter GLOUCESTER brought in by two or three

REGAN
    Ingrateful fox, 'tis he.

CORNWALL
                        [*To Servants*] Bind fast his corky arms.

GLOUCESTER
    What means your graces? Good my friends, consider
    You are my guests. Do me no foul play, friends.

CORNWALL
    [*To Servants*] Bind him, I say—

REGAN
                            Hard, hard! O filthy traitor!

GLOUCESTER
    Unmerciful lady as you are, I am true.   30

CORNWALL
    [*To Servants*] To this chair bind him. [*To GLOUCESTER*] Villain, thou
        shalt find—

                                    [*REGAN plucks his beard*]

34: **white**: white-haired, esteemed; **Naughty**: wicked

36: **quicken**: come to life

37-38: **With robbers'...thus**: You should not abuse my hospitality by handling my face as if you were you thieves trying to rob me.

39: **late**: lately

41: **confederacy**: understanding, allegiance

42: **Late footed**: having recently arrived

42-43: "To whose hands / You have send the lunatic King": Ralph Cosham as Cornwall, Jennifer Harmon as Regan, and the Ensemble in the 2000 Shakespeare Theatre Company production directed by Michael Kahn
Photo: Carol Rosegg

44: **guessingly set down**: conjecturally written

GLOUCESTER
   By the kind gods, 'tis most ignobly done,
   To pluck me by the beard.

REGAN
   So white, and such a traitor!

GLOUCESTER
                      Naughty lady,
   These hairs, which thou dost ravish from my chin   35
   Will quicken, and accuse thee. I am your host.
   With robbers' hands my hospitable favors
   You should not ruffle thus. What will you do?

CORNWALL
   Come, sir, what letters had you late from France?

REGAN
   Be simple, answerer, for we know the truth.   40

CORNWALL
   And what confederacy have you with the traitors
   Late footed in the kingdom?

REGAN
                   To whose hands
   You have sent the lunatic King. Speak.

GLOUCESTER
   I have a letter guessingly set down,
   Which came from one that's of a neutral heart,   45
   And not from one opposed.

CORNWALL
               Cunning.

REGAN
                    And false.

tracks 25-27

47–90:
Samantha Bond as Regan, Rob Edwards as Cornwall, and
Clive Merrison as Gloucester
Sara Kestelman as Regan, Jack Klaff as Cornwall, and
Alec McCowen as Gloucester

48: **charged at peril**: ordered at risk of death

50: **tied to th' stake**: powerless and surrounded by danger; **stand the course**: suffer the attacks

54: **anointed**: sanctified, holy; sovereigns were anointed with holy oil at coronation; **rash**: slash violently (the First Folio reads "stick")

56-57: **would have quenched the fires**: would have risen high enough to drench the stars in the sky with water

58: **holped**: helped

58: **holped...rage**: appears only in the First Quarto, the First Folio reads "holp the heavens to rain"

59: **stern**: dire

60: **turn the key**: unlock the gate and let them in

61: **All...subscribe**: I acknowledge and support all cruel creatures

62: **The wingèd vengeance**: God's divine revenge carried out by one of his winged angels, sweeping down from heaven like birds of prey

65: **will think**: wants, aspires

66: Stage Direction: *CORNWALL pulls out one of GLOUCESTER's eyes*: Brendan O'Hea as Cornwall and Richard O'Callaghan as Gloucester in the 2005 Chichester Festival Theatre production directed by Steven Pimlott

Photo: Donald Cooper

CORNWALL
    Where hast thou sent the King?

GLOUCESTER
                                        To Dover.

REGAN
    Wherefore to Dover? Wast thou not charged at peril—

CORNWALL
    Wherefore to Dover?—Let him first answer that.

GLOUCESTER
    I am tied to th' stake, and I must stand the course.   50

REGAN
    Wherefore to Dover, sir?

GLOUCESTER
    Because I would not see thy cruel nails
    Pluck out his poor old eyes, nor thy fierce sister
    In his anointed flesh rash boarish fangs.
    The sea, with such a storm as his buoyed head   55
    In hell-black night endured, would have buoyed up
    And quenched the stellèd fires. Yet, poor old heart,
    He holped the heavens to rage.
    If wolves had at thy gate howled that stern time,
    Thou shouldst have said "Good porter, turn the key;   60
    All cruels I'll subscribe." But I shall see
    The wingèd vengeance overtake such children.

CORNWALL
    See't shalt thou never.—Fellows, hold the chair.—
    Upon those eyes of thine I'll set my foot.

GLOUCESTER
    He that will think to live till he be old,   65
    Give me some help!—O cruel! O ye gods!
        [CORNWALL pulls out one of GLOUCESTER's eyes and stamps on it]

tracks 25-27

47–90:
Samantha Bond as Regan, Rob Edwards as Cornwall,
and Clive Merrison as Gloucester
Sara Kestelman as Regan, Jack Klaff as Cornwall,
and Alec McCowen as Gloucester

67: **One side...too**: One eye will remind you of the other's loss; i.e., best to take them both out.

72-73: **If you...quarrel**: Even if you were old and venerable (wise old men wore beards) I'd still challenge your authority in these actions.

73: **What do you mean?**: What on earth do you think you are doing or intend to do? (The First Quarto assigns the question to the servant.)

68-78: Scene: Peter Brook's 1962 RSC production cut the part of the servant who attempts to save Gloucester after his blinding altogether.

74: **villein**: servant

75: **take the chance of anger**: take the risks of an angry fight that could lead to bloodshed

76: **stand up thus**: behave so impudently

76: Stage Direction: ***She...behind***: This stage direction appears only in the First Quarto.

77-78: **Yet...him**: Nevertheless, my death will have not been in vain, since you still have one eye left to see to it that Cornwall suffers for my death.

REGAN
[*To CORNWALL*] One side will mock another; t'other, too.

CORNWALL
[*To GLOUCESTER*] If you see vengeance—

SERVANT
                                        Hold your hand, my lord.
I have served you ever since I was a child,
But better service have I never done you   70
Than now to bid you hold.

REGAN
                        How now, you dog!

SERVANT
If you did wear a beard upon your chin
I'd shake it on this quarrel. [*To CORNWALL*] What do you mean?

CORNWALL
My villein!

SERVANT
Why then, come on, and take the chance of anger.   75
                                [They draw and fight]

REGAN
[*To another servant*] Give me thy sword. A peasant stand up thus!
                        She takes a sword and runs at him behind

SERVANT
[*To GLOUCESTER*] O, I am slain, my lord! Yet have you one eye left
To see some mischief on him.
                                [REGAN stabs him again]
                O!
                                        [He dies]

47–90:
Samantha Bond as Regan, Rob Edwards as Cornwall,
and Clive Merrison as Gloucester
Sara Kestelman as Regan, Jack Klaff as Cornwall,
and Alec McCowen as Gloucester

79: Scene: Some directors have staged this scene with Gloucester lying on the ground during the blinding; others have him tied to a chair. In certain productions, the cruelty of this scene has been amplified by having Cornwall or Regan do ghoulish things with Gloucester's eyes once they've been gouged out, such as playing catch with them or smashing them in their hands. In Brook's 1962 RSC production, Cornwall (Tony Church) brought a kind of fascistic sadism to the role, calmly grinding his shining boot spur into Gloucester's eyes, as if he were merely putting out a cigarette underfoot.

80: **luster**: the glimmer in your eyes
82: **nature**: filial love
83: **quit**: requite, revenge yourself

83: "Out, treacherous villain!": Sally Dexter as Regan and Norman Rodway as Gloucester in the 1990 Royal Shakespeare Company production directed by Nicholas Hytner
Photo: Donald Cooper

95-103: **I'll never care...heaven help him**: These last nine lines, showing the servants not only expressing sympathy for Gloucester but also deciding to follow him, appear only in the First Quarto.

CORNWALL

Lest it see more, prevent it. Out, vile jelly!

[He pulls out GLOUCESTER's other eye]

Where is thy luster now?

GLOUCESTER

All dark and comfortless. Where's my son Edmund?
Edmund, enkindle all the sparks of nature
To quit this horrid act.

REGAN

Out, treacherous villain!
Thou call'st on him that hates thee. It was he
That made the overture of thy treasons to us,   85
Who is too good to pity thee.

GLOUCESTER

O, my follies! Then Edgar was abused.
Kind gods, forgive me that, and prosper him!

REGAN

[To SERVANTS] Go thrust him out at gates, and let him smell
His way to Dover. *[To CORNWALL]* How is't, my lord? How look you?   90

CORNWALL

I have received a hurt. Follow me, lady.
[To SERVANTS] Turn out that eyeless villain. Throw this slave
Upon the dunghill.

Exit [one or more with GLOUCESTER
and the body]

Regan, I bleed apace.
Untimely comes this hurt. Give me your arm.

Exeunt [CORNWALL and REGAN]

SECOND SERVANT

I'll never care what wickedness I do   95
If this man come to good.

97: **old course of death**: die of natural causes

99: **Bedlam**: the lunatic released from the insane asylum, i.e., poor Tom

100-101: **His...thing**: He is a rogue and a lunatic, and therefore has the freedom to do what ever we ask of him.

THIRD SERVANT
                    If she live long
And in the end meet the old course of death,
Women will all turn monsters.

SECOND SERVANT
Let's follow the old Earl and get the Bedlam
To lead him where he would. His roguish madness   100
Allows itself to any thing.

THIRD SERVANT
Go thou. I'll fetch some flax and whites of eggs
To apply to his bleeding face. Now heaven help him!

                                        Exeunt

[King Lear

Act 4

0: Location: A clearing

Watercolor scene sketch from the promptbook for Charles Kean's 1858 production
Courtesy of the Folger Shakespeare Library

1-2: **Yet...flattered**: It is better to be openly reviled for being a beggar, than to be constantly reviled behind one's back and flattered to one's face—an indictment of the manner in which many people behave at court
2: **worst**: at one's worst; at the very bottom
3: **dejected**: disconsolate
4: **Stands...fear**: stands in hope and has no fear that things will get worse
5-6: **The lamentable...laughter**: i.e., A change from the best brings sadness; a change from the worst brings joy.
6-9: **Welcome...thy blasts**: from the First Folio
9: **Owes...blasts**: has no obligation to your strong winds
10: **poorly led**: guided by someone who is feeble and poor
11-12: **But that...age**: i.e., Were it not that life's unpredictable changes of fortune compelled us to hate life, none of us would ever acquiesce to old age and death.
20: **I stumbled when I saw**: i.e., I was blind to the truth (of Edgar's love) when I could see.
21-22: **Our...commodities**: i.e., Our wealth may give us a sense of security, but it is our insignificant flaws that turn out to be the most valuable.

Act 4, Scene 1]

Enter EDGAR [as a Bedlam beggar]

EDGAR
    Yet better thus, and known to be contemned
    Than still contemned and flattered. To be worst,
    The low'st and most dejected thing of Fortune,
    Stands still in esperance, lives not in fear.
    The lamentable change is from the best;   5
    The worst returns to laughter. Welcome, then,
    Thou unsubstantial air that I embrace.
    The wretch that thou hast blown unto the worst
    Owes nothing to thy blasts.
                    Enter GLOUCESTER led by an OLD MAN
    Who's here? My father, poorly led? World, world, O world!   10
    But that thy strange mutations make us hate thee,
    Life would not yield to age.
                        [EDGAR stands aside]

OLD MAN
    [To GLOUCESTER] O my good lord, I have been your tenant
    And your father's tenant this fourscore—

GLOUCESTER
    Away, get thee away, good friend, be gone.   15
    Thy comforts can do me no good at all;
    Thee they may hurt.

OLD MAN
    Alack, sir, you cannot see your way.

GLOUCESTER
    I have no way, and therefore want no eyes.
    I stumbled when I saw. Full oft 'tis seen   20
    Our means secure us, and our mere defects

23: The...wrath: the one who nourished your deceived father's anger

Costume rendering for the Old Man from the 1959 production at the Shakespeare Memorial Theatre in Stratford-upon-Avon directed by Glen Byam Shaw

Rare Book and Special Collection Library, University of Illinois at Urbana-Champaign

28-29: The worst...worst: i.e., As long as we are able to say how bad things are, they can get even worse.

33: A has some reason: i.e., he is not completely insane

38: wanton: recklessly cruel

Prove our commodities. Ah dear son Edgar,
The food of thy abusèd father's wrath—
Might I but live to see thee in my touch
I'd say I had eyes again!

OLD MAN

                     How now? Who's there?   25

EDGAR

[*Aside*] O gods! Who is't can say "I am at the worst"?
I am worse than e'er I was.

OLD MAN

                   'Tis poor mad Tom.

EDGAR

[*Aside*] And worse I may be yet. The worst is not
As long as we can say "This is the worst."

OLD MAN
[*To EDGAR*] Fellow, where goest?   30

GLOUCESTER
Is it a beggarman?

OLD MAN
Madman and beggar too.

GLOUCESTER
A has some reason, else he could not beg
In the last night's storm I such a fellow saw,
Which made me think a man a worm. My son   35
Came then into my mind, and yet my mind
Was then scarce friends with him. I have heard more since.
As flies to wanton boys are we to th' gods;
They kill us for their sport.

39: **How...be?**: i.e., How is it possible that he has been so transformed?

40-41: **Bad is...others**: i.e., What an awful business it is that I must continue to deceive my grief-stricken father, even though doing so is rather irritating for all of us.

43: **Then prithee, get thee gone.**: appears only in the First Quarto

44: **wilt o'ertake us**: catch up to us

45: **for ancient love**: i.e., out of respect for the longstanding landlord/tenant relationship from which you and I have both benefited

48: **'Tis the time's plague**: i.e., it is indicative of the sickness of our state

50: **Above the rest**: most importantly; above all

52: **Come on't what will**: regardless of what I get out of it

53: **dance it farther**: maintain this disguise any longer (the First Folio reads "daub")

EDGAR

[Aside] How should this be?
Bad is the trade that must play fool to sorrow,   40
Ang'ring itself and others.

[He comes forward]

Bless thee, master!

GLOUCESTER
Is that the naked fellow?

OLD MAN

Ay, my lord.

GLOUCESTER
Then prithee, get thee gone. If for my sake
Thou wilt o'ertake us hence a mile or twain
I' th' way toward Dover, do it for ancient love,   45
And bring some covering for this naked soul,
Who I'll entreat to lead me.

OLD MAN

Alack, sir, he is mad.

GLOUCESTER
'Tis the time's plague when madmen lead the blind.
Do as I bid thee; or rather do thy pleasure.
Above the rest, be gone.   50

OLD MAN
I'll bring him the best 'parel that I have,
Come on't what will.

[Exit]

GLOUCESTER

Sirrah, naked fellow!

EDGAR
Poor Tom's a-cold. *[Aside]* I cannot dance it farther.

GLOUCESTER
Come hither, fellow.

59-62: **Five fiends...master.**: appears only in the First Quarto

59-61: **Obidicut...mowing**: the names of devils and their traits as listed in Harnsett's *Declaration* (see note 3.4.97)

61: **mowing**: mouthing; **since**: ever since then

64: **Have...strokes**: have weakened us to the point that we are vulnerable to each of Fortune's punches

66: **superfluous and lust-dieted**: excessive and luxuriously fed

67: **That...ordinance**: who opposes your divine laws

67-68: **that...feel**: who refuses to see the truth because he has not suffered enough to feel anything

69: **distribution**: equal allocation of all wealth

72: **bending**: overhanging

73: **confinèd**: 1) obscure; perhaps a sea so deep it will never reveal its secrets, and 2) enclosed; the Straits of Dover are surrounded by its cliffs and the shores of France; **looks in the confinèd deep**: peers into the secretive depths of the sea below (the English Channel)

76: **about me**: around me, in my possession

EDGAR
              [*Aside*] And yet I must.
    [*To GLOUCESTER*] Bless thy sweet eyes, they bleed.   55

GLOUCESTER
    Know'st thou the way to Dover?

EDGAR
    Both stile and gate, horseway and footpath. Poor Tom hath been
    scared out of his good wits. Bless thee, goodman, from the foul
    fiend. Five fiends have been in Poor Tom at once, as Obidicut of
    lust, Hobbididence prince of dumbness, Mahu of stealing, Modo of   60
    murder, Flibbertigibbet of mocking and mowing, who since pos-
    sesses chambermaids and waiting-women. So bless thee, master.

GLOUCESTER
    Here, take this purse, thou whom the heavens' plagues
    Have humbled to all strokes. That I am wretched
    Makes thee the happier. Heavens deal so still.   65
    Let the superfluous and lust-dieted man
    That stands your ordinance, that will not see
    Because he does not feel, feel your power quickly.
    So distribution should undo excess,
    And each man have enough. Dost thou know Dover?   70

EDGAR
    Ay, master.

GLOUCESTER
    There is a cliff whose high and bending head
    Looks saucily in the confinèd deep.
    Bring me but to the very brim of it
    And I'll repair the misery thou dost bear   75
    With something rich about me. From that place
    I shall no leading need.

EDGAR
    Give me thy arm. Poor Tom shall lead thee.
                        [*Exit EDGAR guiding GLOUCESTER*]

0: Location: Before the Duke of Albany's Palace

Set design for the 1959 production at the Shakespeare Memorial Theatre in Stratford-upon-Avon directed by Glen Byam Shaw

Rare Book and Special Collection Library, University of Illinois at Urbana-Champaign

2: **Not met**: has not met
8: **sot**: fool
13: **cowish**: cow-like, cowardly
14: **undertake**: hazard, take responsibility (for)
14-15: **He'll...answer**: i.e., He will not seriously take insults that would compel him to defend himself
15-16: **Our...effects**: i.e., The plot we hatched during our journey (to have Edmund supplant Albany) may come to fruition.
16: **brother**: brother-in-law, i.e., Cornwall
17: **musters**: gathering of the troops; **powers**: soldiers
18; **change arms at home**: exchange weapons, i.e. give up women's work and become the master of the house; **distaff**: staff used for spinning thread, i.e., woman's work
20: **like**: likely
24: **Would...air**: would give you an erection
25: **Conceive**: comprehend what I'm saying, with sexual implications (impregnate)

Act 4, Scene 2]

Enter at one door GONORIL and Bastard [EDMUND]

GONORIL

Welcome, my lord. I marvel our mild husband
Not met us on the way.

[Enter at another door Steward OSWALD]
Now, where's your master?

OSWALD

Madam, within; but never man so changed.
I told him of the army that was landed;
He smiled at it. I told him you were coming;   5
His answer was, "The worse." Of Gloucester's treachery
And of the loyal service of his son
When I informed him, then he called me sot,
And told me I had turned the wrong side out.
What he should most defy seems pleasant to him;   10
What like, offensive.

GONORIL

[*To EDMUND*] Then shall you go no further.
It is the cowish terror of his spirit
That dares not undertake. He'll not feel wrongs
Which tie him to an answer. Our wishes on the way   15
May prove effects. Back, Edmund, to my brother.
Hasten his musters and conduct his powers.
I must change arms at home, and give the distaff
Into my husband's hands. This trusty servant
Shall pass between us. Ere long you are like to hear,   20
If you dare venture in your own behalf,
A mistress's command. Wear this. Spare speech.
Decline your head. This kiss, if it durst speak,
Would stretch thy spirits up into the air.

[She kisses him]

Conceive, and fare you well.   25

26: **Yours in the ranks of death**: i.e., I will remain true to you even in death.

27: **man and man**: i.e., Albany, her husband, and Edmund, her lover

29: **My fool...body**: 1) my husband, who is a fool, controls my body, or 2) my foolish lust for Edmund now controls my body

30: **worth the whistling**: deserving of men's sexual attraction

32-59: **I fear...why does he so?"**: appears only in the First Quarto

32: **fear your disposition**: mistrust your nature

33: **contemns**: despises, disdains

34: **bordered certain**: securely kept in bounds

35: **sliver and disbranch**: tear off and break from

36: **material sap**: the stock from which she was nurtured

37: **to deadly use**: to a destructive end; **The text**: this sermon you are preaching

39: **savor but themselves**: relish only filthy things

42: **head-lugged bear**: an angry bear dragged by a chain around his neck

43: **madded**: made mad, driven insane

44: **brother**: brother-in-law, i.e., Cornwall

EDMUND
　Yours in the ranks of death.

GONORIL
　　　　　　　　My most dear Gloucester.

　　　　　　　　　　　　　　　[Exit EDMUND]

　O, the difference of man and man!
　To thee a woman's services are due;
　My fool usurps my body.

OSWALD
　　　　　　　　Madam, here comes my lord.

　　　　　　　　　　　　　　Exit
　　　　　　　　　　　[Enter ALBANY]

GONORIL
　I have been worth the whistling.

ALBANY
　　　　　　　　　O Gonoril,　　　　　　30
　You are not worth the dust which the rude wind
　Blows in your face. I fear your disposition.
　That nature which contemns its origin
　Cannot be bordered certain in itself.
　She that herself will sliver and disbranch　　35
　From her material sap perforce must wither,
　And come to deadly use.

GONORIL
　　　　　　　　No more. The text is foolish.

ALBANY
　Wisdom and goodness to the vile seem vile;
　Filths savor but themselves. What have you done?
　Tigers, not daughters, what have you performed?　　40
　A father, and a gracious agèd man,
　Whose reverence even the head-lugged bear would lick,
　Most barbarous, most degenerate, have you madded.
　Could my good-brother suffer you to do it—

46: **If that**: If; **visible spirits**: angels

Costume rendering for Gonoril by Susan Tsu from the 2004 Oregon Shakespeare Festival production directed by James Edmondson

Courtesy of the Oregon Shakespeare Festival

50: **Milk-livered**: white-livered, i.e., spineless, cowardly (cowardice was believed to have come from the whiteness or lack of blood in the liver)

52-53: **discerning...suffering**: able to distinguish between insults that should be refuted and those that should be tolerated

53-59: **that not...does he so**: appears only in the First Quarto

55: **Where's thy drum?**: i.e., Why have you not prepared yourself for battle?

56: **noiseless**: without martial sounds, i.e., peaceful, unprepared for war

57: **plumèd helm**: feather-topped helmet; **flaxen biggins**: white linen nightcap

60-61: **Proper...woman**: i.e., Those deformities that commonly distort the facial features of the devil are even more hideous looking when they distort a woman's face.

62-69: **Thou changèd...SECOND GENTLEMAN**: appears only in the First Quarto

62: **self-covered**: disguised or hidden under a fiendish exterior

63: **Bemonster**: make monstrous or hideous; **Were't my fitness**: i.e., if it were suitable for me

67: **doth shield thee**: protects you (Albany cannot attack her because she is female)

68: **mew**: an exclamation of disgust, here aimed at mocking Albany's masculinity

A man, a prince by him so benefacted?   45
If that the heavens do not their visible spirits
Send quickly down to tame these vile offenses,
It will come,
Humanity must perforce prey on itself,
Like monsters of the deep.

GONORIL
                    Milk-livered man,   50
That bear'st a cheek for blows, a head for wrongs;
Who hast not in thy brows an eye discerning
Thine honor from thy suffering; that not know'st
Fools do those villains pity who are punished
Ere they have done their mischief. Where's thy drum?   55
France spreads his banners in our noiseless land,
With plumèd helm thy flaxen biggins threats,
Whiles thou, a moral fool, sits still and cries
"Alack, why does he so?"

ALBANY
                    See thyself, devil.
Proper deformity seems not in the fiend   60
So horrid as in woman.

GONORIL
                    O vain fool!

ALBANY
Thou changèd and self-covered thing, for shame
Bemonster not thy feature. Were't my fitness
To let these hands obey my blood,
They are apt enough to dislocate and tear   65
Thy flesh and bones. Howe'er thou art a fiend,
A woman's shape doth shield thee.

GONORIL
Marry, your manhood mew—

                              Enter SECOND GENTLEMAN

73: **bred**: employed in his household; **thralled with remorse**: enthralled, deeply moved by regret

74: **Opposed against**: objecting to; **bending his sword**: directing his sword

76: **Flew on him**: attacked him

78: **plucked him after**: sent him to his death

79: **above**: i.e., in heaven

80: **justicers**: (heavenly) judges; **nether**: earthly

84: **One way**: in one way; i.e., now that Cornwall is dead, Edmund can claim the throne as Duke of Gloucester

85: **my Gloucester**: Edmund

86-87: **May all...life**: i.e., my fantasies of having the whole kingdom and Edmund to myself may come crashing down on me

88: **tart**: bitter

ALBANY
  What news?

SECOND GENTLEMAN
  O my good lord, the Duke of Cornwall's dead,   70
  Slain by his servant going to put out
  The other eye of Gloucester.

ALBANY
                              Gloucester's eyes?

SECOND GENTLEMAN
  A servant that he bred, thralled with remorse,
  Opposed against the act, bending his sword
  To his great master who, thereat enraged,   75
  Flew on him, and amongst them felled him dead,
  But not without that harmful stroke which since
  Hath plucked him after.

ALBANY
  This shows you are above,
  You justicers, that these our nether crimes   80
  So speedily can venge. But O, poor Gloucester!
  Lost he his other eye?

SECOND GENTLEMAN
                         Both, both, my lord.
  [*To GONORIL*] This letter, madam, craves a speedy answer.
  'Tis from your sister.

GONORIL
                         [*Aside*] One way I like this well;
  But being widow, and my Gloucester with her,   85
  May all the building in my fancy pluck
  Upon my hateful life. Another way
  The news is not so tart.—I'll read and answer.
                                                       [*Exit*]

89: **his son**: i.e., Edmund; **his**: i.e., Gloucester's

90: **hither**: to Albany's castle

91: **back again**: on the way back from (Albany's palace)

ALBANY
    Where was his son when they did take his eyes?

SECOND GENTLEMAN
    Come with my lady hither.

ALBANY
                            He is not here.   90

SECOND GENTLEMAN
    No, my good lord; I met him back again.

ALBANY
    Knows he the wickedness?

SECOND GENTLEMAN
    Ay, my good lord; 'twas he informed against him,
    And quit the house on purpose that their punishment
    Might have the freer course.

ALBANY
                            Gloucester, I live   95
    To thank thee for the love thou showd'st the King,
    And to revenge thy eyes.—Come hither, friend.
    Tell me what more thou knowest.
                                                    Exeunt

0: Location: The French camp near Dover

0-54: The entire scene appears only in the First Quarto.

Set design for the 1959 production at the Shakespeare Memorial Theatre in Stratford-upon-Avon directed by Glen Byam Shaw

Rare Book and Special Collection Library, University of Illinois at Urbana-Champaign

1: **gone back**: returned to France

3: **imperfect in the state**: unsettled in state matters

5: **imports**: foreshadows

10: **pierce**: move

12: **trilled**: trickled

14: **who**: which

Act 4, Scene 3]

Enter KENT [disguised] and FIRST GENTLEMAN

KENT
Why the King of France is so suddenly gone back; know you the
reason?

FIRST GENTLEMAN
Something he left imperfect in the state
Which, since his coming forth, is thought of, which
Imports to the kingdom so much fear and danger   5
That his personal return was most required
And necessary.

KENT
Who hath he left behind him general?

FIRST GENTLEMAN
The Maréchal of France, Monsieur la Far.

KENT
Did your letters pierce the Queen to any demonstration of grief?   10

FIRST GENTLEMAN
Ay, sir. She took them, read them in my presence,
And now and then an ample tear trilled down
Her delicate cheek. It seemed she was a queen
Over her passion who, most rebel-like,
Sought to be king o'er her.

KENT
                              O, then it moved her.   15

17: **express her goodliest**: cast her in the best light

19: **like, a better way**: similar to that, but better

20-21: **seemed...eyes**: seemed unaware that she was crying

23: **a rarity**: something precious, like a jewel

24: **become it**: be so attractive (when grief-stricken)

25: **heaved**: breathed with great difficulty

31: **clamor mastered**: having gotten control over her cries of grief

33: **conditions**: characters

34: **one self**: the same; **mate and make**: i.e., father and mother

35: **issues**: children

36: **King**: the King of France; **returned**: returned to his kingdom

FIRST GENTLEMAN
    Not to a rage. Patience and sorrow strove
    Who should express her goodliest. You have seen
    Sunshine and rain at once; her smiles and tears
    Were like, a better way. Those happy smilets
    That played on her ripe lip seemed not to know   20
    What guests were in her eyes, which parted thence
    As pearls from diamonds dropped. In brief,
    Sorrow would be a rarity most beloved
    If all could so become it.

KENT
                Made she no verbal question?

FIRST GENTLEMAN
    Faith, once or twice she heaved the name of "father"   25
    Pantingly forth as if it pressed her heart,
    Cried "Sisters, sisters, shame of ladies, sisters,
    Kent, father, sisters, what, i' th' storm, i' th' night?
    Let piety not be believed!" There she shook
    The holy water from her heavenly eyes   30
    And clamor mastered, then away she started
    To deal with grief alone.

KENT
                It is the stars,
    The stars above us, govern our conditions,
    Else one self mate and make could not beget
    Such different issues. You spoke not with her since?   35

FIRST GENTLEMAN
    No.

KENT
    Was this before the King returned?

FIRST GENTLEMAN
                No, since.

38: **better tune**: more stable state of mind

40: **yield**: agree, consent

41: **sovereign**: overpowering, like a king; **elbows him**: prods or compels him (to remember)

42: **turned her**: forced her (to seek)

43: **foreign casualties**: chances or opportunities abroad

46: **Detains him from**: keeps him from (seeing)

47: **powers**: armies

48: **afoot**: on the march

50: **dear cause**: important objective

51: **wrap me up**: occupy me

52-53: **grieve...acquaintance**: regret having talked with me

KENT

    Well, sir, the poor distressèd Lear's i' th' town,
    Who sometime in his better tune remembers
    What we are come about, and by no means
    Will yield to see his daughter.

FIRST GENTLEMAN

                    Why, good sir?   40

KENT

    A sovereign shame so elbows him. His own unkindness,
    That stripped her from his benediction, turned her
    To foreign casualties, gave her dear rights
    To his dog-hearted daughters—these things sting
    His mind so venomously that burning shame   45
    Detains him from Cordelia.

FIRST GENTLEMAN

                  Alack, poor gentleman!

KENT

    Of Albany's and Cornwall's powers you heard not?

FIRST GENTLEMAN

    'Tis so; they are afoot.

KENT

    Well, sir, I'll bring you to our master Lear,
    And leave you to attend him. Some dear cause   50
    Will in concealment wrap me up a while.
    When I am known aright you shall not grieve
    Lending me this acquaintance. I pray you go
    Along with me.

                                        Exeunt

0: **Location**: The French Camp

0: Stage Direction: ***DOCTOR***: the First Quarto specifies "Doctor" here and at line 11
3: **fumitor**: fumitory, a poisonous herb
3: **furrow-weeds**: weeds that grow in the furrows of a plowed field
4: **burdocks**: weed-like plant; **cuckoo-flowers**: flowers that bloom in the late spring when the cuckoo sings
5: **Darnel**: grass-like weed; **idle**: useless
6: **sustaining corn**: life-giving grain; **centuries**: troops of one hundred soldiers
8: **man's wisdom**: medical knowledge
9: **his**: of his, i.e., Lear's
10: **outward**: visible, material

10: "He that can help him take all my outward worth": Kristen Bush as Cordelia in the 2007 Public Theater production directed by James Lapine
Photo: Michal Daniel

12: **foster-nurse**: most effective or promising treatment
13: **That to provoke in him**: to induce that in him, i.e., to help him sleep
14: **simples operative**: effective treatments
16: **unpublished virtues**: secret cures
17: **Spring**: grow; **aidant and remediate**: helpful and curative
19: **rage**: madness
20: **wants**: lacks; **means**: i.e., sanity

Act 4, Scene 4]

Enter [Queen] CORDELIA, DOCTOR, and others

CORDELIA
    Alack, 'tis he! Why, he was met even now,
    As mad as the racked sea, singing aloud,
    Crowned with rank fumitor and furrow-weeds,
    With burdocks, hemlock, nettles, cuckoo-flowers,
    Darnel, and all the idle weeds that grow   5
    In our sustaining corn. The centuries send forth.
    Search every acre in the high-grown field,
    And bring him to our eye.

                            [Exit one or more]

                    What can man's wisdom
    In the restoring his bereavèd sense,
    He that can help him take all my outward worth.   10

DOCTOR
    There is means, madam.
    Our foster-nurse of nature is repose,
    The which he lacks. That to provoke in him
    Are many simples operative, whose power
    Will close the eye of anguish.

CORDELIA
                  All blest secrets,   15
    All you unpublished virtues of the earth,
    Spring with my tears, be aidant and remediate
    In the good man's distress!—Seek, seek for him,
    Lest his ungoverned rage dissolve the life
    That wants the means to lead it.   20

                            Enter MESSENGER

22: **preparation**: army

23-24: Scene: **O dear father...I go about**: Jonathan Miller, director of the BBC-TV 1982 production, sought to emphasize some of the play's spiritual themes. When Cordelia says that she is tending to her father's business, there is a sense in which she's also referring to God the Father. The actress, Brenda Blethyn, crosses herself reverently while saying it. Also, Edgar, disguised as Poor Tom, wears a crown of thorns, an allusion to Jesus Christ.

Costume rendering for Cordelia by Susan Tsu from the 2004 Oregon Shakespeare Festival production directed by James Edmondson

Courtesy of the Oregon Shakespeare Festival

26: **importuant**: importunate, pleading

27: **blown**: swollen, prideful

MESSENGER

                       News, madam.   20
The British powers are marching hitherward.

CORDELIA
'Tis known before; our preparation stands
In expectation of them.—O dear father,
It is thy business that I go about;
Therefore great France   25
My mourning and importuant tears hath pitied.
No blown ambition doth our arms incite,
But love, dear love, and our aged father's right.
Soon may I hear and see him!

                                        Exeunt

0: Location: Gloucester's house

Set design for the 1959 production at the Shakespeare Memorial Theatre in Stratford-upon-Avon directed by Glen Byam Shaw

Rare Book and Special Collection Library, University of Illinois at Urbana-Champaign

1: **my brother's powers**: i.e., Albany's armies

4: **spake**: spoke

6: **What might...to him**: i.e., What do my sister's letters impart to him?

8: **is posted**: has gone quickly

9: **ignorance**: stupidity

12: **his**: i.e., Gloucester's

13: **nighted**: dark, blinded to; **descry**: find out

Act 4, Scene 5]

Enter REGAN and Steward [OSWALD]

REGAN
But are my brother's powers set forth?

OSWALD
                      Ay, madam.

REGAN
Himself in person there?

OSWALD
                   Madam, with much ado.
Your sister is the better soldier.

REGAN
Lord Edmund spake not with your lord at home?

OSWALD
No, madam.   5

REGAN
What might import my sister's letters to him?

OSWALD
I know not, lady.

REGAN
Faith, he is posted hence on serious matter.
It was great ignorance, Gloucester's eyes being out,
To let him live. Where he arrives he moves   10
All hearts against us. Edmund, I think, is gone,
In pity of his misery, to dispatch
His nighted life, moreover to descry
The strength o' th' army.

15: **must needs after**: need to follow

18: **charged my duty**: emphasized the importance of obeying her

20: **Transport**: tell me; **Belike**: perhaps

24: **late being**: recent presence

25: **oeillades**: amorous glances

26: **of her bosom**: in her confidence

29: **take this note**: take note of this

30: **have talked**: are in agreement

31: **convenient**: suitable

32: **gather more**: read into or infer

33: **this**: i.e., information, letter, or token of her affection

OSWALD
  I must needs after with my letters, madam.   15

REGAN
  Our troop sets forth tomorrow. Stay with us.
  The ways are dangerous.

OSWALD
                    I may not, madam.
  My lady charged my duty in this business.

REGAN
  Why should she write to Edmund? Might not you
  Transport her purposes by word? Belike   20
  Something, I know not what. I'll love thee much:
  Let me unseal the letter.

OSWALD
                    Madam, I'd rather—

REGAN
  I know your lady does not love her husband.
  I am sure of that, and at her late being here
  She gave strange oeillades and most speaking looks   25
  To noble Edmund. I know you are of her bosom.

OSWALD
  I, madam?

REGAN
  I speak in understanding, for I know't.
  Therefore I do advise you take this note.
  My lord is dead. Edmund and I have talked,   30
  And more convenient is he for my hand
  Than for your lady's. You may gather more.
  If you do find him, pray you give him this,
  And when your mistress hears thus much from you,
  I pray desire her call her wisdom to her.   35
  So, farewell.

38: **Preferment**: reward, promotion

40: **what lady**: The First Folio prints "what party", meaning "which sister".

If you do chance to hear of that blind traitor,
Preferment falls on him that cuts him off.

OSWALD
Would I could meet him, madam. I should show
What lady I do follow.

REGAN

Fare thee well.   40
Exeunt

1: **that same hill**: the hill we discussed earlier (see 4.1.72-74)

Pal Aron as Edgar and David Hargreaves as Gloucester in the 2005 Royal
Shakespeare Company production directed by Bill Alexander

Photo: Donald Cooper

Act 4, Scene 6]

Enter EDGAR [disguised as a peasant, with a staff,
guiding the blind] GLOUCESTER

GLOUCESTER
When shall we come to th' top of that same hill?

EDGAR
You do climb up it now. Look, how we labor.

GLOUCESTER
Methinks the ground is even.

EDGAR
                    Horrible steep.
Hark, do you hear the sea?

GLOUCESTER
              . No, truly.

EDGAR
Why, then your other senses grow imperfect   5
By your eyes' anguish.

GLOUCESTER
                 So may it be indeed.
Methinks thy voice is altered, and thou speak'st
With better phrase and matter than thou didst.

EDGAR
You're much deceived. In nothing am I changed
But in my garments.

GLOUCESTER
             Methinks you're better spoken.   10

13: **choughs**: crow-like birds; **midway air**: the air halfway between the top of the cliff and the sea below

14: **so gross**: as large

15: **samphire**: herb used for pickling

18: **barque**: bark, a small sailing ship

19: **diminished...cock**: shrunk to the size of a cockboat, a small boat that accompanies a large ship

23: **my brain turn**: i.e., I get dizzy

26: **all beneath the moon**: i.e., everything on earth

27: **upright**: up and down

30: **Prosper it**: increase its value

33: **trifle**: play with

EDGAR

Come on, sir, here's the place. Stand still. How fearful
And dizzy 'tis to cast one's eyes so low!
The crows and choughs that wing the midway air
Show scarce so gross as beetles. Halfway down
Hangs one that gathers samphire, dreadful trade!   15
Methinks he seems no bigger than his head.
The fishermen that walk upon the beach
Appear like mice, and yon tall anchoring barque
Diminished to her cock, her cock a buoy
Almost too small for sight. The murmuring surge   20
That on the unnumbered idle pebbles chafes
Cannot be heard, it's so high. I'll look no more,
Lest my brain turn and the deficient sight
Topple down headlong.

GLOUCESTER
                    Set me where you stand.

EDGAR

Give me your hand. You are now within a foot   25
Of th' extreme verge. For all beneath the moon
Would I not leap upright.

GLOUCESTER
                    Let go my hand.
Here, friend, 's another purse; in it a jewel
Well worth a poor man's taking. Fairies and gods
Prosper it with thee! Go thou farther off.   30
Bid me farewell, and let me hear thee going.

EDGAR

Now fare you well, good sir.

                                        [He stands aside]

GLOUCESTER
                    With all my heart.

EDGAR

[*Aside*] Why I do trifle thus with his despair
Is done to cure it.

38: **To quarrel with**: in rebellion against; **opposeless**: irrefutable

39: **snuff**: useless; **of nature**: of my life

42: **conceit**: imagination

44: **Yields**: consents

45: **by this**: by this time

47: **pass**: expire, die

48: **What**: who

50: **precipitating**: falling

51: **shivered**: shattered or cracked

53: **a-length**: in length

57: **chalky bourn**: white cliff (part of the White Cliffs of Dover)

58: **a-height**: on high; **shrill-gorged**: shrill-throated

GLOUCESTER

O you mighty gods,

[He kneels]

This world I do renounce, and in your sights   35
Shake patiently my great affliction off!
If I could bear it longer, and not fall
To quarrel with your great opposeless wills,
My snuff and loathèd part of nature should
Burn itself out. If Edgar live, O bless him!—   40
Now, fellow, fare thee well.

EDGAR

Gone, sir. Farewell.

[GLOUCESTER falls forward]

[Aside] And yet I know not how conceit may rob
The treasury of life, when life itself
Yields to the theft. Had he been where he thought,
By this had thought been past.—Alive or dead?   45
[To GLOUCESTER] Ho, you, sir, friend; hear you, sir? Speak.
[Aside] Thus might he pass indeed. Yet he revives.
[To GLOUCESTER] What are you, sir?

GLOUCESTER

Away, and let me die.

EDGAR

Hadst thou been aught but gossamer, feathers, air,
So many fathom down precipitating   50
Thou hadst shivered like an egg. But thou dost breathe,
Hast heavy substance, bleed'st not, speak'st, art sound.
Ten masts a-length make not the altitude
Which thou hast perpendicularly fell.
Thy life's a miracle. Speak yet again.   55

GLOUCESTER

But have I fallen, or no?

EDGAR

From the dread summit of this chalky bourn.
Look up a-height. The shrill-gorged lark so far
Cannot be seen or heard. Do but look up.

61: **benefit**: consolation

63: **beguile**: charm

71: **whelked**: twisted

72: **happy father**: fortunate old man

73: **clearest**: purest, most righteous

73-74: **who...impossibilities**: who achieved their fame by doing things humans cannot do

76-77: **till..."Enough, enough"**: i.e., until the sources of my suffering cease of their own accord

GLOUCESTER
    Alack, I have no eyes.   60
    Is wretchedness deprived that benefit
    To end itself by death? 'Twas yet some comfort
    When misery could beguile the tyrant's rage
    And frustrate his proud will.

EDGAR
                         Give me your arm.
    Up. So, how now? Feel you your legs? You stand.   65

GLOUCESTER
    Too well, too well.

EDGAR
                This is above all strangeness.
    Upon the crown of the cliff what thing was that
    Which parted from you?

GLOUCESTER
                    A poor unfortunate beggar.

EDGAR
    As I stood here below, methoughts his eyes
    Were two full moons. A had a thousand noses,   70
    Horns whelked and wavèd like the enridgèd sea.
    It was some fiend. Therefore, thou happy father,
    Think that the clearest gods, who made their honors
    Of men's impossibilities, have preserved thee.

GLOUCESTER
    I do remember now. Henceforth I'll bear   75
    Affliction till it do cry out itself
    "Enough, enough," and die. That thing you speak of,
    I took it for a man. Often would it say
    "The fiend, the fiend!" He led me to that place.

80: Stage Direction: *Enter LEAR mad [crowned with weeds and flowers]*: Kevin Kline as Lear in the 2007 Public Theater production directed by James Lapine
Photo: Michal Daniel

81-82: **The safer...thus**: i.e., No one in his right mind would dress himself in such a way.

83: **touch**: arrest; **coining**: minting coins

84: **side-piercing**: heart-rending, an allusion to the suffering of Christ

85: **Nature...respect**: Life offers more examples of human tragedy than art; **press-money**: payment for enlisting

86: **crow-keeper**: laborer hired to keep the crows from eating the grain

86-87: **Draw...yard**: i.e., Draw your bow to the full length of the arrow for me.

88: **do it**: do the trick (to capture the mouse); **gauntlet**: glove thrown down as a challenge; **prove it**: use it to challenge

89: **brown bills**: spears or soldiers carrying spears; **word**: password

90: **Sweet marjoram**: herb thought to ease mental disease

93: **Ha, Gonoril! Ha, Regan!**: appears only in the First Quarto

93: **like a dog**: as a dog fawns on his master, hoping for food

94: **I had...there**: i.e., I had the wisdom of an old man before I could even grow a beard (when I was still young)

94-96: **To say...divinity**: i.e., It goes against the Bible for them to flatter me by agreeing with everything I said. See James 5:12: "let your yea be yea and your nay, nay."

100: **ague-proof**: immune from sickness

EDGAR
    Bear free and patient thoughts.
                    Enter LEAR mad, [crowned with weeds and flowers]
                                    But who comes here?   80
    The safer sense will ne'er accommodate
    His master thus.

LEAR
    No, they cannot touch me for coining. I am the King himself.

EDGAR
    O thou side-piercing sight!

LEAR
    Nature is above art in that respect. There's your press-money. That   85
    fellow handles his bow like a crow-keeper. Draw me a clothier's
    yard. Look, look, a mouse! Peace, peace, this piece of toasted cheese
    will do it. There's my gauntlet. I'll prove it on a giant. Bring up the
    brown bills. O, well flown, bird, in the air. Ha! Give the word.

EDGAR
    Sweet marjoram.   90

LEAR
    Pass.

GLOUCESTER
    I know that voice.

LEAR
    Ha, Gonoril! Ha, Regan! They flattered me like a dog, and told me
    I had white hairs in my beard ere the black ones were there. To say
    "ay" and "no" to every thing that I said "ay" and "no" to was no   95
    good divinity. When the rain came to wet me once, and the wind to
    make me chatter, when the thunder would not peace at my bidding,
    there I found them, there I smelt them out. Go to, they are not men
    of their words. They told me I was everything; 'tis a lie, I am not
    ague-proof.   100

101: **trick**: peculiarity

102: "Ay, every inch a king": Engraving by John Byam Shaw, ca. 1900
Courtesy of the Folger Shakespeare Library

104: **cause**: offense
106: **goes to't**: copulates
107: **Does lecher**: copulates promiscuously
110: **Got...sheets**: begotten lawfully, i.e., by a married couple; **To't, luxury, pell mell**: have sex, lechery, quickly
112: **Whose...snow**: whose icy countenance suggests she is frigid between her legs
113: **That minces**: who acts as if she has; **does shake the head**: moves the head from side to side (showing scorn)
115: **The fitchew...to't**: neither the polecat nor the well-pastured horse has sex
116: **Down from the waist**: from the waist down
117: **centaurs**: mythical creatures whose upper halves are human and whose lower halves are equine
118: **to the girdle**: only from the waist up; **inherit**: possess
122: **civet**: musk perfume (see note 3.4.90)
126: **piece**: 1) masterpiece, and 2) fragment
126-127: **This...naught**: i.e., This great universe shall exhaust itself out of existence.

GLOUCESTER
The trick of that voice I do well remember.
Is't not the King?

LEAR
Ay, every inch a king.

[GLOUCESTER kneels]

When I do stare, see how the subject quakes!
I pardon that man's life. What was thy cause?
Adultery? Thou shalt not die. Die for adultery.   105
No, the wren goes to't, and the small gilded fly
Does lecher in my sight.
Let copulation thrive, for Gloucester's bastard son
Was kinder to his father than my daughters
Got 'tween the lawful sheets. To't, luxury, pell-mell,   110
For I lack soldiers. Behold yon simp'ring dame,
Whose face between her forks presageth snow,
That minces virtue, and does shake the head
To hear of pleasure's name:
The fitchew, nor the soilèd horse goes to't   115
With a more riotous appetite. Down from the waist
They're centaurs, though women all above.
But to the girdle do the gods inherit;
Beneath is all the fiends. There's hell, there's darkness,
There's the sulphury pit, burning, scalding,   120
Stench, consummation. Fie, fie, fie; pah, pah!
Give me an ounce of civet, good apothecary,
To sweeten my imagination.
There's money for thee.

GLOUCESTER
O, let me kiss that hand!

LEAR
Here, wipe it first; it smells of mortality.   125

GLOUCESTER
O ruined piece of nature! This great world
Shall so wear out to naught. Do you know me?

128: **squiny on**: squint at

132: **I would not take this from report**: i.e., I would not have believed this if it had been reported to me; **it is**: and yet, here it is, incredibly enough

135: **case of eyes**: i.e., eye sockets

137: **heavy case**: sad state; **light**: i.e., empty

136-137: "No eyes in your head, nor no money in your purse?": David Hargreaves as Gloucester and Corin Redgrave as Lear in the 2005 Royal Shakespeare Company production directed by Bill Alexander

Photo: Donald Cooper

139: **feelingly**: 1) by means of touch, and 2) painfully

141: **simple**: humble, ordinary

142: **handy-dandy**: i.e., choose whichever hand you like (from a popular children's game)

145: **creature**: poor fellow; **cur**: dog, mongrel

147: **A dog's obeyed in office**: i.e., Even a dog commands obedience when it is in a position of power.

LEAR

    I remember thy eyes well enough. Dost thou squiny on me?
    No, do thy worst, blind Cupid! I'll not love.
    Read thou this challenge. Mark but the penning of't.   130

GLOUCESTER

    Were all the letters suns, I could not see one.

EDGAR

    [*Aside*] I would not take this from report; it is,
    And my heart breaks at it.

LEAR

    [*To GLOUCESTER*] Read.

GLOUCESTER

    What—with the case of eyes?   135

LEAR

    O ho, are you there with me? No eyes in your head, nor no money
    in your purse? Your eyes are in a heavy case, your purse in a light;
    yet you see how this world goes.

GLOUCESTER

    I see it feelingly.

LEAR

    What, art mad? A man may see how this world goes with no eyes;   140
    look with thy ears. See how yon justice rails upon yon simple
    thief. Hark, in thy ear: handy-dandy, which is the thief, which is
    the justice? Thou hast seen a farmer's dog bark at a beggar?

GLOUCESTER

    Ay, sir.

LEAR

    And the creature run from the cur, there thou mightst   145
    Behold the great image of authority.
    A dog's obeyed in office.

148: **beadle**: parish officer whose duty it was to whip beggars and whores

151: **The usurer hangs the cozener**: i.e., The money lender (who can bribe the judge) hangs the con man.

153-158: **Plate sin...accuser's lips.**: from the First Folio

154: **hurtless breaks**: cracks without injury

158: **glass eyes**: 1) spectacles, and 2) eyes made of glass (to replace his)

159: **scurvy**: corrupt, hypocritical

160: **No tears, now.**: appears only in the First Quarto

162: **matter and impertinency**: profundity and insanity

164: **weep**: cry over

164: "If thou wilt weep my fortune, take my eyes": Ted van Griethuysen as Lear and David Sabin as Gloucester in the 2000 Shakespeare Theatre Company production directed by Michael Kahn

Photo: Carol Rosegg

171: **This' a good block**: this (head) is a good mold for a hat. Here, Lear may be referring to the crown of flowers he has just removed from his head (as one removes a hat before entering a church)

172-173: **to shoe...felt**: to use felt padding instead of metal horseshoes (a tactic employed by armies to surprise their enemies)

173: **in proof**: to the test

Thou rascal beadle, hold thy bloody hand.
Why dost thou lash that whore? Strip thine own back.
Thy blood as hotly lusts to use her in that kind   150
For which thou whip'st her. The usurer hangs the cozener.
Through tattered rags small vices do appear;
Robes and furred gowns hides all. Plate sin with gold,
And the strong lance of justice hurtless breaks;
Arm it in rags, a pigmy's straw does pierce it.   155
None does offend, none, I say none. I'll able 'em.
Take that of me, my friend, who have the power
To seal th' accuser's lips. Get thee glass eyes,
And, like a scurvy politician, seem
To see the things thou dost not. No tears, now.   160
Pull off my boots. Harder, harder! So.

EDGAR
[*Aside*] O, matter and impertinency mixed—
Reason in madness!

LEAR
If thou wilt weep my fortune, take my eyes.
I know thee well enough: thy name is Gloucester.   165
Thou must be patient. We came crying hither.
Thou know'st, the first time that we smell the air
We wail and cry. I will preach to thee. Mark me.

GLOUCESTER
Alack, alack, the day!

LEAR
[*Removing his crown of weeds*] When we are born, we cry that we
    are come   170
To this great stage of fools. This' a good block.
It were a delicate stratagem to shoe
A troop of horse with felt; I'll put 't in proof,
And when I have stol'n upon these son-in-laws,
Then kill, kill, kill, kill, kill, kill!   175

Enter three GENTLEMEN

Edwin Forrest as Lear: Photogravure by Gebbie & Co., ca. 1897
Courtesy of the Library of Congress

179: **natural fool of Fortune**: born to be a source of amusement to Fortune
181: **cut to the brains**: mentally ill
183: **seconds**: supporters
184: **of salt**: of salty tears
186: **Ay...Good sir**: appears only in the First Quarto
186: **laying**: keeping down
187: **die bravely**: 1) die courageously, or 2) die in royal finery, but also, 3) copulate vigorously, hence the following reference to bridegroom; **smug**: 1) elegantly dressed, but also, 2) satisfied with himself as a lover
188: **jovial**: 1) majestic like Jove, and 2) jolly
189: **masters**: good sirs
191: **life**: cause for optimism; **an**: if
192: **Sa, sa, sa, sa**: cry used by hunters in pursuit of game
195: **general curse**: i.e., Eve's primordial sin
196: **twain**: 1) Regan and Gonoril, and 2) Adam and Eve; i.e., the two halves of the divided

FIRST GENTLEMAN
  O, here he is. Lay hands upon him, sirs.
  [*To LEAR*] Your most dear daughter—

LEAR
  No rescue? What, a prisoner? I am e'en
  The natural fool of Fortune. Use me well.
  You shall have ransom. Let me have a surgeon;   180
  I am cut to the brains.

FIRST GENTLEMAN
  You shall have anything.

LEAR
  No seconds? All myself?
  Why, this would make a man a man of salt,
  To use his eyes for garden water-pots,   185
  Ay, and laying autumn's dust.

FIRST GENTLEMAN
                              Good sir—

LEAR
  I will die bravely, like a smug bridegroom.
  What, I will be jovial. Come, come,
  I am a king, my masters, know you that?

FIRST GENTLEMAN
  You are a royal one, and we obey you.   190

LEAR
  Then there's life in't. Nay, an you get it, you shall get it with
  running. Sa, sa, sa, sa!
                    Exit running [pursued by two GENTLEMEN.]

FIRST GENTLEMAN
  A sight most pitiful in the meanest wretch,
  Past speaking in a king. Thou hast one daughter
  Who redeems nature from the general curse   195
  Which twain hath brought her to.

197: **gentle**: noble

198: **speed you**: Godspeed, may God bless you

199: **aught**: anything; **toward**: on the horizon

200: **vulgar**: widely spoken of

203: **on speedy foot**: on horseback; **the main**: the majority of the troops

203-204: **descriers...thoughts**: i.e., lookouts expect the army's arrival within hours

208: **worser spirit**: depressive thoughts

210: **father**: honorific term used for older men, but ironic here because Edgar is speaking to his father (see also lines 4.6.72, 242, and 271)

EDGAR
Hail, gentle sir.

FIRST GENTLEMAN
Sir, speed you. What's your will?

EDGAR
Do you hear aught, sir, of a battle toward?

FIRST GENTLEMAN
Most sure and vulgar, everyone hears that,   200
That can distinguish sense.

EDGAR
But, by your favor, how near's the other army?

FIRST GENTLEMAN
Near and on speedy foot, the main; descriers
Stands on the hourly thoughts.

EDGAR
                              I thank you, sir. That's all.

FIRST GENTLEMAN
Though that the Queen on special cause is here,   205
Her army is moved on.

EDGAR
                    I thank you, sir.
                                        Exit [GENTLEMAN]

GLOUCESTER
You ever gentle gods, take my breath from me.
Let not my worser spirit tempt me again
To die before you please.

EDGAR
Well pray you, father.   210

210: **what**: who

211: **tame**: weak, vulnerable

212: **known**: personally experienced; **feeling**: heartfelt

213: **Am pregnant to**: have the capacity to offer

214: **'biding**: nearby dwelling

215: **benison**: blessing

216: **boot**: reward; **to boot**: in addition; **proclaimed prize**: one who has been publicly declared to have a price on his head; **happy**: fortunate

217: **framed flesh**: born

219: **thyself remember**: pray for yourself

220: **friendly**: welcome, longed for

222: **published**: proclaimed

224: **Like**: the same

225: **Ch'ill**: "I will" (Edgar speaks in a rustic dialect to represent peasant speech); **vurther 'cagion**: further occasion, more cause than this

GLOUCESTER

         Now, good sir, what are you?   210

EDGAR

A most poor man, made tame to Fortune's blows,
Who by the art of known and feeling sorrows
Am pregnant to good pity. Give me your hand,
I'll lead you to some 'biding.

GLOUCESTER

            [*Rising*] Hearty thanks.
The bounty and the benison of heaven   215
To send thee boot to boot.

                Enter Steward [OSWALD]

OSWALD

         A proclaimed prize! Most happy!
That eyeless head of thine was first framed flesh
To raise my fortunes. Thou most unhappy traitor,
Briefly thyself remember. The sword is out
That must destroy thee.

GLOUCESTER

         Now let thy friendly hand   220
Put strength enough to't.

OSWALD

        [*To EDGAR*] Wherefore, bold peasant,
Darest thou support a published traitor? Hence,
Lest the infection of his fortune take
Like hold on thee. Let go his arm.

EDGAR

Ch'ill not let go, sir, without vurther 'cagion.   225

OSWALD

Let go, slave, or thou diest.

227: **go your gate**: go your own way; **An chud**: if I could

228: **swaggered**: intimidated, bullied

228-229: **it would...vortnight**: i.e., I would not have survived more than a fortnight (a few weeks, though "fortnight" means two weeks).

229-230: **che vor' ye**: I warrant you

230: **costard**: head (literally, apple)

233: **no...foins**: i.e., your thrusts mean nothing to me

234: **Villain**: serf

236: **about me**: on my person

238: **Upon...party**: on the British side (of the conflict)

239: **serviceable**: officious

244: **sorrow**: sorrowful

245: **deathsman**: executioner

246: **Leave**: by your leave, with your permission; **wax**: wax seal on the letter

247: **rip**: 1) rip open, or 2) rip out

EDGAR

Good gentleman, go your gate. Let poor volk pass. An chud have
been swaggered out of my life, it would not have been so long as
'tis by a vortnight. Nay, come not near the old man. Keep out, che
vor' ye, or I'll try whether your costard or my baton be the   230
harder; I'll be plain with you.

OSWALD

Out, dunghill!

They fight

EDGAR

Chill pick your teeth, sir. Come, no matter for your foins.
[EDGAR knocks him down]

OSWALD

Slave, thou hast slain me. Villain, take my purse.
If ever thou wilt thrive, bury my body,   235
And give the letters which thou find'st about me
To Edmund, Earl of Gloucester. Seek him out
Upon the British party. O, untimely death! Death!

He dies

EDGAR

I know thee well—a serviceable villain,
As duteous to the vices of thy mistress   240
As badness would desire.

GLOUCESTER

What, is he dead?

EDGAR

Sit you down, father. Rest you.
[GLOUCESTER sits]

Let's see his pockets. These letters that he speaks of
May be my friends. He's dead; I am only sorrow
He had no other deathsman. Let us see.   245
Leave, gentle wax; and manners, blame us not.
To know our enemies' minds, we'd rip their hearts;
Their papers is more lawful.

250: **him**: i.e., Albany; **want not**: is not lacking

251: **fruitfully**: plentifully, successfully; **There is nothing done**: i.e., nothing will have been accomplished

253: **supply the place**: take his place; **for your labor**: 1) as payment for your efforts, and 2) as the place for your sexual labors

255: **and for...venture**: i.e., and willing to risk her own fortune for you

256: **O indistinguished...wit**: i.e., how indiscriminate women are in choosing who they bring to their bed to sate their appetites. (Given Edgar's disgust with Gonoril's adulterous plans, "space" is clearly intended here to refer to the vagina.)

259: **Thee I'll rake up**: i.e., I'll merely cover your body (a burial in an unmarked grave suitable for a felon or someone of low status); **post unsanctified**: sinful messenger

260: **in...time**: at the right moment

261: **ungracious**: depraved; **strike the sight**: amaze the eyes

262: **Of the...Duke**: of Albany, the target of this murderous plot; **For him 'tis well**: i.e., it is fortunate for him

264: **How...sense**: how resilient my loathsome mental faculties must be

265: **stand up**: am still standing; **ingenious feeling**: conscious awareness

267: **fencèd**: fenced off

268: **wrong imaginations lose**: delusional thoughts should forget

271: **bestow**: safely lodge

[*Reads the letter*]
Let our reciprocal vows be remembered. You have many opportu-
nities to cut him off. If your will want not, time and place will be   250
fruitfully offered. There is nothing done if he return the conqueror;
then am I the prisoner, and his bed my jail, from the loathed
warmth whereof, deliver me, and supply the place for your labor.
     Your—wife, so I would say—your affectionate
     servant, and for you her own for venture, Gonoril.   255
O indistinguished space of woman's wit –
A plot upon her virtuous husband's life,
And the exchange my brother!—Here in the sands,
Thee I'll rake up, the post unsanctified
Of murderous lechers, and in the mature time   260
With this ungracious paper strike the sight
Of the death-practiced Duke. For him 'tis well
That of thy death and business I can tell.

                [Exit with the body]

GLOUCESTER
   The King is mad. How stiff is my vile sense,
   That I stand up and have ingenious feeling   265
   Of my huge sorrows! Better I were distraught;
   So should my thoughts be fencèd from my griefs,
   And woes by wrong imaginations lose
   The knowledge of themselves.

          A drum afar off. [Enter EDGAR.]

EDGAR
            Give me your hand.
   Far off methinks I hear the beaten drum.   270
   Come, father, I'll bestow you with a friend.

         Exit [EDGAR, guiding GLOUCESTER]

0: Location: The French camp

Set design for the 1959 production at the Shakespeare Memorial Theatre in Stratford-upon-Avon directed by Glen Byam Shaw

Rare Book and Special Collection Library, University of Illinois at Urbana-Champaign

3: **every measure fail me**: all my efforts (to match your goodness) will fail

5: **my reports**: reports of my service to Lear

6: **Nor more, nor clipped**: i.e., neither more nor less; **suited**: dressed

7: **weeds**: ragged cloths

9: **Yet...intent**: were I to reveal my true identity now, my well-made plan would be cut short

10: **My boon**: the favor I seek from you; **know**: acknowledge

11: **meet**: suitable

Act 4, Scene 7]

[Soft music.] Enter CORDELIA, and KENT [disguised].

CORDELIA
O thou good Kent,
How shall I live and work to match thy goodness?
My life will be too short, and every measure fail me.

KENT
To be acknowledged, madam, is o'erpaid.
All my reports go with the modest truth,   5
Nor more, nor clipped, but so.

CORDELIA
                                        Be better suited.
These weeds are memories of those worser hours.
I prithee put them off.

KENT
                                Pardon me, dear madam.
Yet to be known shortens my made intent.
My boon I make it that you know me not   10
Till time and I think meet.

CORDELIA
                                Then be't so, my good lord.
                        [Enter DOCTOR and FIRST GENTLEMAN]
How does the King?

DOCTOR
                        Mad'm, sleeps still.

14: **untuned**: discordant; **wind up**: tune up, as in the tightening of a string on a lute
15: **child-changèd**: changed by (the cruelty of) his children
18: **I' th' sway**: under the control; **arrayed**: arranged comfortably
22: **temperance**: self-control, tranquility
22-23: **Very well...music there!**: appears only in the First Quarto

LOVDER THE MVSIC THERE   ACT IV SCENE VII

23: "Louder the music there!": Engraving by John Byam Shaw, ca. 1900
Courtesy of the Folger Shakespeare Library

24: **restoration**: recuperation
27: **reverence**: wisdom, venerable condition

CORDELIA
O you kind gods,
Cure this great breach in his abusèd nature;
The untuned and hurrying senses, O wind up
Of this child-changèd father!

DOCTOR
So please your Majesty   15
That we may wake the King? He hath slept long.

CORDELIA
Be governed by your knowledge, and proceed
I' th' sway of your own will. Is he arrayed?

FIRST GENTLEMAN
Ay, madam. In the heaviness of his sleep
We put fresh garments on him.   20

DOCTOR
Good madam, be by when we do awake him.
I doubt not of his temperance.

CORDELIA
Very well.

DOCTOR
Please you draw near. Louder the music there!
[LEAR is discovered asleep.]

CORDELIA
O my dear father, restoration hang
Thy medicine on my lips, and let this kiss   25
Repair those violent harms that my two sisters
Have in thy reverence made!

KENT
Kind and dear princess!

28: **Had you**: Even if you had; **white flakes**: locks of gray hair

29: **Had challenged**: would have demanded

31-34: **To stand...thin helm?**: appears only in the First Quarto

31: **deep**: deep-sounding; **dread-bolted**: dreadful and filled with lightning bolts

33: **cross-lightning**: zigzag lightning; **watch**: keep the watch; go sleepless; *perdu*: sentinel *perdu* (French), an isolated sentinel in a dangerous area

34: **thin helm**: thin helmet, i.e., balding head

36: **Against**: in front of; **fain**: compelled

37: **rogues forlorn**: forsaken beggars

40: **concluded all**: come to an end all at once

42–73

Rosalind Iden as Cordelia and Donald Wolfit as Lear

Julia Ford as Cordelia and Trevor Peacock as Lear

45: **wheel of fire**: a hellish torment for the sinful (from the myth of Ixion, a murderer condemned to have his crime purged by a fire); **that**: so that

48: **far wide**: 1) wide of the mark, and 2) lost and wandering afar

48: "You're a spirit, I know. Where did you die?": Ted van Griethuysen as Lear, Monique Holt as Cordelia, and the Ensemble in the 2000 Shakespeare Theatre Company production directed by Michael Kahn

Photo: Carol Rosegg

tracks 28-30

CORDELIA

 Had you not been their father, these white flakes
 Had challenged pity of them. Was this a face
 To be exposed against the warring winds,   30
 To stand against the deep dread-bolted thunder
 In the most terrible and nimble stroke
 Of quick cross-lightning, to watch—poor *perdu*—
 With this thin helm? Mine injurer's mean'st dog,
 Though he had bit me, should have stood that night   35
 Against my fire. And wast thou fain, poor father,
 To hovel thee with swine and rogues forlorn
 In short and musty straw? Alack, alack,
 'Tis wonder that thy life and wits at once
 Had not concluded all! [*To DOCTOR*] He wakes. Speak to him.   40

DOCTOR

 Madam, do you; 'tis fittest.

CORDELIA

 [*To LEAR*] How does my royal lord? How fares your Majesty?

LEAR

 You do me wrong to take me out o' th' grave.
 Thou art a soul in bliss, but I am bound
 Upon a wheel of fire, that mine own tears   45
 Do scald like molten lead.

CORDELIA

        Sir, do you know me.

LEAR

 You're a spirit, I know. Where did you die?

CORDELIA

 [*To DOCTOR*] Still, still far wide!

DOCTOR

 He's scarce awake. Let him alone a while.

42−73
Rosalind Iden as Cordelia and Donald Wolfit as Lear
Julia Ford as Cordelia and Trevor Peacock as Lear

51: **abused**: confused, ill treated by my own senses

52: **another thus**: another person so bewildered

55: Scene: **O look upon me, sir**: Edwin Forrest's (1806-1872) Lear begged for salvation, and Tommaso Salvini (1829-1915) played Lear as humiliated and self-reproachful. In Peter Brook's 1971 film, Paul Scofield appeared to be shrunken, broken, and older, and John Gielguid's (1904-2000) Lear appeared bewildered and sullen.

58: **fond**: senile

60: **Not an hour more nor less**: from the First Folio

63: **mainly**: completely

64: **skill**: mental acuity

LEAR

    Where have I been? Where am I? Fair daylight?   50
    I am mightily abused. I should e'en die with pity
    To see another thus. I know not what to say.
    I will not swear these are my hands. Let's see;
    I feel this pin prick. Would I were assured
    Of my condition.

CORDELIA

                [*Keeling*] O look upon me, sir,   55
    And hold your hands in benediction o'er me.
    No, sir, you must not kneel.

LEAR

                Pray do not mock.
    I am a very foolish, fond old man,
    Fourscore and upward,
    Not an hour more nor less, and to deal plainly,   60
    I fear I am not in my perfect mind.
    Methinks I should know you, and know this man;
    Yet I am doubtful, for I am mainly ignorant
    What place this is, and all the skill I have
    Remembers not these garments, nor I know not   65
    Where I did lodge last night. Do not laugh at me,
    For, as I am a man, I think this lady
    To be my child, Cordelia.

CORDELIA

                And so I am, I am.

LEAR

    Be your tears wet? Yes, faith. I pray, weep not.
    If you have poison for me, I will drink it.   70
    I know you do not love me, for your sisters
    Have, as I do remember, done me wrong.
    You have some cause; they have not.

CORDELIA

                No cause, no cause.

75: **abuse me**: 1) deceive me, and also 2) hurt me (by reminding me that I gave away my kingdom)
76: **rage**: frenzy, distemper

Costume rendering for the Doctor from the 1959 production at the Shakespeare Memorial Theatre in Stratford-upon-Avon directed by Glen Byam Shaw
Rare Book and Special Collection Library, University of Illinois at Urbana-Champaign

77-78: **and yet...he has lost**: appears only in the First Quarto

78: **even o'er**: go over in his memory

80: **further settling**: he is further settled

85-95: **Holds it...battle's fought**: appears only in the First Quarto

85: **Holds it true**: i.e., does it still hold true

87: **conductor**: leader

LEAR
    Am I in France?

KENT
    In your own kingdom, sir.

LEAR
                        Do not abuse me.   75

DOCTOR
    Be comforted, good madam. The great rage
    You see is cured in him, and yet it is danger
    To make him even o'er the time he has lost.
    Desire him to go in; trouble him no more
    Till further settling.   80

CORDELIA
    [*To LEAR*] Will't please your Highness walk?

LEAR
    You must bear with me.
    Pray you now, forget and forgive. I am old
    And foolish.
                        Exeunt. Manet KENT and [FIRST] GENTLEMAN.

FIRST GENTLEMAN
    Holds it true, sir, that the Duke   85
    Of Cornwall was so slain?

KENT
                        Most certain, sir.

FIRST GENTLEMAN
    Who is conductor of his people?

KENT
                        As 'tis said,
    The bastard son of Gloucester.

91: **look about**: assess the situation carefully; **powers of the kingdom**: i.e., British armies

93: **arbitrement**: arbitration by force of arms; **like**: likely

94: **My point...wrought**: my fate (literally, the period at the end of my life's sentence) will be thoroughly determined

95: **Or**: Either; **as**: according to how

FIRST GENTLEMAN
                              They say Edgar,
   His banished son, is with the Earl of Kent
   In Germany.

KENT
                        Report is changeable.   90
   'Tis time to look about. The powers of the kingdom
   Approach apace.

FIRST GENTLEMAN
   The arbitrement is like to be bloody. Fare you well, sir.
                                                          [Exit]

KENT
   My point and period will be throughly wrought,
   Or well or ill, as this day's battle's fought.   95
                                                          Exit

[King Lear

Act 5

0: Location: The British camp near Dover

Watercolor scene sketch from the promptbook for Charles Kean's 1858 production
Courtesy of the Folger Shakespeare Library

1: **Know**: Inquire; **last purpose hold**: most recent plan (to fight) remains firm
2: **since**: since then; **advised by aught**: influenced by anything
3: **abdication**: resignation
4: **self-reproving**: self-recrimination; **his constant pleasure**: the decision he has settled on
5: **man**: i.e., Oswald; **miscarried**: gone amiss
6: **doubted**: feared
9: **honored**: honorable
11: **forfended place**: forbidden place, i.e., the place on her body forbidden to him by injunctions against adultery
12-14: **That thought...call hers**: appears only in the First Quarto
12: **abuses**: degrades
13: **conjunct and bosomed**: sexually intimate
14: **As far as we call hers**: as fully as a man can be with a woman

Act 5, Scene 1]

Enter EDMUND, REGAN, and their powers

EDMUND
    Know of the Duke if his last purpose hold,
    Or whether since he is advised by aught
    To change the course. He's full of abdication
    And self-reproving. Bring his constant pleasure.

[Exit one or more]

REGAN
    Our sister's man is certainly miscarried.   5

EDMUND
    'Tis to be doubted, madam.

REGAN
                    Now, sweet lord,
    You know the goodness I intend upon you.
    Tell me but truly—but then speak the truth—
    Do you not love my sister?

EDMUND
                    Ay, honored love.

REGAN
    But have you never found my brother's way   10
    To the forfended place?

EDMUND
    That thought abuses you.

REGAN
                I am doubtful
    That you have been conjunct and bosomed with her,
    As far as we call hers.

15: **endure**: tolerate

16: **familiar**: intimate

17: **Fear me not**: you need not worry about me in such matters

18-19: **[*Aside*]...and me**: appears only in the First Quarto

20: **bemet**: met

22: **rigor of our state**: i.e., harshness of our governance

23-28: **Where I...speak nobly**: appears only in the First Quarto

23: **cry out**: rebel; **Where**: when; **honest**: honorable

24: **For**: as for

25: **touches us as**: concerns us insomuch as

26: **Yet bolds...fear**: i.e., Not only does it embolden the King, but I fear it encourages others as well.

27: **make oppose**: stir up opposition

28: **Why...reasoned**: i.e., Why are we reasoning about why we should fight, when we should be fighting?

30: **domestic poor particulars**: petty household squabbles

32: **ensign of war**: commissioned officers

EDMUND
                No, by mine honor, madam.

REGAN
  I never shall endure her. Dear my lord,   15
  Be not familiar with her.

EDMUND
  Fear me not. She and the duke her husband!
                Enter ALBANY and GONORIL with troops

GONORIL
  [*Aside*] I had rather lose the battle than that sister
  Should loosen him and me.

ALBANY
  [*To REGAN*] Our very loving sister, well bemet,   20
  For this I hear: the King is come to his daughter,
  With others whom the rigor of our state
  Forced to cry out. Where I could not be honest
  I never yet was valiant. For this business,
  It touches us as France invades our land;   25
  Yet bold's the King, with others whom I fear.
  Most just and heavy causes make oppose.

EDMUND
  Sir, you speak nobly.

REGAN
                Why is this reasoned?

GONORIL
  Combine together 'gainst the enemy;
  For these domestic poor particulars   30
  Are not to question here.

ALBANY
  Let us then determine with the ensign of war
  On our proceedings.

33-34: **I shall...your tent**: appears only in the First Quarto

36: **convenient**: appropriate

37: **I know the riddle**: i.e., I see all too clearly why she insists that I accompany her: she doesn't want me to be alone with Edmund.

40: **this letter**: Gonoril's letter to Edmund (removed from Oswald after he was killed; see line 4.6.236)

43: **prove**: demonstrate in combat

44: **avouchèd**: acknowledged; **miscarry**: die in battle

46: **machination**: plotting (to kill you)

EDMUND

                I shall attend you
Presently at your tent.

[Exit with his powers]

REGAN

             Sister, you'll go with us?

GONORIL

No.   35

REGAN

'Tis most convenient. Pray you go with us.

GONORIL

[*Aside*] O ho, I know the riddle! [*To REGAN*] I will go.
               Enter EDGAR [disguised as a peasant]

EDGAR

[*To ALBANY*] If e'er your grace had speech with man so poor,
Hear me one word.

ALBANY

          [*To the others*] I'll overtake you.
             [Exeunt. Manet ALBANY and EDGAR]

                 Speak.

EDGAR

Before you fight the battle, ope this letter.   40
If you have victory, let the trumpet sound
For him that brought it. Wretched though I seem,
I can produce a champion that will prove
What is avouchèd there. If you miscarry,
Your business of the world hath so an end,   45
And machination ceases. Fortune love you—

ALBANY

Stay till I have read the letter.

51: **o'erlook**: glance at

53: **guess**: assessment

54: **discovery**: reconnoitering

55: **We...time**: i.e., We will be prepared for whatever happens.

57: **jealous**: wary

58: **adder**: poisonous snake

62: **hardly**: with difficulty; **carry...side**: fulfill my half of our reciprocal vows of love

64: **countenance**: support, authority

66: **taking off**: killing

69: **Shall**: they shall

69-70: **my state...debate**: i.e., I must maintain my position with force not with words

EDGAR
    I was forbid it.
    When time shall serve, let but the herald cry,
    And I'll appear again.   50

ALBANY
    Why, fare thee well. I will o'erlook the paper.

                                      [Exit EDGAR]
                                    Enter EDMUND

EDMUND
    The enemy's in view; draw up your powers.
                  [EDMUND offers ALBANY a paper]
    Here is the guess of their great strength and forces
    By diligent discovery; but your haste
    Is now urged on you.

ALBANY
                    We will greet the time.   55
                                      [Exit]

EDMUND
    To both these sisters have I sworn my love,
    Each jealous of the other as the stung
    Are of the adder. Which of them shall I take?—
    Both?—one?—or neither? Neither can be enjoyed,
    If both remain alive. To take the widow   60
    Exasperates, makes mad, her sister Gonoril,
    And hardly shall I carry out my side,
    Her husband being alive. Now then, we'll use
    His countenance for the battle, which being done,
    Let her that would be rid of him devise   65
    His speedy taking off. As for the mercy
    Which he intends to Lear and to Cordelia,
    The battle done, and they within our power,
    Shall never see his pardon; for my state
    Stands on me to defend, not to debate.   70
                                        Exit

0: Location: The battlefield

6: "King Lear hath lost, he and his daughter ta'en:" John Wood as Lear and Alex Kingston as Cordelia in the 1991 Royal Shakespeare Company production directed by Nicholas Hytner

Photo: Donald Cooper

0: Stage Direction: ***Alarum***: trumpet call to arms
1: **father**: venerated old man (see note 4.6.210)
2: **host**: source of shelter
4: Stage Direction: ***Alarum and retreat***: trumpet call for withdrawal
11: **Ripeness is all**: i.e., Timing is everything (we do not leave this world till it is our time).
12: **And that's true too**: from the First Folio

Act 5, Scene 2]

Alarum. Enter the powers of France over the stage led by
CORDELIA with her father in her hand. Then enter EDGAR
[disguised as a peasant, guiding] GLOUCESTER.

EDGAR
  Here, father, take the shadow of this bush
  For your good host; pray that the right may thrive.
  If ever I return to you again
  I'll bring you comfort.

                                                    Exit

GLOUCESTER
                        Grace go with you, sir.
                 Alarum and retreat. [Enter EDGAR.]

EDGAR
  Away, old man. Give me thy hand. Away.   5
  King Lear hath lost, he and his daughter ta'en.
  Give me thy hand. Come on.

GLOUCESTER
  No farther, sir. A man may rot even here.

EDGAR
  What, in ill thoughts again? Men must endure
  Their going hence even as their coming hither.   10
  Ripeness is all. Come on.

GLOUCESTER
  And that's true too.

                    [Exit EDGAR, guiding GLOUCESTER]

0: Location: The British Camp

1: **Good guard**: guard them well
2: **their greater pleasures**: the desires of those in command
3: **That are**: to those who are; **censure**: judge

3-4: "We are not the first / Who with best meaning have incurred the worst": Corin Redgrave as Lear and Sîan Brooke as Cordelia in the 2005 Royal Shakespeare Company production directed by Bill Alexander
Photo: Donald Cooper

6: **Fortune**: the goddess of luck; see also lines 1.1.274, 2.1.39, 2.2.155-56, 4.6.211, and 5.3.173
7: **Shall...sisters**: i.e., Are we not even allowed to talk to Gonoril and Reagan before they put us in jail?
13: **gilded butterflies**: beautifully attired courtiers
16: **take upon 's**: try to solve, assume responsibility for
17: **God's spies**: divine observers of the world who watch events unfold from heaven; **wear out**: live longer than
18-19: **pacts...moon**: i.e., alliances and cliques that are aligned with those who are in power and constantly in a state of flux

Act 5, Scene 3]

Enter EDMUND with LEAR and CORDELIA prisoners,
[a CAPTAIN, and soldiers]

EDMUND
Some officers take them away. Good guard
Until their greater pleasures best be known
That are to censure them.

CORDELIA
                     [*To LEAR*] We are not the first
Who with best meaning have incurred the worst.
For thee, oppressèd King, am I cast down,   5
Myself could else outfrown false Fortune's frown.
Shall we not see these daughters and these sisters?

LEAR
No, no, no, no. Come, let's away to prison.
We two alone will sing like birds i' th' cage.
When thou dost ask me blessing, I'll kneel down   10
And ask of thee forgiveness; so we'll live,
And pray, and sing, and tell old tales, and laugh
At gilded butterflies, and hear poor rogues
Talk of court news, and we'll talk with them too—
Who loses and who wins, who's in, who's out,   15
And take upon 's the mystery of things
As if we were God's spies; and we'll wear out
In a walled prison pacts and sects of great ones
That ebb and flow by th' moon.

EDMUND
                     [*To Soldiers*] Take them away.

Set design for the 1959 production at the Shakespeare Memorial Theatre in
Stratford-upon-Avon directed by Glen Byam Shaw

Rare Book and Special Collection Library, University of Illinois at Urbana-Champaign

21: The gods...incense: i.e., The gods themselves will not accept Cordelia's sacrificial
rites, but will perform them for her.

22-23: He that...foxes: i.e., Only someone from heaven, bringing a firebrand (a burning
stick used to break up a lead of foxes), can separate us from each other again.

24-25: The goodyear...weep: i.e., The years to follow will be kind to us and will
destroy our enemies before they have had a chance cause us any more pain

28: advanced: promoted

31: Are as the time is: must adapt to the rigors of the times

32: a sword: i.e., a warrior

32: great employment: important task

32-33: Thy...bear question: there is no room for debate within the important task

35: write "happy": i.e., consider yourself fortunate

37-38: I cannot...I'll do't.: appears only in the First Quarto

39: strain: lineage

41: opposites: enemies

LEAR

[*To CORDELIA*] Upon such sacrifices, my Cordelia,   20
The gods themselves throw incense. Have I caught thee?
He that parts us shall bring a brand from heaven
And fire us hence like foxes. Wipe thine eyes.
The goodyear shall devour 'em, flesh and fell,
Ere they shall make us weep. We'll see 'em starve first. Come.   25
                        [Exeunt. Manet EDMUND and CAPTAIN]

EDMUND

Come hither, captain. Hark.
Take thou this note. Go follow them to prison.
One step I have advanced thee; if thou dost
As this instructs thee, thou dost make thy way
To noble fortunes. Know thou this: that men   30
Are as the time is. To be tender-minded
Does not become a sword. Thy great employment
Will not bear question. Either say thou'lt do't,
Or thrive by other means.

CAPTAIN

                        I'll do't, my lord.

EDMUND

About it, and write "happy" when thou hast done.   35
Mark, I say, instantly, and carry it so
As I have set it down.

CAPTAIN

                        I cannot draw a cart,
Nor eat dried oats. If it be man's work, I'll do't.
                                                          Exit.
                Enter Duke [of ALBANY], the two ladies [GONORIL
                and REGAN, another CAPTAIN and] others.

ALBANY

[*To EDMUND*] Sir, you have showed today your valiant strain,
And fortune led you well. You have the captives   40
That were the opposites of this day's strife.

46: **retention**: imprisonment
47: **age**: advanced age; **title**: royal status
48: **pluck the common bosom**: appeal to the sympathy of the common people
49: **impressed lances**: lancers (soldiers) whom we have recruited
50: **Queen**: i.e., Cordelia, now Queen of France
52: **further space**: a later date
53: **session**: interrogation, trial
53-58: **At this time...fitter place**: appears only in the First Quarto
55-56: **And...sharpness**: i.e., and even the most virtuous of conflicts are reviled by those who have suffered their dire consequences
59: **subject of**: subordinate in
60: **list**: please
61: **pleasure**: desire, objective; **demanded**: taken up, asked about
62: **powers**: troops
64: **immediate**: most pressing
65: **hot**: fast

66-67:"In his own grace he doth exalt himself / More than in your advancement": Rosalind Cash as Gonoril, Ellen Holly as Regan, and the Ensemble in the 1973 Public Theater production directed by Edwin Sherin
Photo: George E. Joseph

67: **your advancement**: the promotions you confer

We do require then of you, so to use them
As we shall find their merits and our safety
May equally determine.

EDMUND
                    Sir, I thought it fit
To send the old and miserable King   45
To some retention and appointed guard,
Whose age has charms in it, whose title more,
To pluck the common bosom on his side
And turn our impressed lances in our eyes
Which do command them. With him I sent the Queen,   50
My reason all the same, and they are ready
Tomorrow, or at further space, to appear
Where you shall hold your session. At this time
We sweat and bleed. The friend hath lost his friend,
And the best quarrels in the heat are cursed   55
By those that feel their sharpness.
The question of Cordelia and her father
Requires a fitter place.

ALBANY
                    Sir, by your patience,
I hold you but a subject of this war,
Not as a brother.

REGAN
                    That's as we list to grace him.   60
Methinks our pleasure should have been demanded
Ere you had spoke so far. He led our powers,
Bore the commission of my place and person,
The which immediate may well stand up
And call itself your brother.

GONORIL
                    Not so hot.   65
In his own grace he doth exalt himself
More than in your advancement.

68: **me invested**: myself appointed; **compeers**: compares favorably to
69: **the most**: the most with which you could invest him
70: **prove**: prove to be
71: **asquint**: with a squint, i.e., furtively, suspiciously
73: **From...stomach**: i.e., with tremendous anger
74: **patrimony**: inheritance
75: **Dispose...thine**: from the First Folio
75: **The walls is thine**: I surrender all of me, body and soul, to you. (Given the sexualized banter between the two sisters, and Gonoril's subsequent question in line 77, Regan is literally offering Edmund her walls, i.e., her vaginal walls.)
77: **enjoy**: have sex with

Costume rendering for Gonoril from the 1959 production at the Shakespeare Memorial Theatre in Stratford-upon-Avon directed by Glen Byam Shaw
Rare Book and Special Collection Library, University of Illinois at Urbana-Champaign

78: **The...will**: i.e., You have no say in this matter.
79: **Half-blooded fellow**: illegitimate bastard

REGAN

                      In my right
  By me invested, he compeers the best.

GONORIL

  That were the most if he should husband you.

REGAN

  Jesters do oft prove prophets.

GONORIL

                      Holla, holla—   70
  That eye that told you so looked but asquint.

REGAN

  Lady, I am not well, else I should answer
  From a full-flowing stomach. [*To EDMUND*] General,
  Take thou my soldiers, prisoners, patrimony.
  Dispose of them, of me. The walls is thine.   75
  Witness the world that I create thee here
  My lord and master.

GONORIL

              Mean you to enjoy him, then?

ALBANY

  The let-alone lies not in your goodwill.

EDMUND

  Nor in thine, lord.

ALBANY

           Half-blooded fellow, yes.

EDMUND

  Let the drum strike and prove my title good.   80

82: **in thine attaint**: 1) as your companion in corruption, and 2) as an accuser in this effort to attaint you (i.e., to strip you of your civil rights)

83: **subcontracted**: contracted, engaged

86: **contradict**: oppose; **banns**: public announcement of a proposed marriage

87: **make your love to me**: i.e., petition me for permission

88: **An interlude**: a play, i.e., what a farce this is, how melodramatic you all are (from the First Folio)

89: **Let the trumpet sound**: from the First Folio

92: **prove it on thy heart**: i.e., kill you

93: **in nothing less**: in no respect less guilty

96: **What**: whoever

97: **villain-like he lies**: 1) lie dead like a villain (in an unmarked grave), and 2) tell lies like a villain

100: **firmly**: violently

ALBANY
  Stay yet, hear reason. Edmund, I arrest thee
  On capital treason, and in thine attaint
  This gilded serpent. [*To REGAN*] For your claim, fair sister,
  I bar it in the interest of my wife.
  'Tis she is subcontracted to this lord,   85
  And I, her husband, contradict the banns.
  If you will marry, make your love to me.
  My lady is bespoke.—

GONORIL
                    An interlude!

ALBANY
  Thou art armed, Gloucester. Let the trumpet sound.
  If none appear to prove upon thy head   90
  Thy heinous, manifest, and many treasons,

                                    [He throws down a glove]

  There is my pledge. I'll prove it on thy heart,
  Ere I taste bread, thou art in nothing less
  Than I have here proclaimed thee.

REGAN
  Sick, O sick!

GONORIL
                    [*Aside*] If not, I'll ne'er trust poison.   95

EDMUND [*To ALBANY, throwing down a glove*]
  There's my exchange. What in the world he is
  That names me traitor, villain-like he lies.
  Call by thy trumpet. He that dares, approach;
  On him, on you—who not?—I will maintain
  My truth and honor firmly.   100

ALBANY
  A herald, ho!

102: **A herald, ho, a herald!**: appears only in the First Quarto
103: **Trust to thy single virtue**: i.e., rely on your own strength alone
104: **levied**: financed
110: **Sound, trumpet!**: appears only in the First Quarto
111: **quality or degree**: noble birth or rank; **host**: roster
114-115: **Sound...Again!**: appears only in the First Quarto

Costume rendering for the Herald from the 1959 production at the Shakespeare Memorial Theatre in Stratford-upon-Avon directed by Glen Byam Shaw

Rare Book and Special Collection Library, University of Illinois at Urbana-Champaign

EDMUND
  A herald, ho, a herald!

                                          [Enter HERALD]

ALBANY
  [To EDMUND] Trust to thy single virtue, for thy soldiers,
  All levied in my name, have in my name
  Took their discharge.   105

REGAN
  This sickness grows upon me.

ALBANY
  She is not well. Convey her to my tent.
                          [Exit one or more with REGAN]
                          [Enter a HERALD and a trumpeter]
  Come hither, herald. Let the trumpet sound,
  And read out this.

SECOND CAPTAIN
  Sound, trumpet!   110
                                          [Trumpeter sounds]

HERALD
  *[Reads] If any man of quality or degree in the host of the army will
  maintain upon Edmund, supposed Earl of Gloucester, that he's a
  manifold traitor, let him appear at the third sound of the trumpet.
  He is bold in his defense.*

EDMUND
  Sound!
                                          [Trumpeter sounds]
                    Again!   115
      Enter EDGAR, [armed,] at the third sound, a trumpet before him.

ALBANY
  [To HERALD] Ask him his purposes, why he appears
  Upon this call o' th' trumpet.

117: **What**: who

120: **canker-bit**: chewed full of holes, as caterpillars do to the leaves of plants

122: **cope**: confront

128: **profession**: rank as a knight

129: **Maugre**: in spite of

130: **victor-sword and fire-new fortune**: victory in battle and newly-minted fortune

131: **heart**: courage

134: **upward**: top

135: **descent**: lowest extreme

136: **toad-spotted**: 1) venomous, and 2) having a spotty or checkered past; **Say thou no**: if you deny it

137: **bent**: inclined, prepared

HERALD

                        [To EDGAR] What are you?
Your name and quality, and why you answer
This present summons?

EDGAR

                    O, know, my name is lost,
By treason's tooth bare-gnawn and canker-bit.   120
Yet ere I move't, where is the adversary
I come to cope withal?

ALBANY

                Which is that adversary?

EDGAR

What's he that speaks for Edmund, Earl of Gloucester?

EDMUND

Himself. What sayst thou to him?

EDGAR

                  Draw thy sword,
That if my speech offend a noble heart   125
Thy arm may do thee justice. Here is mine.

                        [He draws his sword]

Behold, it is the privilege of my tongue,
My oath, and my profession. I protest,
Maugre thy strength, youth, place, and eminence,
Despite thy victor-sword and fire-new fortune,   130
Thy valour and thy heart, thou art a traitor,
False to thy gods, thy brother, and thy father,
Conspirant 'gainst this high illustrious prince,
And from the extremest upward of thy head
To the descent and dust beneath thy feet   135
A most toad-spotted traitor. Say thou no,
This sword, this arm, and my best spirits are bent
To prove upon thy heart, whereto I speak,
Thou liest.

139: **wisdom**: prudence

141: **tongue some say**: speech somewhat indicates

142: **What safe...demand**: from the First Folio

143: **right of knighthood**: chivalric right to refuse combat with an unknown person of uncertain rank

144: **toss...head**: confront you directly with those crimes of which you accuse me

145: **hell-hated**: hated as much as hell is hated

147: **give...way**: deliver them directly to your heart

148: **Where...ever**: they (the charges of treason you have leveled at me) will forever be applied to you (after I defeat you); **speak**: sound

149: **Save**: spare (Albany wants Edmund to live to be put on trial for his crimes); **practice**: trickery

151: **opposite**: opponent

152: **cozened and beguiled**: deceived and misled

153: **stopple it**: stop it up

155: **no tearing**: i.e., do not destroy the evidence (the letter plotting Albany's death)

EDMUND
                    In wisdom I should ask thy name,
But since thy outside looks so fair and warlike,   140
And that thy tongue some say of breeding breathes,
What safe and nicely I might well demand
My right of knighthood I disdain and spurn.
Here do I toss those treasons to thy head,
With the hell-hated lie o'erturn thy heart,   145
Which, for they yet glance by and scarcely bruise,
This sword of mine shall give them instant way
Where they shall rest forever. Trumpets, speak!
                    [Flourish. They fight. EDMUND is vanquished.]

ALBANY
Save him, save him!

GONORIL
                    This is mere practice, Gloucester.
By the law of arms thou art not bound to answer   150
An unknown opposite. Thou art not vanquished,
But cozened and beguiled.

ALBANY
                    Stop your mouth, dame,
Or with this paper shall I stopple it.
[To EDMUND] Hold, sir, thou worse than anything, read thine
     own evil.
[To GONORIL] Nay, no tearing, lady. I perceive you know't.   155

GONORIL
Say if I do, the laws are mine, not thine.
Who shall arraign me for't.

ALBANY
                    Most monstrous!
O, Know'st thou this paper?

GONORIL
                    Ask me not what I know.
                                                        Exit

159: **Govern**: restrain

163: **fortune on**: victory over

164: **charity**: forgiveness

168: **pleasant vices**: sins of pleasure

170: **got**: begot you

173: **The wheel...circle**: 1) Everything has come around to where it began, 2) my crimes have received their appropriate punishment, and 3) the wheel of fortune has turned. See also 1.1.274, 2.1.39, 2.2.155-56, 4.6.211, and 5.3.6.

174: **gait**: bearing

Costume rendering for Albany from the 1959 production at the Shakespeare Memorial Theatre in Stratford-upon-Avon directed by Glen Byam Shaw

ALBANY

  Go after her. She's desperate. Govern her.

                                      [Exit one or more]

EDMUND

  What you have charged me with, that have I done,   160

  And more, much more. The time will bring it out.

  'Tis past, and so am I. [*To EDGAR*] But what art thou,

  That hast this fortune on me? If thou beest noble,

  I do forgive thee.

EDGAR

              Let's exchange charity.

  I am no less in blood than thou art, Edmund.   165

  If more, the more ignobly thou hast wronged me.

  My name is Edgar, and thy father's son.

  The gods are just, and of our pleasant vices

  Make instruments to scourge us.

  The dark and vicious place where thee he got   170

  Cost him his eyes.

EDMUND

  Thou hast spoken truth.

  The wheel is come full circle. I am here.

ALBANY

  [*To EDGAR*] Methought thy very gait did prophesy

  A royal nobleness. I must embrace thee.   175

  Let sorrow split my heart if I did ever hate

  Thee or thy father!

EDGAR

  Worthy prince, I know't.

ALBANY

               Where have you hid yourself?

  How have you known the miseries of your father?

180: **List**: listen to

182: **The bloody proclamation to escape**: i.e., the proclamation (my death sentence) that caused me to escape

183: **followed me so near**: was never very far from thoughts

185: **shift**: change

187: **habit**: disguise

188: **rings**: i.e., eye sockets

189: **precious stones**: i.e., sparkling, jewel-like eyes

193: **success**: outcome

195: **my pilgrimage**: the story of my disguised exile; **flawed**: weakened, broken

202: **dissolve**: i.e., dissolve into tears

203-220: **This would...a slave**: appears only in the First Quarto

203: **a period**: the limit

204: **such as**: those who

204-206: **but another...extremity**: i.e., yet one more sad circumstance remains to be elaborated which, adding as it does more sorrow to what was already too much, brought much more and exceeded the limit

207: **big in clamor**: loud in lamenting (all that had happened)

EDGAR

    By nursing them, my lord. List a brief tale,   180
    And when 'tis told, O that my heart would burst!
    The bloody proclamation to escape
    That followed me so near—O, our lives' sweetness,
    That with the pain of death would hourly die
    Rather than die at once!—taught me to shift   185
    Into a madman's rags, to assume a semblance
    That very dogs disdained; and in this habit
    Met I my father with his bleeding rings,
    The precious stones new-lost; became his guide,
    Led him, begged for him, saved him from despair;   190
    Never—O father!—revealed myself unto him
    Until some half hour past, when I was armed.
    Not sure, though hoping, of this good success,
    I asked his blessing, and from first to last
    Told him my pilgrimage; but his flawed heart—   195
    Alack, too weak the conflict to support—
    'Twixt two extremes of passion, joy and grief,
    Burst smilingly.

EDMUND

                This speech of yours hath moved me,
    And shall perchance do good. But speak you on—
    You look as you had something more to say.   200

ALBANY

    If there be more, more woeful, hold it in,
    For I am almost ready to dissolve,
    Hearing of this.

EDGAR

                This would have seemed a period
    To such as love not sorrow; but another
    To amplify, too much would make much more,   205
    And top extremity.
    Whilst I was big in clamor came there in a man
    Who, having seen me in my worst estate,
    Shunned my abhorred society; but then, finding

212: **As**: as if; **threw...father**: threw himself on my father Gloucester's corpse

215: **puissant**: powerful; **strings of life**: heartstrings

217: **tranced**: entranced, dazed

219: **enemy king**: i.e., Lear, the king who had banished him (and thus could be thought of as Kent's enemy)

221-222: **What kind...bloody knife**: appears only in the First Quarto

222: **smokes**: steams (as with the heat of fresh blood)

223: **O, she's dead!**: from the First Folio

224: **Who, man?**: appears only in the First Quarto

227: **contracted**: betrothed

Who 'twas that so endured, with his strong arms   210
He fastened on my neck and bellowed out
As he'd burst heaven; threw him on my father,
Told the most piteous tale of Lear and him
That ever ear received, which in recounting
His grief grew puissant and the strings of life   215
Began to crack. Twice then the trumpets sounded,
And there I left him tranced.

ALBANY

                    But who was this?

EDGAR

Kent, sir, the banished Kent, who in disguise
Followed his enemy king, and did him service
Improper for a slave.   220
                Enter [SECOND GENTLEMAN] with a bloody knife.

SECOND GENTLEMAN

Help, help, O, help!

ALBANY

                    What kind of help?
What means that bloody knife?

SECOND GENTLEMAN

                         It's hot, it smokes.
It came even from the heart of—O, she's dead!

ALBANY

Who, man? Speak.

SECOND GENTLEMAN

Your lady, sir, your lady; and her sister   225
By her is poisoned—she hath confessed it.

EDMUND

I was contracted to them both; all three
Now marry in an instant.

229-234: **Produce...urges**: appears only in the First Quarto

234: **The compliment...urges**: i.e., the ceremonial reception demanded by common courtesy

236: **Aye good night**: farewell forever

237: Scene: **Great thing of us forgot!**: Audiences have often found something darkly humorous about this line in performance.

239: **object**: horrific sight (of all the dead)

245: **Despite**: in spite; **Quickly send**: quickly send a messenger

246: **writ**: written order of execution

ALBANY
      Produce their bodies, be they alive or dead.
      This justice of the heavens, that makes us tremble,   230
      Touches us not with pity.

                                    Enter KENT [as himself]

EDGAR
      Here comes Kent, sir.

ALBANY
      O, 'tis he; the time will not allow
      The compliment that very manners urges.

KENT
      I am come to bid my king and master   235
      Aye good night. Is he not here?

ALBANY
      Great thing of us forgot!—
      Speak, Edmund; where's the King, and where's Cordelia?
                  The bodies of GONORIL and REGAN are brought in.
      Seest thou this object, Kent?

KENT
      Alack, why thus?

EDMUND
                        Yet Edmund was beloved.   240
      The one the other poisoned for my sake,
      And after slew herself.

ALBANY
      Even so.—Cover their faces.

EDMUND
      I pant for life. Some good I mean to do,
      Despite of my own nature. Quickly send,   245
      Be brief in it, to th' castle; for my writ
      Is on the life of Lear and on Cordelia.
      Nay, send in time.

258–279
Paul Scofield as Lear, David Burke as Kent, Richard McCabe as Edgar,
and Peter Blythe as Albany
Sir John Gielgud as Lear

249: **office**: duty (to carry out the execution)
256: **fordid herself**: undid or destroyed herself, i.e., committed suicide

257: Scene: ***Enter LEAR***: Edmund Kean (1787-1833) staggered in carrying Cordeila; John Gielgud (1904-2000) carried her vigorously over one shoulder. In Peter Brook's 1971 film, Paul Scofield appeared to be strong physically but seemed broken emotionally and spiritually. Tommaso Salvini (1829-1915) and Orson Welles (1915-1985) dragged Cordelia's body behind them.

257: Stage Direction: ***Enter LEAR with CORDELIA in his arms***: Ted van Griethuysen as Lear and Monique Holt as Cordelia,in the 2000 Shakespeare Theatre Company production directed by Michael Kahn
Photo: Carol Rosegg

260: **heaven's...crack**: i.e., the skies would open up and rain down tears
263: **stone**: i.e., the mirror's surface
264: **Is...end**: i.e., Is this all that comes of our efforts and hopes in life?

ALBANY
                    Run, run, O run!

EDGAR
    To who, my lord?—Who hath the office? Send
    Thy token of reprieve.   250

EDMUND
    Well thought on! Take my sword. The captain,
    Give it the captain.

ALBANY
                    Haste thee for thy life.
                                        [Exit SECOND CAPTAIN]

EDMUND
    He hath commission from thy wife and me
    To hang Cordelia in the prison, and
    To lay the blame upon her own despair,   255
    That she fordid herself.

ALBANY
    The gods defend her!—Bear him hence a while.
                            [Exeunt some with EDMUND.]
                    [Enter LEAR with CORDELIA in his arms,
                        followed by the SECOND CAPTAIN.]

LEAR
    Howl, howl, howl, howl! O, you are men of stones.
    Had I your tongues and eyes, I would use them so
    That heaven's vault should crack. She's gone forever.   260
    I know when one is dead and when one lives.
    She's dead as earth.
                                        [He lays her down.]
                    Lend me a looking-glass.
    If that her breath will mist or stain the stone,
    Why, then she lives.

KENT
                    Is this the promised end?

258–279
Paul Scofield as Lear, David Burke as Kent, Richard McCabe as Edgar, and Peter Blythe as Albany
Sir John Gielgud as Lear

265: **horror**: i.e., the Apocalypse
265: **Fall and cease**: i.e., We sin and we die. Given the religious context, Albany could be describing human history in biblical terms: the Fall (from Eden) and the resulting end (the Apocalypse).

"King Lear Weeping over the Dead Body of Cordelia": Painting (1786-1788)
James Barry (1741-1806)

277: **falchion**: light sword
278: **skip**: run in terror
279: **same crosses spoil me**: i.e., comparable adversities exhaust me (also a reference to Christ bearing the cross)
280: **I'll...straight**: i.e., I'll be able to recognize you momentarily

EDGAR
    Or image of that horror?

ALBANY
                        Fall and cease.   265

LEAR
    This feather stirs. She lives. If it be so,
    It is a chance which does redeem all sorrows
    That ever I have felt.

KENT
                    [*Kneeling*] Ah, my good master!

LEAR
    Prithee, away.

EDGAR
                    'Tis noble Kent, your friend.

LEAR
    A plague upon you, murderous traitors all.   270
    I might have saved her; now she's gone forever.—
    Cordelia, Cordelia, stay a little. Ha?
    What is't thou sayst?—Her voice was ever soft,
    Gentle, and low, an excellent thing in women.—
    I killed the slave that was a-hanging thee.   275

SECOND CAPTAIN
    'Tis true, my lords, he did.

LEAR
                        Did I not, fellow?
    I have seen the day with my good biting falchion
    I would have made them skip. I am old now,
    And these same crosses spoil me. [*To KENT*] Who are you?
    Mine eyes are not o' the best, I'll tell you straight.   280

281-282: **If Fortune...behold**: i.e., If the goddess Fortune were to celebrate the lives of two people who had suffered the greatest fall from good luck to bad, Lear would be one of them.

283: **This...sight**: 1) my eyes are failing me, and 2) I can barely recognize you

284: **Caius**: the name Kent used when he disguised himself (this is its only mention in the play)

288: **I'll...straight**: i.e., I'll process that information momentarily

289: **difference**: i.e., the initial conflict between Lear and Cordelia; **decay**: the current deterioration of Lear's health and fortune

292: **So think I, too**: appears only in the First Quarto

293: **desperately**: in despair

KENT

    If Fortune bragged of two she loved or hated,
    One of them we behold.

LEAR

    This is a dull sight. Are not you Kent?

KENT

    The same, your servant Kent. Where is your servant Caius?

LEAR

    He's a good fellow, I can tell you that.   285
    He'll strike, and quickly too. He's dead and rotten.

KENT

    No, my good lord, I am the very man—

LEAR

    I'll see that straight.

KENT

    That from your first of difference and decay
    Have followed your sad steps.

LEAR

                    You're welcome hither.   290

KENT

    Nor no man else. All's cheerless, dark, and deadly.
    Your eldest daughters have fordone themselves,
    And desperately are dead.

LEAR

               So think I, too.

ALBANY

    He knows not what he sees; and vain it is
    That we present us to him.   295

295: **very bootless**: in vain

296: **trifle**: small matter

298: **decay**: 1) decay of Lear, and 2) decay of the kingdom (from the ravages of war)

299: **for**: as for

302: **With...honors**: with whatever benefit and such further distinctions as your honorable conduct in this conflict

306: **poor fool**: Lear is using the word "fool" here as a term of endearment to refer to Cordelia.

306: Scene: **And my poor fool is hanged**: Akira Kurosawa's *Ran* (1984) follows the fortunes of King Hidetora, who has three sons. At the film's climax, Hidetora and his loyal son, Saburo, are ambushed. The father cradles his bleeding son's corpse in his arms:

310: **O...O!**: appears only in the First Quarto

311-312: **Do you...there**: from the First Folio

314: "Look up, my lord": the Ensemble in the 2000 Shakespeare Theatre Company production directed by Michael Kahn

Photo: Carol Rosegg

EDGAR

Very bootless.   295

Enter another CAPTAIN

THIRD CAPTAIN
   [*To ALBANY*] Edmund is dead, my lord.

ALBANY

That's but a trifle here. –

You lords and noble friends, know our intent.
What comfort to this great decay may come
Shall be applied; for us, we will resign
During the life of this old Majesty   300
To him our absolute power; [*To EDGAR and KENT*] you to your rights
With boot and such addition as your honors
Have more than merited. All friends shall taste
The wages of their virtue, and all foes
The cup of their deservings.—O see, see!   305

LEAR
   And my poor fool is hanged. No, no, no life.
   Why should a dog, a horse, a rat have life,
   And thou no breath at all? O, thou wilt come no more,
   Never, never, never, never, never.—Pray you, undo
   This button. Thank you, sir. O, O, O, O!   310
   Do you see this? Look on her. Look, her lips,
   Look there, look there.

EDGAR
   He faints. [*To LEAR*] My lord, my lord!

KENT
   [*To LEAR*] Break, heart, I prithee break.

EDGAR

[*To LEAR*] Look up, my lord.

315: **Vex...ghost**: i.e., Disturb not his spirit as it moves on to the afterlife.

316: **rack**: 1) torture device, and 2) perhaps a pun on wreck, as in shipwreck, referring to the disastrous wreck of Lear's life

317: Scene: *[LEAR dies]*: In Peter Brook's 1962 RSC production, Paul Scofield played Lear's final dying moments as if acknowledging the stark truth that there was no God. Half-smiling, half-weeping, Scofield's Lear seemed keenly aware of the cosmic farce in which he had been accorded the lead role.

At least some cues for performing Lear's final moments are to be found in the two extant versions of the play themselves. In the Quarto, for example, Lear's last utterance begins with his dying groan, "O, o, o, o," and is followed by the following final words: "Break heart, I prithee break." Lear, on the verge of death here, seems to be hastening his own heart to bring the suffering of his life to an end. In the Folio version of the play, published some fifteen years later, Kent is given the line, "Break heart, I prithee break," and Lear's final words are: "Do you see this? Look on her. Look, her lips, / Look there, look there." As such, Lear in this later version dies in a sort of ecstasy, thinking that Cordelia's lips are moving and that she is still alive. In Nahum Tate's famous Restoration adaptation of the play, the Folio's version of Lear's dying words authorized Tate to rewrite the play's ending altogether so that both Lear and Cordelia live happily ever after.

319: **but usurped his life**: only forcibly borrowed his existence from God

321: **general woe**: official mourning period and funeral ceremonies

322: **the gored state**: our country, which has been maimed and bloodied by war

323: **journey**: journey to the afterlife

KENT

    Vex not his ghost. O, let him pass. He hates him   315
    That would upon the rack of this tough world
    Stretch him out longer.

                                    [LEAR dies]

EDGAR

                O, he is gone, indeed.

KENT

    The wonder is he hath endured so long.
    He but usurped his life.

ALBANY

    [To Attendants] Bear them from hence. Our present business   320
    Is general woe. *[To KENT and EDGAR]* Friends of my soul, you twain
    Rule in this kingdom, and the gored state sustain.

KENT

    I have a journey, sir, shortly to go:
    My master calls, and I must not say no.

ALBANY

    The weight of this sad time we must obey,   325
    Speak what we feel, not what we ought to say.
    The oldest hath borne most. We that are young
    Shall never see so much, nor live so long.

                         [Exeunt carrying the bodies]

A Voice Coach's Perspective on Speaking Shakespeare

KEEPING SHAKESPEARE PRACTICAL

Andrew Wade

tracks 34-35

Introduction to Speaking Shakespeare: Derek Jacobi
Speaking Shakespeare: Andrew Wade with Myra Lucretia Taylor

Why, you might be wondering, is it so important to keep Shakespeare practical? What do I mean by practical? Why is this the way to discover how to speak the text and understand it?

Plays themselves are not simply literary events—they demand interpreters in the deepest sense of the word, and the language of Shakespeare requires, therefore, not a vocal demonstration of writing techniques but an imaginative response to that writing. The key word here is imagination. The task of the voice coach is to offer relevant choices to the actor so that the actor's imagination is titillated, excited by the language, which he or she can then share with an audience, playing on that audience's imagination. Take the word "IF"—it is only composed of two letters when written, but if you say it aloud and listen to what it implies, then your reaction, the way the word plays through you, can change the perception of meaning. "Iffffffff"... you might hear and feel it implying "possibilities," "choices," "questioning," "trying to work something out." The saying of this word provokes active investigation of thought. What an apt word to launch a play: "If music be the food of love, play on" (Act 1, Scene 1 in *Twelfth Night, or What You Will*). How this word engages the listener and immediately sets up an involvement is about more than audibility. How we verbalize sounds has a direct link to meaning and understanding. In the words of Touchstone in *As You Like It,* "Much virtue in if."

I was working with a company in Vancouver on *Macbeth,* and at the end of the first week's rehearsal—after having explored our voices and opening out different pieces of text to hear the possibilities of the rhythm, feeling how the meter affects the thinking and feeling, looking at structure and form— one of the actors admitted he was also a writer of soap operas and that I had completely changed his way of writing. Specifically, in saying a line like, "The multitudinous seas incarnadine / Making the green one red" he heard the complexity of meaning revealed in the use of polysyllabic words becoming monosyllabic, layered upon the words' individual dictionary definitions. The writer was reminded that merely reproducing the speech of everyday life was nowhere near as powerful and effective as language that is shaped.

Do you think soap operas would benefit from rhyming couplets? Somehow this is difficult to imagine! But, the writer's comments set me thinking. As I am constantly trying to find ways of exploring the acting process, of opening out actors' connection with language that isn't their own, I thought it would be a good idea to involve writers and actors in some practical work on language. After talking to Cicely Berry (Voice Director, the Royal Shakespeare Company) and Colin Chambers (the then RSC Production Adviser), we put together a group of writers and actors who were interested in taking part. It was a fascinating experience all round, and it broke down barriers and misconceptions.

The actors discovered, for instance, that a writer is not coming from a very different place as they are in their creative search; that an idea or an image may result from a struggle to define a gut feeling and not from some crafted, well-formed idea in the head. The physical connection of language to the body was reaffirmed. After working with a group on Yeats' poem *Easter 1916,* Ann Devlin changed the title of the play she was writing for the Royal Shakespeare Company to *After Easter.* She had experienced the poem read aloud by a circle of participants, each voice becoming a realization of the shape of the writing. Thus it made a much fuller impact on her and caused her thinking to shift. Such practical exchanges, through language work and voice, feed and stimulate my work to go beyond making sure the actors' voices are technically sound.

It is, of course, no different when we work on a Shakespeare play. A similar connection with the language is crucial. Playing Shakespeare, in many ways, is crafted instinct. The task is thus to find the best way to tap into someone's imagination. As Peter Brook put it, "People forget that a text is dumb. To make it speak, one must create a communication machine. A living network, like a nervous system, must be made if a text which comes from far away is to touch the sensibility of the present."

This journey is never to be taken for granted. It is the process that every text must undergo every time it is staged. There is no definitive rehearsal that would solve problems or indicate ways of staging a given play. Again, this is where creative, practical work on voice can help forge new meaning by offering areas of exploration and challenge. The central idea behind my work comes back to posing the question, "How does meaning change by speaking out aloud?" It would be unwise to jump hastily to the end process for, as Peter Brook says, "Shakespeare's words are records of the words that he wanted spoken, words issuing from people's mouths, with pitch, pause and rhythm and gesture as part of their meaning. A word does not start as a word—it is the end product which begins as an impulse, stimulated by attitude and behavior which dictates the need for expression" (1).

PRACTICALLY SPEAKING

Something happens when we vocalize, when we isolate sounds, when we start to speak words aloud, when we put them to the test of our physicality, of our anatomy. We expose ourselves in a way that makes taking the language back more difficult. Our body begins a debate with itself, becomes alive with the vibrations of sound produced in the mouth or rooted deep in the muscles that aim at defining sound. In fact, the spoken words bring into play all the senses, before sense and another level of meaning are reached.

"How do I know what I think, until I see what I say," Oscar Wilde once said. A concrete illustration of this phrase was reported to me when I was leading a workshop recently. A grandmother said the work we had done that day reminded her of what her six-year-old grandson had said to his mother while they were driving through Wales: "Look, mummy, sheep! Sheep! Sheep!" "You don't have to keep telling us," the mother replied, but the boy said, "How do I know they're there, if I don't tell you?!"

Therefore, when we speak of ideas, of sense, we slightly take for granted those physical processes which affect and change their meaning. We tend to separate something that is an organic whole. In doing so, we become blind to the fact that it is precisely this physical connection to the words that enables the actors to make the language theirs.

The struggle for meaning is not just impressionistic theater mystique; it is an indispensable aspect of the rehearsal process and carries on during the life of every production. In this struggle, practical work on Shakespeare is vital and may help spark creativity and shed some light on the way meaning is born into language. After a performance of *More Words*, a show devised and directed by Cicely Berry and myself, Katie Mitchell (a former artistic director of The Other Place in Stratford-upon-Avon) gave me an essay by Ted Hughes that echoes with the piece. In it, Ted Hughes compares the writing of a poem—the coming into existence of words—to the capture of a wild animal. You will notice that in the following passage Hughes talks of "spirit" or "living parts" but never of "thought" or "sense." With great care and precaution, he advises, "It is better to call [the poem] an assembly of living parts moved by a single spirit. The living parts are the words, the images, the rhythms. The spirit is the life which inhabits them when they all work together. It is impossible to say which comes first, parts or spirit."

This is also true of life in words, as many are connected directly to one or several of our senses. Here Hughes talks revealingly of "the five senses," of "word," "action," and "muscle," all things which a practical approach to language is more likely to allow one to perceive and do justice to.

Words that live are those which we hear, like "click" or "chuckle," or which we see, like "freckled" or "veined," or which we taste, like "vinegar" or "sugar," or touch, like "prickle" or "oily," or smell, like "tar" or "onion," words which belong to one of the five senses. Or words that act and seem to use their muscles, like "flick" or "balance" (2).

In this way, practically working on Shakespeare to arrive at understanding lends itself rather well, I think, to what Adrian Noble (former artistic director of the RSC) calls "a theater of poetry," a form of art that, rooted deeply in its classical origins, would seek to awaken the imagination of its audiences through love and respect for words while satisfying our eternal craving for myths and twice-told tales.

This can only be achieved at some cost. There is indeed a difficult battle to fight and hopefully to win: "the battle of the word to survive." This phrase was coined by Michael Redgrave at the beginning of the 1950s, a period when theater began to be deeply influenced by more physical forms, such as mime (3). Although the context is obviously different, the fight today is of the same nature.

LISTENING TO SHAKESPEARE

Because of the influence of television, our way of speaking as well as listening has changed. It is crucial to be aware of this. We can get fairly close to the way *Henry V* or *Hamlet* was staged in Shakespeare's time; we can try also to reconstruct the way English was spoken. But somehow, all these fall short of the real and most important goal: the Elizabethan ear. How did one "hear" a Shakespeare play? This is hardest to know. My personal view is that we will probably never know for sure. We are, even when we hear a Shakespeare play or a recording from the past, bound irrevocably to modernity. The Elizabethan ear was no doubt different from our own, as people were not spoken to or entertained in the same way. A modern voice has to engage us in a different way in order to make us truly listen in a society that seems to rely solely on the belief that image is truth, that it is more important to show than to tell.

Sometimes, we say that a speech in Shakespeare, or even an entire production, is not well-spoken, not up to standard. What do we mean by that? Evidently, there are a certain number of "guidelines" that any actor now has to know when working on a classical text. Yet, even when these are known, actors still have to make choices when they speak. A sound is not a sound without somebody to lend an ear to it: rhetoric is nothing without an audience.

There are a certain number of factors that affect the receiver's ear. These can be cultural factors such as the transition between different acting styles or the level of training that our contemporary ear has had. There are also personal and emotional factors. Often we feel the performance was not well-spoken because, somehow, it did not live up to our expectations of how we think it should have been performed. Is it that many of us have a self-conscious model, perhaps our own first experience of Shakespeare, that meant something to us and became our reference point for the future (some treasured performance kept under glass)? Nothing from then on can quite compare with that experience.

Most of the time, however, it is more complex than nostalgia. Take, for example, the thorny area of accent. I remind myself constantly that audibility is not embedded in Received Pronunciation or Standard American. The familiarity that those in power have with speech and the articulate confidence gained from coming from the right quarters can lead us all to hear certain types of voices as outshining others. But, to my mind, the role of theater is at least to question these assumptions so that we do not perpetuate those givens but work towards a broader tolerance.

In Canada on a production of *Twelfth Night*, I was working with an actor who was from Newfoundland. His own natural rhythms in speaking seemed completely at home with Shakespeare's. Is this because his root voice has direct links back to the voice of Shakespeare's time? It does seem that compared to British dialects, which are predominantly about pitch, many North American dialects have a wonderful respect and vibrancy in their use of vowels. Shakespeare's language seems to me very vowel-aware. How useful it is for an actor to isolate the vowels in the spoken words to hear the music they produce, the rich patterns, their direct connection to feelings. North Americans more easily respond to this and allow it to feed their speaking. I can only assume it is closer to how the Elizabethans spoke.

In *Othello* the very names of the characters have a direct connection to one vowel in particular. All the male names, except the Duke, end in the sound OH: Othello, Cassio, Iago, Brabantio, etc. Furthermore, the sound OH ripples through the play both consciously and unconsciously. "Oh" occurs repeatedly and, more interestingly, is contained within other words: "so," "soul," and "know." These words resonate throughout the play, reinforcing another level of meaning. The repetition of the same sounds affects us beyond what we can quite say.

Vowels come from deep within us, from our very core. We speak vowels before we speak consonants. They seem to reveal the feelings that require the consonants to give the shape to what we perceive as making sense.

Working with actors who are bilingual (or ones for whom English is not the native language) is fascinating because of the way it allows the actor to have an awareness of the cadence in Shakespeare. There seems to be an objective perception to the musical patterns in the text, and the use of alliteration and assonance are often more easily heard not just as literary devices, but also as means by which meaning is formed and revealed to an audience.

Every speech pattern (i.e., accent, rhythm) is capable of audibility. Each has its own music, each can become an accent when juxtaposed against another. The point at which a speech pattern becomes audible is in the dynamic of the physical making of those sounds. The speaker must have the desire to get through to a listener and must be confident that every speech pattern has a right to be heard.

SPEAKING SHAKESPEARE

So, the way to speak Shakespeare is not intrinsically tied to a particular sound; rather, it is how a speaker energetically connects to that language. Central to this is how we relate to the form of Shakespeare. Shakespeare employs verse, prose, and rhetorical devices to communicate meaning. For example, in *Romeo and Juliet*, the use of contrasts helps us to quantify Juliet's feelings: "And learn me how to lose a winning match," "Whiter than new snow upon a raven's back." These extreme opposites, "lose" and "winning," "new snow" and "raven's back," are her means to express and make sense of her feelings.

On a more personal note, I am often reminded how much, as an individual, I owe to Shakespeare's spoken word. The rather quiet and inarticulate schoolboy I once was found in the speaking and the acting of those words a means to quench his thirst for expression.

NOTES:

(1) Peter Brook, *The Empty Space* (Harmondsworth: Penguin, 1972)

(2) Ted Hughes, *Winter Pollen* (London: Faber and Faber, 1995)

(3) Michael Redgrave, *The Actor's Ways and Means*
    (London: Heinemann, 1951)

In the Age of Shakespeare

Thomas Garvey

One of the earliest published pictures of Shakespeare's birthplace, from an original watercolor by Phoebe Dighton (1834)

The works of William Shakespeare have won the love of millions since he first set pen to paper some four hundred years ago, but at first blush, his plays can seem difficult to understand, even willfully obscure. There are so many strange words: not fancy, exactly, but often only half-familiar. And the very fabric of the language seems to spring from a world of forgotten assumptions, a vast network of beliefs and superstitions that have long been dispelled from the modern mind.

In fact, when "Gulielmus filius Johannes Shakespeare" (Latin for "William, son of John Shakespeare") was baptized in Stratford-on-Avon in 1564, English itself was only just settling into its current form; no dictionary had yet been written, and Shakespeare coined hundreds of words himself. Astronomy and medicine were entangled with astrology and the occult arts; democracy was waiting to be reborn; and even educated people believed in witches and fairies, and that the sun revolved around the Earth. Yet somehow Shakespeare still speaks to us today, in a voice as fresh and direct as the day his lines were first spoken, and to better understand both their artistic depth and enduring power, we must first understand something of his age.

REVOLUTION AND RELIGION

Shakespeare was born into a nation on the verge of global power, yet torn by religious strife. Henry VIII, the much-married father of Elizabeth I, had

From *The Book of Martyrs* (1563), this woodcut shows the Archbishop of Canterbury being burned at the stake in March 1556

Map of London ca. 1625

defied the Pope by proclaiming a new national church, with himself as its head. After Henry's death, however, his daughter Mary reinstituted Catholicism via a murderous nationwide campaign, going so far as to burn the Archbishop of Canterbury at the stake. But after a mere five years, the childless Mary also died, and when her half-sister Elizabeth was crowned, she declared the Church of England again triumphant.

In the wake of so many religious reversals, it is impossible to know which form of faith lay closest to the English heart, and at first, Elizabeth was content with mere outward deference to the Anglican Church. Once the Pope hinted her assassination would not be a mortal sin, however, the suppression of Catholicism grew more savage, and many Catholics—including some known in Stratford—were hunted down and executed, which meant being hanged, disemboweled, and carved into quarters. Many scholars suspect that Shakespeare himself was raised a Catholic (his father's testament of faith was found hidden in his childhood home). We can speculate about the impact this religious tumult may have had on his plays. Indeed, while explicit Catholic themes, such as the description of Purgatory in *Hamlet*, are rare, the larger themes of disguise and double allegiance are prominent across the canon. Prince Hal offers false friendship to Falstaff in the histories, the heroines of the comedies are forced to disguise themselves as men, and the action of the tragedies is driven by double-dealing villains. "I am not what I am," Iago tells us (and himself) in *Othello*, summing up in a single stroke what may have been Shakespeare's formative social and spiritual experience.

If religious conflict rippled beneath the body politic like some ominous undertow, on its surface the tide of English power was clearly on the rise. The defeat of the Spanish Armada in 1588 had established Britain as a global power; by 1595 Sir Walter Raleigh had founded the colony of Virginia (named for the Virgin Queen), and discovered a new crop, tobacco, which would inspire a burgeoning international trade. After decades of strife and the threat of invasion, England enjoyed a welcome stability. As the national coffers grew, so did London; over the course of Elizabeth's reign, the city would nearly double in size to a population of some 200,000.

Hornbook from Shakespeare's lifetime

A 1639 engraving of a scene from a royal state visit of Marie de Medici depicts London's packed, closely crowded half-timbered houses.

FROM COUNTRY TO COURT

The urban boom brought a new dimension to British life—the mentality of the metropolis. By contrast, in Stratford-on-Avon, the rhythms of the rural world still held sway. Educated in the local grammar school, Shakespeare was taught to read and write by a schoolmaster called an "abecedarian", and as he grew older, he was introduced to logic, rhetoric, and Latin. Like most schoolboys of his time, he was familiar with Roman mythology and may have learned a little Greek, perhaps by translating passages of the New Testament. Thus while he never attended a university, Shakespeare could confidently refer in his plays to myths and legends that today we associate with the highly educated.

Beyond the classroom, however, he was immersed in the life of the countryside, and his writing all but revels in its flora and fauna, from the wounded deer of *As You Like It* to the herbs and flowers which Ophelia scatters in *Hamlet*. Pagan rituals abounded in the rural villages of Shakespeare's day, where residents danced around maypoles in spring, performed "mummers' plays" in winter, and recited rhymes year-round to ward off witches and fairies.

The custom most pertinent to Shakespeare's art was the medieval "mystery play," in which moral allegories were enacted in country homes and village squares by troupes of traveling actors. These strolling players—usually four men and two boys who played the women's roles—often lightened the moralizing with bawdy interludes in a mix of high and low feeling, which would become a defining feature of Shakespeare's art. Occasionally even a professional troupe, such as Lord Strange's Men, or the Queen's Men, would arrive in town, perhaps coming straight to Shakespeare's door (his father was the town's bailiff) for permission to perform.

Rarely, however, did such troupes stray far from their base in London, the nation's rapidly expanding capital and cultural center. The city itself had existed since the time of the Romans (who built the original London Bridge), but it was not until the Renaissance that its population spilled beyond its ancient walls and began to grow along (and across) the Thames, by whose banks the Tudors had built their glorious palaces. It was these two contradictory worlds—a modern metropolis cheek-by-jowl with a medieval court—that provided the two very different audiences who applauded Shakespeare's plays.

Londoners both high and low craved distraction. Elizabeth's court constantly celebrated her reign with dazzling pageants and performances that required a local pool of professional actors and musicians. Beyond the graceful landscape of the royal parks, however, the general populace was packed into little more than a square mile of cramped and crooked streets where theatrical entertainment was frowned upon as compromising public morals.

Just outside the jurisdiction of the city fathers, however, across the twenty arches of London Bridge on the south bank of the Thames, lay the wilder district of "Southwark." A grim reminder of royal power lay at the end of the bridge—the decapitated heads of traitors stared down from pikes at passersby. Once beyond their baleful gaze, people found the amusements they desired, and their growing numbers meant a market suddenly existed for daily entertainment. Bear-baiting and cockfighting flourished, along with taverns, brothels, and even the new institution of the theater.

Southwark, as depicted in Hollar's long view of London (1647). Blackfriars is on the top right and the labels of Bear-baiting and the Globe were inadvertently reversed.

THE ADVENT OF THE THEATRE

The first building in England designed for the performance of plays—called, straightforwardly enough, "The Theatre"—was built in London when Shakespeare was still a boy. It was owned by James Burbage, father of Richard Burbage, who would become Shakespeare's lead actor in the acting company The Lord Chamberlain's Men. "The Theatre," consciously or unconsciously, resembled the yards in which traveling players had long plied their trade—it was an open-air polygon, with three tiers of galleries surrounding a canopied stage in a flat central yard, which was ideal for the athletic competitions the building also hosted. The innovative arena must have found an appreciative audience, for it was soon joined by the Curtain, and then the Rose, which was the first theater to rise in Southwark among the brothels, bars, and bear-baiting pits.

Even as these new venues were being built, a revolution in the drama itself was taking place. Just as Renaissance artists turned to classical models for inspiration, so English writers looked to Roman verse as a prototype for the new national drama. "Blank verse," or iambic pentameter (that is, a poetic line with five alternating stressed and unstressed syllables), was an adaptation of Latin forms, and first appeared in England in a translation of Virgil's *Aeneid*. Blank verse was first spoken on stage in 1561, in the now-forgotten *Gorboduc*, but it was not until the brilliant Christopher Marlowe (born the same year as Shakespeare) transformed it into the "mighty line" of such plays as *Tamburlaine* (1587) that the power and flexibility of the form made it the baseline of English drama.

Marlowe—who, unlike Shakespeare, had attended college—led the "university wits," a clique of hard-living free thinkers who in between all manner of exploits managed to define a new form of theater. The dates of Shakespeare's arrival in London are unknown—we have no record of him in Stratford after 1585—but by the early 1590s he had already absorbed the essence of Marlowe's invention, and begun producing astonishing innovations of his own.

While the "university wits" had worked with myth and fantasy, however, Shakespeare turned to a grand new theme, English history—penning the three-part saga of *Henry VI* in or around 1590. The trilogy was such a success that Shakespeare became the envy of his circle—one unhappy competitor, Robert Greene, even complained in 1592 of "an upstart crow...beautified with our feathers...[who is] in his own conceit the only Shake-scene in a country."

Such jibes perhaps only confirmed Shakespeare's estimation of himself, for he began to apply his mastery of blank verse in all directions, succeeding at tragedy (*Titus Andronicus*), farce (*The Comedy of Errors*), and romantic comedy (*The Two Gentlemen of Verona*). He drew his plots from everywhere: existing poems, romances, folk tales, even other plays. In fact a number of Shakespeare's dramas (*Hamlet* included) may be revisions of earlier texts owned by his troupe. Since copyright laws did not exist, acting companies usually kept their texts close to their chests, only allowing publication when a play was no longer popular, or, conversely, when a play was *so* popular (as with *Romeo and Juliet*) that unauthorized versions had already been printed.

Demand for new plays and performance venues steadily increased. Soon, new theaters (the Hope and the Swan) joined the Rose in Southwark, followed shortly by the legendary Globe, which opened in 1600. (After some trouble with their lease, Shakespeare's acting troupe, the Lord

pendeth on to meane a ftay. Bafe minded men all thꝛee
of you,if by my miferie you be not warnd:foꝛ vnto none
of you (like mee) fought thofe burres to cleaue : thofe
Puppets (J meane)that fpake from our mouths, thofe
Anticks garnifht in our colours. Js it not ftrange,that
J,to whom they all haue beene beholding: is it not like
that you,to whome they all haue beene beholding, fhall
(were yee in that cafe as J am now) bee both at once of
them foꝛfaken : Yes truft them not : foꝛ there is an vp-
ftart Crow, beautified with our feathers, that with his
Tygers hart wrapt in a Players hyde, fuppofes he is as
well able to bombaft out a blanke verfe as the beft of
you : and beeing an abfolute Iohannes fac totum, is in
his owne conceit the onely Shake-fcene in a countrey.
O that J might intreat your rare wits to be imploied in
moꝛe pꝛofitable courfes : ὰ let thofe Apes imitate your
paft excellence, and neuer moꝛe acquaint them with
your admired inuentions. J knowe the beft hufband of

Greene's insult, lines 9–14

Chamberlain's Men, had disassembled "The Theatre" and transported its timbers across the Thames, using them as the structure for the Globe.) Shakespeare was a shareholder in this new venture, with its motto "All the world's a stage," and continued to write and perform for it as well. Full-length plays were now being presented every afternoon but Sunday, and the public appetite for new material seemed endless.

The only curb on the public's hunger for theater was its fear of the plague—for popular belief held the disease was easily spread in crowds. Even worse, the infection was completely beyond the powers of Elizabethan medicine, which held that health derived from four "humors" or internal fluids identified as bile, phlegm, blood, and choler. Such articles of faith, however, were utterly ineffective against a genuine health crisis, and in times of plague, the authorities' panicked response was to shut down any venue where large crowds might congregate. The theaters would be closed for lengthy periods in 1593, 1597, and 1603, during which times Shakespeare was forced to play at court, tour the provinces, or, as many scholars believe, write what would become his famous cycle of sonnets.

The Next Stage

Between these catastrophic closings, the theater thrived as the great medium of its day; it functioned as film, television, and radio combined as well as a venue for music and dance (all performances, even tragedies, ended with a dance). Moreover, the theater was the place to see and be seen; for a penny

Famous scale model of the Globe completed by Dr. John Cranford Adams in 1954. Collectively, 25,000 pieces were used in constructing the replica. Dr. Adams used walnut to imitate the timber of the Globe, plaster was placed with a spoon and medicine dropper, and 6,500 tiny "bricks" measured by pencil eraser strips were individually placed on the model.

you could stand through a performance in the yard, a penny more bought you a seat in the galleries, while yet another purchased you a cushion. The wealthy, the poor, the royal, and the common all gathered at the Globe, and Shakespeare designed his plays—with their action, humor, and highly refined poetry—not only to satisfy their divergent tastes but also to respond to their differing points of view. In the crucible of Elizabethan theater, the various classes could briefly see themselves as others saw them, and drama could genuinely show "the age and body of the time his form and pressure," to quote Hamlet himself.

In order to accommodate his expanding art, the simplicity of the Elizabethan stage had developed a startling flexibility. The canopied platform of the Globe had a trap in its floor for sudden disappearances, while an alcove at the rear, between the pillars supporting its roof, allowed for "discoveries" and interior space. Above, a balcony made possible the love scene in *Romeo and Juliet*; while still higher, the thatched roof could double as a tower or rampart. And though the stage was largely free of scenery, the costumes were sumptuous—a theater troupe's clothing was its greatest asset. Patrons were used to real drums banging in battle scenes and real cannons firing overhead (in fact, a misfire would one day set the Globe aflame).

With the death of Elizabeth, and the accession of James I to the throne in 1603, Shakespeare only saw his power and influence grow. James, who considered himself an intellectual and something of a scholar, took over the patronage of the Lord Chamberlain's Men, renaming them the King's Men; the troupe even marched in his celebratory entrance to London. At this pinnacle of both artistic power and prestige, Shakespeare composed *Othello*, *King Lear*, and *Macbeth* in quick succession, and soon the King's Men acquired a new, indoor theater in London, which allowed the integration of more music and spectacle into his work. At this wildly popular venue, Shakespeare developed a new form of drama that scholars have dubbed "the romance," which combined elements of comedy and tragedy in a magnificent vision that would culminate in the playwright's last masterpiece, *The Tempest*. Not long after this final innovation, Shakespeare retired to Stratford a wealthy and prominent gentleman.

Beyond the Elizabethan Universe

This is how Shakespeare fit into his age. But how did he transcend it? The answer lies in the plays themselves. For even as we see in the surface of his drama the belief system of England in the sixteenth century, Shakespeare himself is always questioning his own culture, holding its ideas up to the light and shaking them, sometimes hard. In the case of the Elizabethan faith in astrology, Shakespeare had his villain Edmund sneer, "We make guilty of our disasters the sun, the moon, and stars; as if we were villains on necessity." When pondering the medieval code of chivalry, Falstaff decides, "The better part of valor is discretion." The divine right of kings is questioned in *Richard II*, and the inferior status of women—a belief that survived even the crowning of Elizabeth—appears ridiculous before the brilliant examples of Portia (*The Merchant of Venice*), and Rosalind (*As You Like It*). Perhaps it is through this constant shifting of perspective, this relentless sense of exploration, that the playwright somehow outlived the limits of his own period, and became, in the words of his rival Ben Jonson, "not just for an age, but for all time."

track 36

Conclusion of the Sourcebooks Shakespeare **KING LEAR**
Sir Derek Jacobi

About the Online Teaching Resources

The Sourcebooks Shakespeare is committed to supporting students and edu-cators in the study of Shakespeare. A web site with additional articles and essays, extended audio, a forum for discussions, as well as other resources can be found (starting in August 2006) at www.sourcebooksshakespeare.com. To illustrate how the Sourcebooks Shakespeare may be used in your class, Jeremy Ehrlich, the head of education at the Folger Shakespeare Library, contributed an essay called "Working with Audio in the Classroom." The fol-lowing is an excerpt:

One possible way of approaching basic audio work in the classroom is shown in the handout [on the site]. It is meant to give some guidance for the first-time user of audio in the classroom. I would urge you to adapt this to the particular circumstances and interests of your own students.

To use it, divide the students into four groups. Assign each group one of the four technical elements of audio – volume, pitch, pace, and pause – to fol-low as you play them an audio clip or clips. In the first section, have them record what they hear: the range they encounter in the clip and the places where their element changes. In the second section, have them suggest words for the tone of the passage based in part on their answers to the first. Sec-tions three and four deal with tools of the actor. Modern acting theory finds the actor's objective is his single most important acting choice; an actor may then choose from a variety of tactics in order to achieve that objective. Thus, if a character's objective on stage is to get sympathy from his scene partner, he may start out by complaining, then shift to another tactic (asking for sym-pathy directly? throwing a tantrum?) if the first tactic fails. Asking your stu-dents to try to explain what they think a character is trying to get, and how she is trying to do it, is a way for them to follow this process through closely. Finally, the handout asks students to think about the meaning (theme) of the passage, concluding with a traditional and important tool of text analysis.

As you can see, this activity is more interesting and, probably, easier for students when it's used with multiple versions of the same piece of text. While defining an actor's motivation is difficult in a vacuum, doing so in relation to another performance may be easier: one Othello may be more

concerned with gaining respect, while another Othello may be more concerned with obtaining love, for instance. This activity may be done outside
of a group setting, although for students doing this work for the first time I
suggest group work so they will be able to share answers on some potentially
thought-provoking questions...

For the complete essay, please visit www.sourcebooksshakespeare.com.

Acknowledgments

The series editors wish to give heartfelt thanks to the advisory editors of the series, David Bevington and Peter Holland, for their ongoing support, timely advice, and keen brilliance.

We are incredibly grateful to the community of Shakespeare scholars for their generosity in sharing their talents, collections, and even their address books. We would not have been able to put together such an august list of contributors without their help. Our sincere thanks go to our text editor, Douglas Brooks, for his brilliant work, and to Bradley Ryner, Tom Garvey, Doug Lanier, and Andrew Wade for their marvelous essays. We are also grateful to William Proctor Williams for his continuing guidance.

Our research was aided immensely by the wonderful staff at Shakespeare archives and libraries around the world: the staff at The Shakespeare Birthplace Trust; Jeremy Ehrlich, Bettina Smith, and everyone at the Folger Shakespeare Library; and Gene Rinkel, Bruce Swann, and Tim Cole from the Rare Books and Special Collections Library at the University of Illinois. These individuals were instrumental in helping us gather audio: Justyn Baker, Janet Benson, Barbara Brown, Nelda Gil, Liz Cooper and Josh Flanagan for the Olivier audio. The following are the talented photographers who shared their work with us: Donald Cooper, George Joseph, Michal Daniel, and Carol Rosegg. Thank you to Jessica Talmage at the Mary Evans Picture Library and to Tracey Tomaso at Corbis. We appreciate all your help. Extra appreciation goes to Doug Lanier for all his guidance and the use of his personal Shakespeare collection.

From the world of drama, the following shared their passion with us and helped us develop the series into a true partnership between the artistic and academic communities. We are indebted to: Liza Holtmeier, Lauren Beyea, and the team from the Shakespeare Theatre Company; Amy Richard from the Oregon Shakespeare Festival; Nancy Becker of The Shakespeare Society; and Myra Lucretia Taylor.

With respect to the audio, we extend our heartfelt thanks to our narrating team: our director, John Tydeman, our esteemed narrator, Sir Derek Jacobi, and the staff of Motivation Studios. John has been a wonderful, generous resource to us and we look forward to future collaborations. We owe a debt of gratitude to Nicolas Soames for introducing us and for being unfailingly helpful. Thank you to Joe Plummer for his excellent work on the audio analysis. Thanks also to the "Speaking Shakespeare" team: Andrew Wade and Myra Lucretia Taylor for that wonderful recording, and Steve Alvarado and the team at Dubway Studios. Thank you to Paul Estby for mastering the entire CD.

We would also like to thank Tanya Gough, the proprietor of The Poor Yorick Shakespeare Catalog, for all her efforts on behalf of the series. Our personal thanks for their kindness and unstinting support go to our friends and our extended families.

Finally, thanks to everyone at Sourcebooks who contributed their talents in realizing The Sourcebooks Shakespeare–in particular: Todd Green, Todd Stocke, Megan Dempster, and Melanie Thompson. Special mention to Nikki Braziel and Elizabeth Lhost, assistants extraordinaire for the Sourcebooks Shakespeare.

So, thanks to all at once and to each one (*Macbeth,* 5.7.104)

Audio Credits

In all cases, we have attempted to provide archival audio in its original form. While we have tried to achieve the best possible quality on the archival audio, some audio quality is the result of source limitations. Archival audio research by Marie Macaisa. Audio analysis by Joe Plummer. Narration script by Marie Macaisa. Narration recording and audio engineering by Motivation Sound Studios, London, UK. Mastering by Paul Estby. Recording for "Speaking Shakespeare" by Dubway Studios, New York City, USA.

Narrated by Sir Derek Jacobi
Directed by John Tydeman
Produced by Marie Macaisa

The following are under license from Naxos of America www.naxosusa.com
℗ HNH International Ltd. All rights reserved.
Tracks 4, 7, 9, 10, 14, 18, 21, 24, 27, 32

The following are selections from The Complete Arkangel Shakespeare ℗ 2003, with permission of The Audio Partners Publishing Corporation. All rights reserved. Unabridged audio dramatizations of all 38 plays. For more information, visit www.audiopartners.com/shakespeare.
Tracks 3, 6, 17, 23, 26, 30

The following are under license from IPC Media. All rights reserved.
Tracks 20, 29

The following are under license from Granada International. All rights reserved.
Tracks 12, 15

The following are under license from the Sir John Gielgud Charitable Trust. All rights reserved.
Track 33

Photo Credits

Every effort has been made to correctly attribute all the materials reproduced in this book. If any errors have been made, we will be happy to correct them in future editions. Photos are credited on the pages in which they appear.

Images from the 1959 production at the Shakespeare Memorial Theatre in Stratford-upon-Avon directed by Glen Byam Shaw are courtesy of the Rare Book and Special Collections Library, University of Illinois at Urbana-Champaign.

Photos from the Shakespeare Theatre Company's 2000 production directed by Michael Kahn are © 2000 Carol Rosegg.

Photos from the Public Theater's 1973 production directed by Edwin Sherin are © 1973 George E. Joseph; from its 2007 production directed by James Lapine are © 2007 Michal Daniel.

Photos from the Royal Shakespeare Company's 1991 production directed by Nicholas Hytner are © 1991 Donald Cooper; from its 1993 production directed by Adrian Noble are © 1993 Donald Cooper; from its 1999 production directed by Yukio Ninagawa are © 1999 Donald Cooper; from its 2005 production directed by Bill Alexander are © 2005 Donald Cooper; from its 2007 production directed by Trevor Nunn are © 2007 Donald Cooper.

Photos from the Oregon Shakespeare Festival's 2004 production directed by James Edmondson are courtesy of the Oregon Shakespeare Festival.

Photos from the 1999 Shakespeare's Globe production directed by Annete Leday are © 1999 Donald Cooper.

Photos from the 1997 Old Vic production directed by Peter Hall are © 1997 Donald Cooper.

Engravings by John Byam Shaw and watercolor sketches from Charles Kean's 1858 promptbook are courtesy of the Folger Shakespeare Library.

William Shakespeare's signature (on the title page) courtesy of Mary Evans Picture Library. Other images from the Mary Evans Picture Library used in the text are credited on the pages in which they appear.

Images from "In the Age of Shakespeare" courtesy of The Folger Shakespeare Library.

About the Contributors

TEXT EDITOR
Douglas A. Brooks is Associate Professor of English at Texas A&M University and the Editor of *Shakespeare Yearbook*. He is the author of *From Playhouse to Printing House: Drama and Authorship in Early Modern England* (Cambridge UP, 2000) and the editor of two collections of essays, *Printing and Parenting in Early Modern England* (Ashgate Publishing Co., 2005) and *Milton and the Jews*, forthcoming Cambridge UP. Brooks has published essays in *Medieval and Renaissance Drama in England*, *Shakespeare Studies*, *ELR*, *Philological Quarterly*, *Genre*, *Renaissance Drama*, *Studies in English Literature*, and *Poetics Today*. He is presently completing a book entitled *The Gutenberg Father in Early Modern England*.

SERIES EDITORS
Marie Macaisa spent twenty years in her first career: high tech. She has a bachelor's degree in computer science from the Massachusetts Institute of Technology, a master's degree in artificial intelligence from the University of Pennsylvania, and worked for many years on the research and development of innovative applications of computer technology. She became the series editor of *The Sourcebooks Shakespeare* in 2003. She contributed the *Cast Speaks* essays for previous volumes and is the producer of the accompanying audio CDs.

Dominique Raccah is the founder, president, and publisher of Sourcebooks. Born in Paris, France, she has a bachelor's degree in psychology and a master's in quantitative psychology from the University of Illinois. She also serves as series editor of *Poetry Speaks* and *Poetry Speaks to Children*.

ADVISORY BOARD
David Bevington is the Phyllis Fay Horton Distinguished Service Professor in the Humanities at the University of Chicago. A renowned text scholar, he has edited several Shakespeare editions including the *Bantam Shakespeare* in individual paperback volumes, *The Complete Works of Shakespeare*

(Longman, 2003), and *Troilus and Cressida* (Arden, 1998). He teaches courses in Shakespeare, renaissance drama, and medieval drama.

Peter Holland is the McMeel Family Chair in Shakespeare Studies at the University of Notre Dame. One of the central figures in performance-oriented Shakespeare criticism, he has also edited many Shakespeare plays, including *A Midsummer Night's Dream* for the Oxford Shakespeare series. He is also general editor of Shakespeare Survey and co-general editor (with Stanley Wells) of Oxford Shakespeare Topics. Currently he is completing a book, *Shakespeare on Film*, and editing *Coriolanus* for the Arden 3rd series.

ESSAYISTS

Thomas Garvey has been acting, directing, or writing about Shakespeare for over two decades. A graduate of the Massachusetts Institute of Technology, he studied acting and directing with the MIT Shakespeare Ensemble, where he played Hamlet, Jacques, Iago, and other roles, and directed *All's Well That Ends Well* and *Twelfth Night*. He has since directed and designed several other Shakespearean productions, as well as works by Chekhov, Ibsen, Sophocles, Beckett, Moliere, and Shaw. Mr. Garvey has written on theatre for the *Boston Globe* and other publications.

Douglas Lanier is an associate professor of English at the University of New Hampshire. He has written many essays on Shakespeare in popular culture, including "Shakescorp Noir" in *Shakespeare Quarterly* 53.2 (Summer 2002) and "Shakespeare on the Record" in *The Blackwell Companion to Shakespeare in Performance* (edited by Barbara Hodgdon and William Worthen, Blackwell, 2005). His book *Shakespeare and Modern Popular Culture* (Oxford University Press) was published in 2002. He is currently working on a book-length study of cultural stratification in early modern British theater.

Bradley D. Ryner is an Assistant Professor of English at Arizona State University. His work has appeared in the journals *English Studies* and *Shakespeare* (both published by Routledge), and *The Oxford Companion to Shakespeare* (edited by Michael Dobson and Stanley Wells). He is working on a book manuscript that examines the conventions for representing economic systems on the English Renaissance stage. An essay on *Cymbeline* derived from this project is scheduled to appear in a collection to be published by Palgrave.

Andrew Wade was head of voice for the Royal Shakespeare Company from 1990 to 2003 and voice assistant director from 1987 to 1990. During this time he worked on 170 productions and with more than 80 directors. Along with Cicely Berry, Andrew recorded *Working Shakespeare* and the DVD series on *Voice and Shakespeare*, and he was the verse consultant for the movie *Shakespeare In Love*. In 2000, he won a Bronze Award from the New York International Radio Festival for the series *Lifespan*, which he co-directed and devised. He works widely teaching, lecturing, and coaching throughout the world.

AUDIO CONTRIBUTORS

Sir Derek Jacobi (Series Narrator) is one of Britain's foremost actors of stage and screen. One of his earliest Shakespearean roles was Cassio to Sir Laurence Olivier's Othello in Stuart Burge's 1965 movie production. More recent roles include Hamlet in the acclaimed BBC Television Shakespeare production in 1980, the Chorus in Kenneth Branagh's 1989 film of *Henry V*, and Claudius in Branagh's 1996 movie *Hamlet*. He has been accorded numerous honors in his distinguished career, including a Tony award for Best Actor in *Much Ado About Nothing* and a BAFTA (British Academy of Film and Television) for his landmark portrayal of Emperor Claudius in the blockbuster television series *I, Claudius*. He was made a Knight of the British Empire in 1994 for his services to the theatre.

John Tydeman (Series Director) was the Head of Drama for BBC Radio for many years and is the director of countless productions, with 15 Shakespeare plays to his credit. Among his numerous awards are the Prix Italia, Prix Europa, UK Broadcasting Guild Best Radio Programme (*When The Wind Blows* by Raymond Briggs), and the Sony Personal Award for services to radio. He has worked with most of Britain's leading actors and dramatists and has directed for the theatre, television, and commercial recordings. He holds an M.A. from Cambridge University.

Joe Plummer (Audio Analyst) is the Director of Education for the Williamstown Theatre Festival and Assistant Professor of Shakespearean Performance with Roger Rees at Fordham University's Lincoln Center Campus. He has taught several Master classes on Shakespeare and performance at Williams College, the National Shakespeare Company and Brandeis University, and also teaches privately. Joe is currently the Artist-In-Residence and Director of Educational Outreach for The Shakespeare Society in New York City and is the founder and Producing Artistic Director of poortom productions, the only all-male Shakespeare Company in the US. He has performed extensively in New York and in regional theaters.